TACTICAL GUIDE TO ONLINE MARKETING

TACTICAL GUIDE TO ONLINE MARKETING

Tig Tillinghast

3340-TILL

Library of Congress Number: 2001119451
ISBN #: Hardcover 1-4010-3693-7
Softcover 1-4010-3692-9

This book was printed in the United States of America.

To order additional copies of this book, contact:

Tactical Guides Publishing
Boston, MA
www.tacticalguide.com

CONTENTS

13340-TILL

PREFACE

This book came together over the course of eight years of working in online media—from the early days of online services and failed interactive television test beds, to the success of the Internet banner and the advent of popular rich media. In that time, the marketing industry developed enough of a framework to make online media buying a set process, with specific players, who have very specific expectations and policies. Not all of it works rationally. Much of what folks do in the online media business looks silly to an outsider. Truth be told, it looks pretty silly to the insiders. This book seeks to guide readers through those processes—both the strategic decisions and the tactical issues—to get practical results.

This book was written with three audiences in mind:

- People working in interactive media today who hope to learn something new, perhaps about types of online marketing they haven't yet performed
- Traditional media people who want to gain a good grasp of both the strategic and tactical issues of the online media
- And, finally, marketing majors coming into their first jobs dealing with online media

I've always wanted to be able to hand a book to my new employees to get them partly up to speed on the frenetic online media space. Most marketing books approach the topic at a very high level, skipping basic tactics. I hope this book suffices as part of the missing link, introducing readers to the step-by-step processes that underlie all our strategies.

The three savviest online experts I know were coerced into reading the manuscript of the book, and they made many greatly needed comments. I thank Tom Hespos, Laura Mitrovich and Jim Meskauskas. They deserve the credit for reducing the number of errors and omissions. More importantly, these three have, through their own writings, helped buyers maintain a healthy cynicism that improves and grows the interactive media industry much faster than would any form of mindless boosterism.

The Tactical Guide to Interactive Media will be out of date after just a few weeks on the shelves. Readers can see updates on the companion website, www.tacticalguide.com, and can place themselves on the email list for notification of the next edition (expected in the second half of 2002) by sending an email to edition2@tacticalguide.com. Email feedback on this book's content is also welcomed at editorial@tacticalguide.com.

It's my hope that people reading this book will gain two things. I hope they gain some confidence in their own abilities to grapple with the industry and work with its existing structures and processes. And I hope they will begin to understand that we know but a small portion of the science of online marketing.

The people just entering into the industry today will be the true parents of interactive media. We who preceded them created only the very basest of tools and structures. They will be the ones who figure out the mechanics of the new measurements, opportunities and the new structures that need to be created to exploit them.

Tig Tillinghast
Cambridge, MA, October 2001

ADVERTISING BASICS

The premise of advertising holds that markets can be influenced by the presentation of messages.

More particularly, it holds that showing carefully crafted messages to appropriate audiences will result in a profitable change of belief or behavior. In other words, people can be manipulated. Here are some recent examples:

- A major car manufacturer spends $100 million (written $100MM in the industry) to tell skeptical people that its poorly manufactured cars have great quality. This makes car shoppers, who would not have otherwise bothered to test drive one of these cars, stop by the local dealership.
- A company launches a new flavor of fruit drink that would seem extremely disgusting to most people who haven't tasted it. A print campaign showing kids drinking it down with great satisfaction, all the sweeter because it makes adults squeamish. The ads create a beverage fad.
- People who have high interest rate mortgages find a flyer in the mail on how they can refinance their loan. With no cost to themselves, they can start making lower monthly house payments. Five percent of the people receiving the flyer go through with the transaction, making the campaign pay for itself 15 times over.

Advertising works, at least sometimes. And some media are better than others for different types of objectives.

"Media" is the broad term we use for any place we can put an ad. We tend to divvy up the media world into specific types, like

13340-TILL

television, Internet, print, direct mail, outdoor and radio. In fact, media people tend to divvy themselves up in the same way. Few individuals work across more than two or three media. Even ad agencies tend to concentrate on certain types of clients who prefer certain types of media.

That loan refinance campaign mentioned above would have bombed miserably on television because the agency would not have been able to target the necessary highly-qualified audience quite as well. Likewise, the beverage campaign wouldn't have worked in direct mail because the costs would have been too high per person to make money from the sale of a peach-tomato-limeade.

For reasons like these, we tend to see certain types of media attracting certain types of advertisers.

The Internet, though, is a bit of an exception to this. Marketers have found that it can work very well as a direct response medium, attracting high-end product advertising that requires very qualified audiences. Others have found it works well as a branding mechanism, reaching large numbers of people very cheaply. It has become a bit like the elephant in the fable about the three blind men. The blind man feeling the trunk believes the creature to be a tree. The one feeling the tale is convinced it's a snake. The person on the torso believes it to be a boulder. Observers can see a similar spectacle taking place during interactive conferences, where interactive industry experts get together to discuss what everyone else is doing wrong.

The Philosophy of the Ad Markets

Online advertising differs significantly from the traditional media's processes and—frequently—purposes. But you can't really explain online advertising fully without comprehending and comparing the basic traditional media terms and methods. Taking this basic breakdown view of our industry reveals the very philosophical underpinnings of what we do.

While online and offline advertising may differ enormously in form and function, the philosophy of advertising remains the same: a buyer with both a message and a competitive amount of money may buy the opportunity to air the message. This is about as capitalistic as you can get.

Even for the liberal arts students out there, like me, it's pretty simple: it's the essence of supply and demand. The more supply out there, the cheaper the media must be priced to sell. The more demand out there, the higher the media may be priced to sell.

Implicit in this philosophy is the presumption that buyers with the most money *should* win the media opportunities for their message—as opposed to buyers with more compelling message but fewer dollars. Looking from the other side, media sellers *should* allow their goods to be sold to the highest bidder, regardless of message.

We've set up a marketplace of media—much like a stock market—where participants can become players based on two factors: the capital they have and the cleverness with which they invest it. As a buyer or seller, you can't ignore either of these factors. The "invisible hand" of Adam Smith, the guy who first theorized about modern market principles, is ready to lift you up via your intelligent media buying or slap you down to the degree you spend too much for less valuable exposure.

Traditional Advertising Mechanics

In the past, we've measured these media marketplaces with several different types of numbers. The most basic measure of a media buy is the number of impressions purchased—the number of times individuals see an ad. This number will often get broken up into two other numbers: reach and frequency. These define how many individuals saw an ad, and the average number of times they saw it.

To illustrate, to advertise my bird dog training service, I might purchase an ad in two magazines: *Bird Dog Monthly* and *Point*. If

13340-TILL

both of these magazines have 50 subscribers, and these happen to be the very same 50 people, I can say that I purchased 100 impressions, with a reach of 50 and a frequency of 2.

For impressions in the print media, we've used the circulation figure, the number of people who receive a copy of a publication. Some print reps try to augment their circulation figures by claiming that multiple people read the publication. These additional impressions are called pass-along or pass-through. Ad agencies often ignore these pass-along numbers. My own belief is that things tend to even out. It might be true that a couple of additional people see each magazine, but it's also true that only a fraction of readers see any given advertisement.

When a magazine sells media to a buyer, it is always selling a number of impressions equal to that of the circulation. Unless the publication does something fancy, like selective binding (different ads to different people) or regional editions, the sellers are limited to the circulation figures as the ad package. This is why circulation figures are so important in print.

In fact, most publications selling media go ahead and pay a lot of money to have special third-party organizations conduct circulation audits, essentially verification studies to ensure that the publication does indeed have the audience it claims to have. The audience level a seller claims is called the guaranteed circulation.

Buyers generally purchase this media based on the thousands of impressions. Buyers will ask various sites the cost of an ad, then figure out the cost per thousand impressions (CPM) to determine the relative rates.

They will select some media to purchase—after some negotiation—then codify the deal with a contract called an insertion order. If the seller fails to deliver the right number of impressions, they are usually bound by the terms of that insertion order to provide a makegood to account for the discrepancy.

In the broadcast media, we use some more complicated measures, namely ratings and share. These figures show what percentage of the viewing audience at a given time sees a particular ad. A ratings figure of 4.7 means that of all the television-owning households in that market, 4.7 percent of them were reported to have been watching the TV show on which a particular ad appeared.

A 4.7 share would mean that of all the households then watching television, 4.7 percent of them were watching that particular program. This is a type of metric in which some online media people are beginning to take interest.

How Does Online Media Differ?

The online world's markets may work similarly to those of traditional media, but the delivery mechanisms remain so vastly different, that we need to add some new dimensions to the way we think about them.

The online site is free from the fetters of circulation-based or ratings-based packages we see in traditional media. Online, sellers can package up certain areas of the site, certain times of day, or entirely arbitrary numbers of impressions.

Unfortunately, this means online buyers may no longer rely on circulation audits to ensure that they get their money's worth. Where before they knew that the same number of folks who saw the magazine had the potential to see their ad, they now have a very confusing set of different possible measures.

Most commonly, advertisers look directly at impression numbers, as defined by the various technical measures the Web sites produce. And each site may use a slightly different technical measure.

Often the online media get further divvied up by various targeting technologies. Advertisers will buy a certain number of impressions, but only the impressions that happen when the ad appears in a certain context, like when a viewer is doing a search using a very particular search term keyword.

The media deals may be based on measures other than impressions. We can, for instance, pay for each time someone clicks on our ad—what we call cost per clickthrough or CPC. We can also follow that user from the original site where the ad appeared, onto our client's site. This allows us to purchase media based on how many people actually buy something on our client's site, or perhaps perform some other objective measure. We call this type of buying cost per action, or CPA (sometimes referred to as cost per transaction, or CPX).

A word of warning: some folks use a term "CPT" to mean cost per transaction. Most tend to avoid this because it conflicts with another ill-favored term: cost per transfer. Sticking to CPC and CPA should reduce confusion.

To review, purchasing online media is a bit more complex. We can buy not only impressions, but clickthroughs and actions as well. Increasingly, people buy combinations of these, paying a basic impression rate in addition to premiums for either clickthroughs or transactions. Online, we count all of these performance measures separately from the circulation figures of a web site, which we often refer to as the "traffic" numbers.

How do your clients know that all that money they're blowing out the media chute actually has some sort of positive effect on their businesses? In traditional media, they sometimes will look at several numbers to determine a before-and-after effect, but most times, they merely measure the amount of exposure they bought and received. These are the numbers agencies have typically been responsible for collecting and presenting as a "post-buy" report document.

Interactive Media's Role

The fact that we can measure more performance by using online media has led some to conclude that the interactive stuff is best for direct response campaigns and the traditional stuff is best for awareness and branding campaigns—the types of campaigns that usually don't require so much measurement. But these assumptions remind me of the drunk who decides to look for his car keys under the streetlight because it's easier to see there than where he dropped them in the gutter. Just because we can measure direct response results well online doesn't mean the medium performs better or worse relative to other media.

In point of fact, online media can be a more efficient way of conducting a direct response campaign. That efficiency can be exploited if we take advantage of the fact that we can reach people in places and at times when they are about to do things similar to the responses we ask of them. We also have the capability of employing online media as inefficiently as we'd be forced to do using a traditional media for the direct response campaign. It's all a matter of how much we decide to exploit the additional data available online.

On the other side of the issues, a common myth told in offices throughout the industry is that interactive media are inefficient for branding and awareness purposes. In point of fact, study after study has shown that online media are roughly as good at branding as television. When the first study came out showing that online banners worked as well as 30 second TV spots, I was very skeptical. Online media trade groups then sponsored more studies that reported similar results, and I was even more skeptical. But then, over the past few years, more and more clients have done their own branding research with their own campaigns, comparing the results of their interactive and traditional media. A similar ratio of performance pervades all this research: a banner ad and a TV commercial increase brand association by about 40 percent. Print and other media don't come very close to that type of branding success.

This, by itself, doesn't make online media as efficient as traditional media for branding purposes. For that to happen, the prices of the media would also have to be equivalent. Since most online media is priced higher than the equivalent print or TV impressions, we can often give the nod to traditional media for highest branding efficiency. But when we're seeking to target particular

13340-TILL

groups, we can often find them with much less media wastage online, bringing the effective CPM rates down, perhaps even in favor of online media. The superior targeting capabilities of online media make up for the inferiority of its prices—sometimes.

All of this leads us to the conclusion that online media can be either efficient or relatively inefficient for any of these types of campaign objectives. It depends on how we choose to exploit the medium. It is true that we get very good post-buy measurement that is very desirable in direct response campaigns, but that shouldn't by itself limit our use of online media to the ghetto of direct response. And just because it's about as difficult to get branding success measurements online as it is to do offline, this doesn't signify that traditional media will work any better for the other, harder-to-measure, types of objectives, like branding.

Traditional Performance Metrics

Advertisers tend to break up audiences into groups of people—or markets. In a wonderful demonstration of our industry myopia, we call any one particular market segment a "universe."

The two major media measures of the universe are the share of voice (SOV) and the share of market (SOM). The share of voice represents the percentage of impressions your ads comprise within your competitive category's media spending against a particular audience universe. For instance, if the brand and its competitors bought a total of 1,000,000 impressions (usually written as 1MM), and your advertiser's brand was responsible for 120,000 impressions of that (usually written 120M), your share of voice would be 12 percent. The share of market represents the percentage of actual purchase or use your client's product receives versus the competition within the given audience universe.

Agencies like to give themselves pats on the back for showing a high SOV relative to the media spend. This ratio, while suggestive of superior media buying skills, is easily manipulated by agencies. They will sometimes consider the relevant universe to be a group of people other than the ones the competitors deem appropriate. In a case like that, all the different clients in a category may be told that they are receiving a very high SOV relative to their spending. But this will be true only because they are measuring themselves by different criteria. It's reminiscent of the queen in Snow White (the client) asking the mirror (the agency) if she's the "fairest of them all." One mirror will tell one queen she has the most beautiful eyes. Another mirror tells a different queen she has the noblest nose. A third might tell a queen she has the fairest lips. When queens get together and compare notes, they get very agitated.

Generally, the greater our SOV, the greater our SOM, but it doesn't always work out that way. You can usually bet your next expense report check that the company that sees its share of market erode well past its share of voice will fire its agency in the next couple of quarters. I know a guy who actually trades the stocks of agencies specifically with this in mind. And he doesn't do too badly.

Recall is the measure of the percentage of folks who can remember seeing your ad and associate it with the right brand. We usually speak in terms of either unaided recall or aided recall.

Unaided recall goes like this:
Q: "Do you remember seeing any recent beer commercials?"
A: "Er, I dunno."

And aided recall goes more like this:
Q: "More taste?"
A: "Less filling! I saw that Miller beer ad last night during the game."

For the younger readers out there, this could be replaced with the equivalent:
Q: "Waasup?"
A: "Waaaaaasuuuuuuuuup!"

This recall of the creative hopefully leads to an increase in brand association, which means that people not only remember the ad, but they remember which product the ad was representing. Better brand association, in theory, leads to better brand "preference." Technically speaking, preference is a ratio (expressed as a percentage) of the rate of consumer choice of your clients product versus the rate of choice of others. This is truly where the rubber hits the road. You found the target, you got a media message to the target, the creative had a discernable effect on the target. Agencies increasing the preference percentages for their clients' brands seldom need worry about being fired.

In traditional broadcast media, though, these figures have been very difficult to measure. Companies conduct expensive studies on people's opinions on various brands both before and after ads appear. The results are compared to interpolate what effect the advertising had on the people's preferences. This process is too cumbersome, slow and expensive to do with each campaign.

The Online Advantages

In the online world, we have quite a different set of performance information. In fact, we often have a complete record of everyone's interactions with our ad. We know who saw it, who clicked on it, how much stuff they bought, and what profit margin they represent going forward. The trick isn't so much getting this information, as it is linking one event to the next, resolving discrepancies among data sources and engineering a process to digest this information and exploit it usefully in our media context. These are all key areas we shall explore in ensuing chapters.

I want to stress that solving these problems is much more important than attempting to replicate our traditional media performance metrics on the Internet. A lot of traditional agencies waste a lot of time worrying about things like share of voice within a site. That energy would be much better wasted worrying about the return on investment (ROI) given to the client relative to the cost of the media—especially since those numbers are already there to be ferreted out by a competent media buyer.

In the coming sections, the book will cut through the jungle of online metric vines and thistles. In the process of explaining how we can link the observed behaviors online, we'll cover banner servers and other types of technologies that often fail to give us straight answers. We'll explain the technical causes of this, hopefully setting up your expectations as to what can be usefully garnered from the various online measurements.

When Online Advertising Isn't Enough

It happens, and it happens rather frequently. An advertiser runs online ads along side a few other types of media, and the spreadsheet at the end of the day doesn't give the online media the most efficient rating. There might be some print and direct mail. Perhaps some TV. Maybe even some alternative online media like direct email, or online promotions, or an online loyalty program. What to do?

We could take a page from the traditional advertising industry's book, and claim that there are "branding" benefits missing from the spreadsheet numbers. Television and print have come a long way representing that a good part of their value come from a certain *je ne sais quois*. We see the larger online media vendors hyping the studies showing a certain layer of branding clothing the naked direct benefits of online media. I give them full credit, as they seem to show consistent results, but in the end, clients often look to very specific behavioral measures—like which customer bought what.

Some agencies have the luxury of being able to adjust the media mix of a campaign, letting the success in the market determine how much spending goes to which medium, without it affecting the financial interests of the agency. But this isn't available to most. Most often, any particular agency only operates in a limited number of worlds—maybe online media and print. Maybe just online media and traditional promotions marketing. Very few agencies actually retain the multiple media neutrality required to be agnostic about all these choices—it requires a diversity and scale that few agencies achieve without becoming large, overly-bureaucratic companies. This means that agencies become biased toward the budgets they control, and therefor the media in which they work.

The very biggest agency organizations frequently have an implicit policy of pushing clients into the media that make the largest profit margin. "Yes, sir, that $80 million would be best spent on 10 network television contracts." Of course, that did a lot of good to the hundreds of Internet startups that blew through their VC funds on television. And there, but for the grace of common sense, go we.

Most buyers in the industry face a strange, invisible wall. They find a vendor—maybe an online loyalty program vendor or an email marketing program vendor—and they realize that the ROI is superior to throwing more money into the more typical online media of banners. But somehow they can't get their organization to start using these folks. The creatives push back, saying that this isn't part of their job description. The media director doesn't quite know how to put the result figures of this new service in comparison to the other media work. The account folks turn their noses up on something that isn't "mainline" advertising, worried that their peers will see them as matchbook cover marketing hacks. And, not to cast aspersions too broadly, the media buyers themselves tend to want to consider only those options that compare directly with the other media offers they know and use.

Sometimes that invisible wall isn't so invisible. Agencies can become quite conflicted when a client divvies up the different media among different agencies. So when you're agency gets assigned the online media budget, you better darned tooting find that the best way to spend every dime should be online media. Or else. This is the most stifling type of relationship, and it makes agencies somewhat dishonest. We become like lawyers who know our clients are guilty. We become honorable advocates of the wrong, and clients stop seeing us as impartial judges and more as counselors for one type of medium.

I've found that in these situations, the most reasonable listener in all this usually remains the client. The client has the vested interest to spend the money in the best way, regardless of the status of the media.

New forms of online media, online forms of database and direct marketing and other alternatives will sometimes be found to be more efficient than our normal media buys. Even print and television will sometimes be found more efficient. Agencies that try to deny this will only lose their credibility. Clients who respect and reward the agencies who are honest about the most efficient media mix will be rewarded with more value for their money.

THE PLAYERS

The online media industry, like its traditional media counterpart, divides itself into two main camps. There are the buyers and the sellers. In both cases, the camps frequently divide up into owners and agents. On the buy side, these are represented by the advertisers (the owners of the money to be spent) and the ad agencies (the agents). On the sell side of things, these are the site (that owns the media to be sold) and the sales representative, referred to frequently as simply a "rep" (the agents).

Most people conducting online buys reside in the ad agency, and most money spent online is spent through agencies. Some advertisers do maintain in-house staffs to do the media planning and buying directly. Someone graduating today from college and getting job in the online media field would stand a very good chance of winding up at an ad agency. The next likely place would be as a sales rep at a site or rep firm.

In the course of planning and buying, many different types of people will come into contact with one another. To better understand the motives behind each, we will describe some job responsibilities and nuances for the different roles.

The Buyer/Planner's New Role

Not surprisingly, while media departments now enjoy a level of strategic leadership that they lacked previously, the demands on their staffs become more daunting. It takes an exceptional candidate to be able to meet all the criteria set out for new agency hires. I laughed when I saw a friend of mine posting this want ad on a web site recently for a new buyer position. This was supposed to attract people from right out of school:

Media buyer wanted:
- Must lead account and creative teams to ensure execution
- Suggest objectives and design strategies to meet client needs
- Must work with all types of media, including new forms of interactive
- Keep up to date on all new technologies and sites
- Engage media community to get best offers from reps
- Manage all planning processes including negotiating, trafficking, analysis and discrepancy resolution
- Manage client relationship
- Have knowledge of research sources
- Have excellent presentation and writing skills
- Work well under pressure and unreasonable deadlines

I told him that if he found someone out of school who could do all that, they shouldn't be wasted on an ad agency—we should elect the person president. Yet, these are the expectations now foisted on the media department. With luck, a new media planner will find herself in a media department with experienced and sympathetic old hands. It usually doesn't take very long for young staff to grow into these responsibilities, but no one will ever have these skills congenitally.

These expectations have risen, in good part, because more and more departments at the client companies now demand influence on interactive media decisions. These agency media decision makers, then, have greater prominence within the agency because they're now dealing with more and higher-level client contacts.

Once a client web site goes live, the media folks suddenly confront new sets of clients to satisfy. The objectives multiplied to include the likes of:

- Branding
- Product advertising
- Promotion
- Sales
- Fulfillment
- Service
- Data collection
- Relationship building
- Competitive response
- Investor relations
- Public relations
- Press relations
- Recruiting
- Channel building
- Vendor solicitation and service
- Product development
- Legal liability mitigation
- Online co-promotion and partnerships

A key to the success of any interactive project is getting the right players involved at the very beginning, not just to secure their buy-off, but also to create an economy of scale in the education and strategy-building processes. This type of process places the media planners and supervisors in front of the clients' most senior management.

A friend of mine in San Francisco who runs an online agency makes it a policy of working with clients only if they first have or create an "Internet committee" consisting of all players. This man has more reason to require the committee than simply the obvious benefits the client derives. It makes his life slightly more manageable. Otherwise, he finds himself in the dismal position of mediating among internal client departments without the real authority to make decisions.

The role of the planner and buyer expands to include those of an evangelist, a technologist, negotiator, statistician, database manager, salesman and historian. Albeit daunting, it is truly a fun and rewarding job.

Disadvantages of In-House Buyers

Advertisers who decide to conduct their own planning and buying without the help of an agency run a few risks. They can certainly save money, but they often sacrifice a greater deal of efficiency in the process.

As a fee structure, agencies have traditionally charged about another 15 percent of the cost of the media. With online media, this has risen even higher due to the higher level of staffing necessary to manage the more complex and less standardized process. But, because of inefficiencies and infrastructure costs, clients do not find a 15 percent savings by going it alone.

The savings left over after that can prove illusory for several reasons:

- They do not have the negotiating history with the same variety of sites and technology companies as does an ad agency that negotiates on behalf of many different clients
- They cannot provide the same economies of scale the agency can provide to media vehicles
- The in-house staff work only in a narrow product category and remain unfamiliar with new types of media, targeting and technologies growing in other product categories
- Web sites can take advantage of clients' inexperience by offering deals that turn out to be more expensive than ones agencies can competitively bid across more media vendors
- Finally, my own personal experience shows that clients—perhaps because they are not accustomed to these types of contracts—fail to put certain safeguards into the terms of media deals. This has lead to, for instance, the client having to continue buying media at a very high price long after they've realized their mistake.

3340-TILL

That said, there are many advertisers who do just fine purchasing their own media. Especially the advertisers who spend too little to efficiently hire an agency or who purchase a type of media so specialized or targeted that they find themselves more expert in its purchase than an agency media department.

Routing Around the Agency

Sales representatives, finding themselves rejected by agency buyers, sometimes attempt to go directly to the advertiser. Disciplined advertisers disallow this for the twin reasons of preventing their voicemail boxes from becoming filled up with appeals by rejected sites and ensuring that they give their agencies the full moral authority they need to negotiate prices from a position of strength.

While not as popular now in hindsight, a few years ago it became fashionable to conduct very large single media deals with a site. These were called sponsorships or partnerships, and they generally amounted to tens of millions of dollars being spent at one location for what turned out to be terribly uncompetitive rates. During the Internet mania of 1999, some sites would approach advertisers directly with the lure of press releases, temporary stock price rises and momentary fame. Most of those deals today have been abrogated.

The Sell-Side

The people selling the media come in a variety of stripes. The most common is the independent sales rep, employed by a site for the sole purpose of selling that site's media. Other types include:

- Network sales reps, who sell multiple sites and sometimes packages that mix some of several sites' media.

- Ad auction companies that allow sites to sell their media on electronic markets, akin to the NASDAQ.
- Media rep firms that represent a stable of sites, usually spread across a spectrum of different audiences, allowing the their sales reps to push a particular site when a client calls for a certain type of audience. These firms will often deliberately recruit specific sites with the lure of giving them an exclusivity on that special audience. For instance, a network without a kids component might approach SpoiledBrat.com and make such an offer.

Different types of sales reps will be able to offer different types of flexibility, depending on their individual deals with the media companies they sell.

We can generalize that the sales reps selling their own company's media will have more flexibility on price and terms. Sites sold through large networks often prove inflexible because they must conform to the same terms all sites on the network establish. This is also true of other types of site dealings. For instance, networks tend to have much less flexibility with creative formats and special content-oriented deals like sponsorships.

Since rep firms and networks typically take anywhere from 25 percent to 60 percent of the gross media proceeds, sites are understandably reluctant to further discount the rates with these sellers.

As in traditional media, the size of a media vehicle tends to dictate whether or not it employs an in-house sales force. The very small sites, while they would like to outsource this type of business function, do not have the economies of scale to justify a repping service. They will instead often attempt to join an ad network. The rep services, often provided by the very same major repping firms found in traditional media, generally sell the intermediate-sized sites. The very largest sites, like Yahoo!, have an economy of scale that allows them to employ their own reps.

Routing Around the Reps

Especially when a site's media is sold by different sources—perhaps both an internal sales force and a network—buyers will find it desirable to go around the official sales reps to get the media at a lower price.

Sometimes sites will take a portion of the media they normally fail to sell in a given month and hand it over to large networks, to be sold as "remnant media." Buyers purchase these generic batches of media for very low cost, and the networks often will refuse to reveal exactly from which sites this media comes. They are often obligated to refuse to identify the origin of the media because those sites don't want it known that they can be acquired for a small fraction of their normal rate card prices.

A friend of mine told the story of how he once had an expensive financial site on the buy in addition to a large network purchase. He discovered, through having set up a separate click-through page for this campaign, that the network buy must have contained a very large amount of that same financial site, because the clickthrough rate was enormous. He discovered that while he spent $X for a 1MM impressions by buying through the site, he was also receiving 10 MM impressions for only 1/2 $X, coming from a separate remnant buy.

People inexperienced with the wiles of client-agency relationships would expect this to be a great boon to the agency. The buyers had figured out a way—albeit out of sheer luck—to multiply the effective performance of the media budget. But clients generally don't think in those terms. Instead, his agency was castigated for having spent the $X, and was forced to go back and renegotiate the original contract.

A lot of these strange dual price points in the industry reflect its nascent stage and will very likely become smoother over time as the industry continues to mature.

The Middlemen

A slew of companies sits between the buyers and sellers. We'll describe them in more tactical detail as they become relevant in subsequent chapters. They tend to be the companies offering technical and clerical services to help the buyers and sellers transact.

They include the banner serving companies, outfits that produce trafficking automation systems—like Solbright—database and analysis companies, and research firms.

If I were to draw a picture of the whole Internet media industry, I'd draw a line with five sections. On the two outside sections, I'd put the labels "Advertisers" and "Media Vendors." On the sections inside those two, I'd put the labels "Agencies" and "Reps." And in the center would reside these "middlemen" companies, helping inform and smooth the transactions between the two major sides.

ON AGENCIES

This book's readers come from many different backgrounds—marketers, clients, traditional agency people, interactive agency people, people trying to get their start in the industry—many of whom have nothing to do with ad agencies. But each of these groups needs to understand how an interactive ad process works. The most comprehensive way of covering this material is to show it through the eyes of someone in the ad agency.

In the interactive industry, the agencies are the engines under the hood. A client might choose not to employ an agency, but in its place, it will have to simulate one. The roles and responsibilities of the various agency players and processes warrant examination.

What Agencies Do—Partner or Vendor?

Here are the key responsibilities an ad agency performs for clients:

- Help develop over-arching brand and communications strategies
- Develop the most cost-efficient strategies for reaching the right people with the appropriate marketing messages
- Create the marketing messages
- Produce the ads that contain the marketing messages
- Deal with all the clerk work involved with this process, including legal approvals, ad trafficking, production, billing, discrepancy resolution, etc . . .

Agencies and their advertising clients often have different ideas about the role of the agency. Most people who run ad firms will tell you that the agencies are the business partners of the clients, determining the marketing strategies, the long-term branding, which products will be most appropriate to which audiences and sometimes even what new products should be developed.

Most clients consider the agency role to be more clerical in nature. The agencies take the marketing direction from the client's marketing staff and make ads, which then get placed in appropriate media. Clients consider ad agencies to be much like any other specialized business service, like accounting or legal work.

To truly be a partner to a client, the agency would have to be taking a lot into consideration, like all the business school stuff: cost of goods sold, relative margins, diminishing rates of return, government regulation, and about a hundred other things that liberal arts graduates joining ad agencies most often don't care to know.

Most agency folks are good marketers. Just marketers. It's an important piece of the puzzle—perhaps one of the three or four most important pieces of a business—but especially in traditional media, we've been just marketers. That began to change when interactive media came around.

Over the course of the last ten years, as large agencies have done more interactive work, these large agencies have run into the problems of having to deliver more strategic services. In the interactive realm, it was the ad agencies of major corporations that built the first web site and jumpstarted the e-commerce process. In the course of having to deliver on this consulting role, many agencies found that their existing structures weren't very well suited to such work.

It's very difficult to get agency account executives to change their behaviors or their limited roles in the process of marketing clients' goods. In interactive, we wind up selling directly to consumers and other businesses. That means we have to be aware of all sorts of things at the client that we never needed to know

13340-TILL

before, like how much inventory is available of certain products, how much it will cost to make some more, labor issues, exclusive reselling agreements with other parts of the retail channel, etc . . . The very structure of those big ad agencies prevented them from taking all these issues into account.

Another hiccup on the way to e-commerce proved to be the fact that many clients weren't structured well to interact with this new electronic business engine. When agencies start making suggestions about such things as product development and retooling manufacturing facilities, the senior people in various client departments sometimes felt threatened.

Back in the early 90s, before McDonald's Corporation or any other fortune 500 firm had a Web site, I sat in the McDonald's boardroom while the senior most officials from various departments filed in. Represented were marketing, media, operations, product development, legal, real estate, facilities, press relations, customer service, sponsorships and promotions. No one from my agency, in the 15 years they had been marketing McDonald's, had ever met all these people. In fact, as I watched, several of these folks were introducing themselves to one another. Right in front of me, the woman who ran customer service shook hands for the first time with the man who ran media. That site turned out to be the first reason a lot of these department heads found that they had common interests. In the course of the next few years, they were to find that there was a lot they could do on this new medium, but that they would have to work together very closely.

The people who helped manage this process at the ad agencies slowly, and mostly unknowingly, began to add to their responsibilities until they became fairly comprehensive. This is in good part why the agency process that evolved is a good model with which to describe all of the Internet marketing opportunities and tactics.

Why Use an Agency?

The marketing departments of medium-sized and large companies hire ad agencies largely because the agencies can often do two things a little better than their own in-house departments. They can buy better media for less money, and they can produce better creative concepts.

Because ad agencies do both things for many clients at once, they are able to constantly learn about the changing tastes of consumers, the media markets and provide refreshing insight into both the creative and media processes.

On the clerical side, the agency has the infrastructure to handle many media sites all at once, trafficking out different creative sizes and handling all the incoming data.

The Different Departments

Since the 1950s, agencies have divided up their responsibilities into areas of special expertise. The typical agency divvies up into three major departments and several minor ones. The big three are account, creative and media.

The account folks are jacks of all trades but masters of none. They are the managers. They orchestrate the whole process, posing themselves as the primary client contact and making sure that all the many processes finish more or less on time. They are also supposed to be the primary people helping the client with the broad marketing strategy. In theory, they are consulting with media and creative people to digest the best information to come up with insights that the clients will find valuable.

The creative people are responsible for conceptualizing the ads themselves. They write the words and come up with the imagery for advertising. Most frequently, they construct the "roughs" and hire out artists and copywriters with more narrow specialties to produce the finished work. They have a reputation for drinking a lot of latté and taking long lunches, and they tend to get away with a lot more at the agency than the folks wearing suits. An important thing to remember about the creative group is the unspoken hierarchy of status. People who work on network TV ads get more respect than people who create ads for cable and syndicated TV. Those people are, in turn, held in higher esteem than the folks doing print. Who are placed above those doing outdoor billboards, direct mail, matchbook covers, posters and, finally, online banners. As a new medium, online work has yet to win much status among creatives.

The media department is perhaps the most highly organized group. They are responsible for getting the most out of the media dollar. They need to figure out what media to use, negotiate the pricing and other deal elements, analyze results and even make suggestions to the other departments as a result of the analysis. The complexity and the empirical nature of these tasks lead naturally to a very hierarchical structure with many levels and subdivisions of expertise. Because of the media department's particular mission and relevance to things interactive, it is on this department that the book focuses.

Several other groups provide services to the other departments. The creative production department manages the process of making ads. The traffic department makes sure the right TV stations and magazines get the right ads at the right time, in the right sizes. The accounting department does the billing both to the media vendors and to the clients, and makes sure that the media vendors give their clients all the media they're due. Some agencies, generally the larger ones, also have research departments and account planning departments. These groups often drive the creation of the strategy behind the ads and the media buys, but the account groups tend to closely control these departments.

The Rise of the Media Department

The media department has traditionally been an under-appreciated group. They remain responsible for a great deal of the strategy behind marketing, yet they get treated like just another one of the smaller service groups within the agency, like accounting or trafficking. So, it's all the more notable that media departments in ad agencies have become—just in the last couple years—the darlings of the client. It's now media that wins or loses clients, just as much—if not more—than creative departments.

When a big Chicago agency first hired me out of college, they had me slated as an account guy, like they did everyone from my eastern school. I'd have to slog through a year or two of media, but I was marked as someone who would move on to bigger and better things once I'd passed this "training." I'd even get paid about 10 percent more than the people who were doomed to stay forever on the 9th floor in media, but who were doing identical work at the time.

They hired the media folks out of the state schools in the Midwest. I can tell you from personal experience that there are plenty of complete idiots graduating Ivy League schools, and that there are many utterly brilliant people coming out of state schools. But the firm liked things simple. You were either category A or category B, and those in category B were relegated to media.

In some ways, this became a self-fulfilling prophecy. By treating the media folks like second-class employees, the firm made the media job much less attractive. So the smart people in the department left—either for other firms or, more often, for media sales jobs where they'd double their pay. As a result, the remaining people took on the pallor of the Land of the Misfit Agency People.

The boards of directors of the ad agencies seldom had more than one or two media people on them. I know that at my firm, at the time, there was only one. The media departments were given the smallest offices on the lowest floors in the building. I can remember visiting a big firm in Portland, Oregon a few years back for a meeting we had with a common client. Their offices were a central part of that city's downtown restoration—a build-

13340-TILL

ing about which the whole town bragged. So, I was surprised to be led through a series of unfinished catwalks and basement passageways to a small, cramped, hot and noisy little office where they housed the media department. The symbolism was unavoidable: it was as though the creatives feared the media people would pollute their work if they were kept too close.

People reading this book who work in large traditional agencies know what I'm talking about. For all the denials from management, it's an attitude that remains difficult to hide. You can sense the air of superiority from other groups in many subtle ways—the way you're sometimes invited out to lunch; the way your offices always happen to face the alley; the way your group is asked to just "add on" a media plan to existing new business pitches. You are not asked to help with the core client strategies.

To explain all this, we have to remember how departments started out. People who worked in the industry back then are now dead, but you can get a caricature of the old "ad executive" by watching daytime syndicated TV. If you remember Darren from Bewitched, you might remember that his job involved media deals, writing ad copy and taking clients out to dinner. This ad "renaissance man" (and, yes, they were mostly men) was the norm, combining media, creative and account person in to one person. In the middle part of this last century, agencies began to create specialized departments. One of the first was the media group, siphoning off some of the least-liked work for the people who ran the firm.

Importantly, the firms founders saw themselves as fitting into the creative or account departments—not media. People starting up new firms through the 60s and 70s, 80s and 90s were almost all creative or account people. They always figured they could hire someone to do the media. The very top-most media people still weren't equity owners.

And then interactive media happened, and everything got turned on its head.

Media's New Primacy

Media departments came to dominate the interactive space because they lacked both the inertia of other departments and the conflicts of interest that prevented the other agency groups from piling on. While the account folks worried about profitability, and the creative folks worried about being demoted by working on something as low-status as an online ad, the media department seized their opportunity. There were new deals to be done, new standards to figure out. It was a whole lot more fun than buying spot television. The smartest new hires at the agency started to ask their bosses about transferring to the media group.

I remember a conversation I had with the media director back at Leo Burnett in Chicago. I knew he had been recruited decades before for an account position and had decided to stay in media, where he worked during his training. I told him I was considering the same thing. He told me I'd be an idiot. He'd learned in his career that no matter how smart you are, if you're in the media department, you're seen as just a media person. He said that once the interactive stuff began to take off and look interesting, the account and creative people would grab it back and make it theirs.

And, in retrospect, he was both right and wrong. He was right that this is what happened at his agency by the mid-90s. But he was wrong in that most high-spending interactive clients, by that time, had left the large agencies to hire new media agencies run by media people. I've always been an account person myself, but since I ran a few large interactive groups, most people I meet in the industry assume my background was in media.

Those people who quit to start the new agencies such as I-Traffic, Organic, Exile on 7th, Left Field and the like, were not creative executives. They didn't come from the account departments. They were media people, and they ate the lunches of the larger agencies that had previously failed to respect them.

This process can partly be attributed to the idiosyncrasies of the creative and account people themselves. Creatives have been turned off by the lack of richness of the interactive media. They wanted TV-quality production values, and they got instead the moral equivalent of matchbook covers. The account people couldn't figure out why they'd want to divert TV money—on which they made a very predictable margin—and shunt that over to this interactive stuff where they lost money hand over fist. On top of that, trying this new stuff made them feel very insecure. Account people can't position themselves as experts when they work in a medium so immature.

Here's a funny truism about creative and account people: we (I'm one) don't care so much about great marketing so much as we care about putting out great ads. And the ads in one medium appear a whole lot better—in terms of the status conferred upon the agency staff responsible—than the ads in other media.

It's generally accepted among agency people, especially creatives, that there exists a hierarchy of media. And as they advanced through their careers, these folks will climb the ladder of promotions to outdoor on their way to print which would precede radio, and eventually, the vaunted television. This becomes a self-fulfilling culture. The best creatives always want to do what they think is most respected. And most could care less about interactive stuff.

The media people turned out to be different. When interactive media rolled around, the culture of media departments was one of rigid boundaries. Most agencies had a set process, and deviating from this process earned you the ire of the media director. There wasn't a lot of room for creativity in the normal course of the day, which led to a funny trait in media people. Like computer programming engineers, they developed a talent and respect for "tricking" this system. If you could figure out a slightly more efficient manner of buying, or a way to exploit slightly better rates, you could be seen as a hero. So when interactive media arrived, the more ambitious and creative media people took to it like ducks to water.

Back in 1995, clients would dedicate an amount of money to an experimental interactive budget, and the creative people would look at as though they'd been kicked. It was the media people who would jump on it. And this set up a precedent that we'd never quite shake: the media people would define the type of media bought—whether it be banners, interstitials, sound files, online promotions, etc . . . The creatives would have to fit their creative ideas into whatever format the media people determined. And the account people, far from controlling this marketing process, would be left to make sure the creatives actually got their work done in the right format and on time.

At first this control of the process was limited. The banner sizes and different technologies varied so much that creatives wouldn't even agree to start work until everyone knew which sites were on the buy. But this order of battle caused the media departments to have to develop high-level marketing strategies to figure out their buys in the first place.

Smart people, who somehow found themselves working for an ad agency, began to yearn to move over to the media side, particularly the interactive media side. This became a problem for agencies in the late 90s because the brain drain was extreme. The interactive media groups grew so quickly that they had to steal staff from other departments, other agencies, and even other industries. A lot of new sales reps for sites were stolen back into the agency at this time, and they even got pay raises in the process.

It got to a point that a reverse stigma arose in the media department. The "cool" place to work was in media—specifically, interactive media. I can remember having difficulty, when running an interactive shop out of San Francisco in 1997, when some of the young traditional media staff came to me to discuss "the stigma." They were traditional media people who loved what they did, yet they felt somehow belittled by the process going on around them. Because of the strained labor markets, they were paid less even though they tended to be more senior than the interactive hires. But the thing that really stung was the fact that these young new media whippersnappers had an exploratory camaraderie, and they had been able to wrest control of the marketing process from the creative and account people. The traditional people wanted me to mandate similar powers for themselves. I wish I could have. I had to explain to them how there are many things one cannot mandate, among them culture and vigor. Getting traditional media creatives and account people to let the media folks into the strategy process would require a cultural change that is most difficult (I tried, like many before me). It's something that the media folks needed to take forcefully themselves.

Sometimes, when traditional media groups did attempt to take more control, disaster would result when the creatives refused to go along. At my first agency, when such an impasse occurred in the early 90's on the Tropicana account, it resulted in both the media teams travelling to the client's corporate headquarters to give their respective campaign presentations despite their not having resolved the power conflict. The creatives got up to show their nifty new television ads (they always want to do television), and the media folks got up and showed the client their highly-articulated outdoor billboard media campaign. That lead the client to utter the infamous line, "One of you is trying to shove a round peg into the other group's square hole." The results were both predictable: within a few months, the client was working with another agency, and they were doing the television campaign.

As they developed interactive capabilities in the mid 90s, some ad agencies didn't show the flexibility to allow for these natural shifts in power toward the media group. And at those agencies, many employees quit to join the new interactive agencies then popping up. The most talented—and thereby the most frustrated—people left in droves.

The new agencies that concentrated on interactive media were most often started by media folks. This was new. When I worked on the Sony account in 1994 at Leo Burnett as an account guy, I had an intern from the client's media group working for me. I turned around for a couple years, and when I saw him next that same guy had started I-Traffic. This stuff was happening all over the industry.

As clients sunk money into the interactive trend, they didn't tell their agency, "Go spend this on newer and better creative mechanisms." They told their agencies, "Go spend this money on more and better media vehicles."

A study done interactive agency K2 some years ago showed that the biggest factor, by far, in determining successful campaign response was the media selection. Intuitively, many in the online marketing business have assumed that tweaking the media portion of the campaign comprises time better spent than redesigning creative. The K2 study seemed to bear this out.

BUDGETING FOR INTERACTIVE MEDIA

Online Versus Offline

Advertisers need to first determine the rough proportions of where their marketing spending should go. There should be logical rationale as to why an advertiser spends a certain amount on broadcast media versus print versus online advertising. This usually happens in an annual planning process that will often start well before any money changes hands. Most major corporations start planning for the next year in the third quarter.

Most advertisers that spend millions of dollars have a division of labor within their marketing groups, divvying up the tasks by medium. As a result, these media-oriented employees will frequently ask their partners—often an ad agency given the particular media assignment—to help analyze how the media mix might be adjusted to better effect. A cynic would say that this is often an effort for each of these media groups to try to take a larger slice of the media spending pie, using their respective agencies to gin up excuses and research to suggest they should be given more billings.

The appropriate budget level for a particular medium relies on factors like the product category, target audience, and other variables. But even more so, it depends on the political culture of the advertiser.

The truth is that most budgets are divided across media not so much by the rational needs of companies and products, but by the seniority and authority of the people in charge of the various media. This makes the agency's job a bit complex in attempting to separate out a decent chunk of the money for interactive work.

Somewhere, deep in the bowels of the advertiser, there is a group of people very, very concerned with print (or TV, or outdoor, or . . . you get the picture). And they see the commandeering of media dollars as a direct attack on their worth as employees.

Step one is to determine who has the power to make decisions about the budget. At large advertisers these people are most often very senior, perhaps two or three layers of seniority above the person who is normally the client contact with an agency.

Step two is to make sure that senior managers put some scrutiny on their marketing managers. By pointing out the potential for irrational political motives to determine budget levels, the threat will be partly inoculated. When I worked for agencies handling large interactive accounts, I used to roll around a budgeting presentation to various client management types. The presentation contained three elements:

- A quantification of the cost per sale inspired by each medium
- An estimation of the point where each medium begins to show a diminishing rate of returns in terms of advertising effectiveness against a given audience
- A competitive analysis of what other companies were doing with different media in the same industry segment

At the very least, it forced the marketing managers responsible for the traditional media budgets to make up rationale as to why they should earn the brunt of the budget. And once the budgeting process was placed in those rational terms, the interactive media naturally began to gather a greater and greater portion of the budget as it proved its worth.

People on the ad agency side of the business need to consider some of the internal politics of those organizations as well. Over the course of many decades of relative stability in the traditional media markets, agencies have developed structures that tend to reward employees with greater and greater responsibilities. This generally means larger and larger budget allocations. When these budgets go through major shifts—say taking a large chunk of a print budget and putting it into online advertising—this can be perceived as a threat to the career of an account director or a media director. Pains should be taken to ensure all of these stakeholders that any budget allocation should be predicated on market rationale rather than the seniority of the respective manager. Interactive marketing directors sometimes find themselves in a position where they lose budget arguments due largely because of their youth and relative inexperience.

The Product Category

So what is the right percentage? The type of product will determine this in good part. Here are some factors that would tend to increase the percentage we should be spending online:

- The percentage of selling or fulfillment that occurs online
- The degree to which the product's purchasers can be found online
- The importance to the product category of purchaser online research and evaluation
- Audience expectations that the product should be seen online

Likewise, several factors might move dollars over to the traditional media side:

- Product categories may imply certain audiences that are difficult to target online, or otherwise easier to reach traditionally

- The company's CEO may want to make a big traditional media splash to help the stock price (just so everyone's on the same page, this is against Securities and Exchange Commission rules)

The Metric Value

Some companies are able to take the data gleaned from online work—or traditional direct mail work for that matter—and use this learning for future marketing, product development or other reasons.

To the degree that a client has the infrastructure to take advantage of this data, it makes more sense to spend media where this flow of data will be harvested. Direct mail and interactive media do well in this category.

Working on Match.com, a computer dating service account in the late 1990's, my agency discovered that the people who wound up paying subscription fees for the service had several consistent traits that weren't intuitive to us at first. This allowed the client to adapt their marketing—and eventually even the product itself—to this more important audience.

Compensation

Finally, and of course cynically, you don't want your client to be spending many online dollars with you if it isn't willing to pay the premiums necessary to properly do this work.

Online media is more expensive when it comes to agency resources, production, tracking and analysis. Many are the time we've suggested clients not spend online, if they weren't prepared to do it correctly.

To pay for all of this management overhead, it makes sense to spend online only if the campaigns involve more than $50,000. Otherwise, the percentage eaten up by the campaign management becomes too oppressive. It's not often an agency will be able to provide all the planning, buying, management, trafficking and analysis functions in a campaign for fewer than $10,000. When the media budget begins to decline below that $50,000 figure, the overhead costs begin to appear too burdensome to justify spending online.

The Percentages

Ultimately, the budgets for individual campaigns must extend from their specific objectives. Based on previous similar experiences, an agency can then develop best- and worst-case scenarios of response rates (or other objective success criteria). From that, a realistic budget can be estimated to achieve the objectives.

So, factoring in all these influences, I find that most marketing budgets can reasonably find themselves spending between 20 and 60 percent of their marketing dollars online. Retailers and the soap companies might see a proportion much lower than this, and software companies might see it a bit higher.

Agencies often experience a financial conflict of interest in recommending these proportions. When you factor in all the labor costs, agencies make a much, much better margin spending money on network television. It's not surprising that with a staff that wishes to be seen involved in TV work and a corporate management that requires the margins seen in television advertising, the agency view of the world becomes slanted toward the traditional media.

As a generalization, if an advertiser sells product online, or finds its primary target audience reachable online, they will need to re-examine the motives behind budget allocation to interactive of less than 10 percent of their overall spending.

Minimum Weights

This is an issue that comes up frequently: what is the minimum amount of impressions or dollars that should be dedicated to a media buy? Every time a new site comes around, or a new section within a site comes out or perhaps a new targeting mechanism appears within an older site, we face the question of how many impressions will give us a good idea of the way this media performs.

When an advertiser first starts out with online advertising, they will also want to know what minimum weight should be dedicated per campaign. This number can be figured by multiplying the minimum buy figures by the number of buys we determine a campaign needs to have.

To answer these questions, let's suppose we are a new advertiser to the web. Let's further stipulate that we market a product with a broad enough audience that we have to choose from among many sites. In this scenario, we need to purchase enough sites to be able to compare the different types of media to determine which ones we'll want to buy in the future. And we'll need to purchase enough media on each site to get a sufficient sampling.

The first hurdle to leap will be purchasing enough impressions to be statistically significant. This usually turns out to be a low hurdle, as impressions run pretty cheap. We can get tens of thousands of impressions for several hundred dollars.

But buying such a small lot of impressions would make our media "flight" end almost as soon as it began. That wouldn't give us a very good idea of how the media performs over time. This will skew the test. If we buy only 50 M impressions, and they run over the course of ten minutes on a Tuesday night at 3 a.m., we could get some pretty funky performance results. We need to either buy several different lots over the course of a week's time, or purchase enough media to ensure that the site will not have the opportunity to "flush" the buy out too quickly. Most sites do assume that the impressions should be meted out evenly over the course of the contract's term.

Controls are problematic, particularly with unique types of media or new types of media. When trying to test the effective-

13340-TILL

ness of a new manner of geographical targeting, for instance, we need to control that test with another—known—geographical targeting media buy. And this can be a royal pain when we're trying to match up the relative effectiveness of the two buys on a region-by-region basis. You need to purchase an awful lot of media to make sure you get a large enough sample in any one geographical location.

One last factor worth bringing up remains the issue of burn-out, especially in vertical industries and the business-to-business space. When working with a narrow audience within the constraints of a narrow topic, it's quite easy to purchase too much media. We can buy all the relevant sites and wind up getting the same viewers over and over again. This is especially true when employing targeting technologies.

A great example is the keyword buy. While, under normal circumstances, very few viewers might overlap from a site A to a site B, when you purchase a keyword on both sites, you will very likely get a much higher overlap. We call this overlap "duplicated reach."

If you use one of the syndicated research panel companies to attempt to determine the duplicated reach from one site to the next, you could be gravely deceived. They use a methodology that fails to take into account specific targeting, such as keywords.

So, how do we figure out how much media to buy? We apply two tests.

For the first test, we make sure we're purchasing enough media. Are we buying enough impressions to be significant? Does our test remain significant even when we break down all the different targeting pieces? Will the media run over the course of a period of time so that we don't get strange time-of-day and day-of-week problems?

For the second test, we make sure we aren't buying too much media. This is best determined by watching declining response rates, the typical symptom of burn-out.

In most cases, we find that we need to purchase about 10

sites to begin to get an idea of how the different media vehicles compare against one another in efficiency. And on each of those sites, we need to purchase at least $5,000 of media. Some sites even have minimums ranging between $1,000 and $5,000 per month. After conducting the analysis, I usually wind up quoting a minimum campaign media spend of about $50,000, but it does vary by client type and the particular circumstances of a campaign. With fewer than $50,000 it becomes difficult to usefully employ the performance results to determine with precision the success of the various elements.

How Much Should Marketing Services Cost?

Strange partnerships develop in the world of interactive. Ad agencies now compete with interface design firms. Computer programming houses vie against multimedia advertising production firms. Which is all at once very invigorating to these industries, but it begs the question: how much should anyone be paid for a project that will elicit radically different bids?

Most of these different types of companies ask for compensation based on the rates and structures of their respective industries. Programmers submit underestimated hours and associated fees. Design and multimedia firms choose an arbitrary round number for their creative product, trying to guess how much the client is willing to pay. Agencies take educated guesses as to the hours they'll put against managing the process and try to pad the numbers where they can. This all becomes evident when these different types of companies compete against one another for the same piece of business.

Pricing Bedlam

On a project I helped manage for Sun Microsystems, five companies that do Java programming came back with bids ranging from $8,000 to $120,000. At first, I thought some of the competitors misunderstood the scale of the project. But in follow-up conversations with the bidders, it became clear that everyone understood the very specific tasks at hand. The discrepancy came instead from intrinsic cost structures within these very different types of companies.

The small programming houses looked at the project simply as a series of programming objects that had to be repurposed or written anew. Their bids were the cheapest by an order of magnitude.

The web development/multimedia firms saw this as a big creative project against which they would mobilize tens of their staff. Even though all the graphics and copy were already made, they were asking for more than $100,000.

The high bidder told me, "Well, think of it this way. Your client will spend millions on their media, hundreds of thousands on producing a single TV commercial. Why should this be different?"

The multimedia folk tried to price the project not against what it would cost them, but by what they perceived the market normally bears. And if they weren't competing against a different type of company, they just might have won it. As it was, the small programming house won the project.

Some clients find the higher bids tempting when they involve large, brand name companies. The theory holds that these larger companies are more likely to get the project done correctly and on time. My own experience does not bear this out. My anecdotal experience tells me that the very high-end and costly service companies tend to rely greatly on their reputation to justify the prices. On the other end, I've had very poor luck with low bidders with very little experience.

Past experience seems to be the one consistent attribute of the companies that successfully performed various multimedia, programming and production tasks for my own clients. I would much rather hire a company that successfully handled several similar projects than a company with great brand recognition or a surprisingly low price.

IMPORTANCE OF OBJECTIVES

Making a campaign succeed at its objectives is a difficult-yet-rewarding process. Ensuring the advertiser chooses the correct objectives in the first place, alas, can be a harder task, attended by few short-term rewards. Yet marketing departments and their ad agencies must get advertisers to choose specific and useful objectives, or they will find themselves in a budgetary dead end months later, when they have few measurable results to show a relative efficiency against other media.

Some advertisers have their marketing people and their ad agencies move quickly to purchase online media for vague and general objectives, like "creating an online presence" or "conducting online branding." Both of those objectives can be valid, useful things to accomplish, but they most often do not answer specific and real client needs. After campaigns like this take place, it becomes more difficult to justify continued media spending.

For better or worse, campaigns involving measurable objective success tend to be augmented, while campaigns with vague goals and results tend to get cut in the subsequent budgeting discussions. Many times, this is a rational process, but sometimes this becomes unfair to the less tangible, yet valid, types of marketing, such as branding.

This trend results in many interactive agencies and marketing departments concentrating almost exclusively on direct marketing-oriented tasks. Many clients do find that interactive marketing suits their direct response purposes, but that other media remain more efficient for branding purposes. But, more often, the branding baby is figuratively thrown out with the bath water, even as the online media often a highly-targeted audience with a great deal of efficiency.

Regardless of the determined objective, branding does happen. And it can happen both positively and negatively. Several times, clients I've worked with have—especially when refining direct response online creative—discovered that ads have a negative effect on the consumers' image of the client's brand. High-end brands, like DeBeer's Diamonds, Lexus automobiles or Versace clothing will do well to avoid the blinking-price-reduction-type creative that often results from responding to performance metrics limited to clickthroughs and sales.

These branding disasters happen when the media people fail to communicate well enough with the creative people. Very often, the briefing documents given to the creative department properly tell the creative folks what branding limitations they have in putting together a piece of creative. The campaign starts out properly enough, but as it progresses and the media folks start to switch out creatives based on performance, something goes awry. The media people might ask the creative and production departments to make slight changes to the ad based on clickthrough results, and the creative can morph into a branding monster. This happens especially when a sales department at the advertiser company, as opposed to the marketing department, retains a great deal of say in the progress of a campaign. Immediate sales response tactics can conflict with controlled branding strategies.

Often, accustomed to the practices of traditional media, the creative departments don't take much time to check in on campaigns once they start to run. They fail to do so at the peril of the client's brand.

Marketing departments within advertiser companies, and especially the ad agencies they retain, must recognize that they have only limited authority in setting objectives. Many marketing columns and textbooks have been written telling these workers how simple it is to choose from among more useful objectives. But the practical realities in the real-world work environment dictate several often-overlooked limitations. Specifically, processes by which objectives are set depend entirely on two highly-political advertiser company decisions: general corporate strategy and budget allocations.

Pitfalls in Setting Objectives:

- Ad agencies most often find themselves with little control over objective decisions. Most interactive agencies become engaged in the marketing process immediately after the objectives have been set internally at the client. The longer-term the relationship, and the more respected the previous agency performance, the more likely the agency will be allowed into the objective-creation process.

  However, some agencies do suggest completely new campaigns to satisfy novel objectives. While this presents difficulties in approval and funding, clients often appreciate this type of initiative. It can go a long way to gain the respect of a client.
- Marketing departments at the advertiser companies frequently have very limited mandates, giving very little flexibility in the types of objectives they can attempt. It might be that the sales department remains responsible for direct marketing efforts, while the marketing department that interfaces with the agency can only conduct awareness and branding efforts. On the other hand, an advertiser company might retain a separate ad agency to handle print and TV branding, preventing the online agency from delving too deeply into that type of marketing.

  Direct marketing efforts are tricky for a lot of marketers because they necessarily involve different advertiser company departments that otherwise wouldn't interact together. Inventory management, fulfillment staff, production managers and all sorts of other advertiser employees often must be involved in the process for it to work smoothly.

- Even with explicit direction as to which measures will accurately reflect success relative to an objective, some people at the advertiser company will insist on looking at the available direct response metrics. Despite the fact that the marketing group informs other departments that a particular campaign will be judged by a pre- and post-campaign branding study, some people will still insist on comparing the results to other past campaigns based on clickthroughs, leads and sales. Information like this, that can be abused, is best left out of post-buy documents and other published reports.
- Budgeting between different media types and different types of marketing tasks is most often pre-determined by political realities existing at the advertiser company. Over decades, companies have become accustomed to giving the larger budgets to the more senior people who, over time, have graduated through the media types upwards toward television. Taking TV brand budgets and giving them to young Internet upstarts goes against the instincts of many in management. To fund new online efforts, it sometimes seems to management as though they are punishing the groups dealing with other media and the people who lead those groups. To free up these funds, the managers of the traditional media budgets must be engaged in the process and made to understand that money might be shifted not due to a failure on their part, but due to an opportunity in the new media.
- Because an ad agency is denied permission to change the objective of a campaign does not mean it will not be held accountable for that campaign's subsequent failure to help a client. Agencies have a great incentive to make sure objectives make sense and remain realistic: their future billings depend on it.

- Ad agency management, fearing the introduction of agency competition, will very infrequently turn down a client's request to fulfill a campaign, no matter how obvious the folly of the objective. This puts the staff that has to follow through with these projects in a strange position. Agencies who do refuse to participate in certain types of campaigns—knowing them to be folly—will often benefit in subsequent marketing partner evaluations. Despite management fears to the contrary, I've found that clients come back to the marketing partners who have the guts to turn down work.

Steps to Deal with the Pitfalls:

- First, understand who at the advertiser company has the power to set objectives. More often than not, the marketing contacts with which ad agencies interact only have a relatively narrow leeway with campaign objectives. They've been given certain moneys to accomplish certain tasks. Trying to make these types of marketing departments change their objectives radically can only breed resentment toward the agency.
- If the advertiser company shows bias toward giving funds to traditional media, the best solution is to bring the issue up in the very beginning of objective-setting discussions. Once the issue is aired out, subsequent discussions tend to avoid the irrational biases toward one medium or another. It also prevents employees dealing with the different media from growing resentments toward one another.
- Get buy-in from the departments in the advertiser company who benefit most from the type of objective being achieved. If it makes sense to exploit online media for direct response purposes, make sure that the sales and other departments get behind it.

13340-TILL

- When campaigns prove to be successful, sometimes the marketing groups grow frustrated that these programs do not get expanded. The odds of being rewarded with larger subsequent budgets increase when the prospect is brought up before the campaign's successful performance becomes known. Marketers should propose contingent additional budgets that depend on reaching targets. This strategy works especially well with direct response marketing, where marketers can quantitatively establish the profitability of the media buys.
- Make sure all interested parties understand the "blessed" metrics that will be employed to determine success or failure. Sometimes different departments or different levels of a company will make different assumptions about which performance data will be relevant in evaluating a campaign. This information should be agreed upon even before campaign planning begins.
- Conversely, before a campaign begins, explicitly state which performance measures will be ignored. In a perfect world, irrelevant campaign measures—like clickthrough in a campaign dedicated to a direct sales effort—shouldn't even be provided to people beyond the media folks responsible for tabulating the statistics.

Setting Objectives and Metrics for Success

Objectives and the metrics used to measure their accomplishment need to be decided in tandem. They fall into two broad categories: direct response and branding. Here are some examples and the corresponding choices of metrics that we can apply.

Branding: Affecting Brand Image

In both traditional and online media, these types of campaigns typically do not have the benefit of direct success feedback. Accustomed to having plenty of post-buy data to play with, some interactive buyers dislike branding campaigns for this reason. But we can at least show a comparative success relative to branding efforts in other media by comparing the degree to which the media proves efficient relative to a specific target reached.

For instance, an advertiser may pay a CPM of $5 to advertise a cake mix in a general interest magazine. If the advertiser only cares about women older than 34 years of age, then it might find about 3/4 of the impressions were wasted. That gives an effective CPM of $20. Online buys can be compared to these rates by calculating the degree to which the media is correctly targeted. An online media buy with a CPM of $15 would prove the more efficient branding medium, so long as the wastage turned out to be lower than 33 percent.

This all presumes—as has been established in many studies to date—that an impression seen online has the rough equivalent effect as one seen in traditional media. It turns out that, in study after study conducted within many product categories, that this is shown to be true. Frankly, this surprises a lot of people, including even some interactive advocates.

A seminal study done in 1997 by Millward Brown determined that both TV and the Internet banner ad produced about the same rate of recall. About one in ten people would recall an ad and its associated brand a day after one exposure to either a 30-second TV ad or an online banner.

A couple years later, IPSOS-ASI, another highly-respected, independent research firm produced very similar results with a very different methodology. As a study author put it, "Our clients asked us to 'show us something definitive, a side-by-side comparison of the Web and TV.'" They tested more than 300 banner ads across more than 40 brands to conclude that, "What we have is two media, and one is equally effective as the other at getting ads noticed."

Branding: Awareness

In striving to increase awareness online, we can measure both the number of impressions seen by specific targets, and we can also develop rough estimates of the number of unique viewers of a campaign, as well as average frequencies.

Also, the relative efficiency of acquiring impressions among a special target proves a good tool with which we can compare media.

Many advertisers have done offline research to confirm the awareness benefits they receive from their online advertising. In one such study, release in 2000, Travelocity showed that their brand awareness grew 16 percent among those exposed to their ad campaign. Where people were exposed to a higher than average frequency of ad exposure, their brand awareness grew even more When they showed people ads more than four times, the brand awareness grew 44 percent.

When agencies purchase media from certain ad networks, they will sometimes have additional branding measurement options. Doubleclick, for instance, offers a service called Brand Impact, and 24/7 Media offers a variant of Dynamic Logic's AdIndex. These services conduct online polling to help determine branding levels before and after a campaign.

These types of services will help measure the impact of the creative, determining the increase in brand awareness caused by certain numbers of ad exposures. They also measure purchase intent relative to the number of ad exposures—a figure very important to know when trying to determine how much average frequency you want to purchase on a given site.

Direct Response: Driving Traffic

While simply driving traffic to a site sometimes doesn't do an advertiser any good, sometimes the traffic itself is the objective. Sites that sell advertising, for instance, need viewers to come to the homepage. When they do, the site sells the impressions created by the visit. This is one of the simpler campaigns to measure, as the clickthrough figures tend to determine performance quite well.

A campaign's success will be measured by the cost per click, or perhaps the cost per click relative to another medium's efficiency in delivering traffic. Occasionally, the metric will be limited to visitors who come within a very specific period of time. When sites conduct celebrity chats, for instance, they require the ads to have a certain timeliness in their performance.

Direct Response: Customer Acquisition

Getting someone to buy something involves more complicated measures. The impressions and clickthroughs now don't mean much. In fact, it's been proven that clickthrough rates and exposure levels have little correlation to purchasing. To measure the success of a sales-oriented campaign, we must measure sales.

A media director at Carat Interactive, a big shop in Boston, used to like to show a spreadsheet to his new clients that showed how there was often no relationship between the simple measures of impressions and clicks with sales. The graph laid out a composite of his clients' sales with the composite of the clicks and impressions. It looked like a tangle of pillars.

In 2000, AdKnowledge released a study more formally proving this. They showed that the ads with the highest clickthroughs had lower conversion rates from click to sale than the average ads. They found that 62 percent of the time, the ad with the best clickthrough wasn't the one with the best return on investment.

But using sales as a metric becomes difficult because the sales data comes not from the agency or media site, but from the client's site. Marketers frequently find their client data hard to acquire, and often in formats that make the analysis difficult.

If the media planners hope to determine which sites or pieces of creative prove most efficient per sale, they must have the client site data very well integrated with the sites data as well as the agency's pricing data.

This allows the calculation of the several potentially relevant measures:

- Cost per inquiry
- Cost per transaction
- Cost per lead
- Or may be even the cost divided by the average lifetime profit value of a newly-acquired customer

Buyers need to be aware that even these metrics will not entirely measure the benefits of these online campaigns. Confirming what many in the industry suspected, Avenue A released a study in 2000 that showed banner ads raise Web site visits, registrations and sales even with people do not click on an ad. These seemingly ambient visits and transactions generally don't get credited properly to the campaign.

Direct Response: Maximizing Customer Profit

When the data between site, agency and client are exceptionally well consolidated into one database, and only under these conditions, customer profit analysis can be done. This examines the effect on particular ad messages on individuals and types of individuals to determine their effects on sales relative to the necessary media costs.

Proctor & Gamble conducted such a study in 2000, proving that sales rose in one of their snack food brands during a controlled 16-week online campaign. The sales volume increased 19 percent, even though the clickthrough for their ads was a mere 0.27 percent.

Direct Response: Research

Sometimes clients advertise just to learn things about their customers or their messages. This is a form of direct response marketing, requiring a high percentage of people approached to respond with information. The important measurements becomes the rate at which surveys are filled out (because the higher the rate, the more accurate the research will be) as well as the cost per filled survey.

In setting the objectives, the marketers must ensure they are both specific and measurable. And, pending the success or failure of campaigns, they must be revisited over time to make sure the medium's potential gets maximized.

PHASES OF THE AGENCY MEDIA PROCESS

The planning process remains best described from the perspective of an ad agency buyer. While media people in other roles, like marketing managers at client advertisers, will not need to go through all the steps an agency buyer will, they will benefit from understanding the complete process. It will become obvious to the non-agency folks where certain steps can be skipped, such as obtaining client approvals. The process may be broken up into phases:

- Phase 1: Creating briefs from campaign objectives
- Phase 2: Preplanning, to get broad direction for subsequent planning efforts
- Phase 3: Planning
- Phase 4: Negotiating
- Phase 5: Buying
- Phase 6: Trafficking
- Phase 7: Campaign Management
- Phase 8: Analysis

PHASE 1: ESTABLISHING STRATEGY—DEFINING OBJECTIVES

Marketing staff at the advertiser and the more senior people at the agency tend to be the people who help determine objectives and strategies. Often, the media director or media supervisor will work with the account department to determine the strategy that fits both the client's overall campaign objectives and those on which the online media budget will focus.

In traditional media, the creative staff tends to have more input in the strategy forming process, but they tend to have less influence in the online strategy determination. This is in part because the creatives tend to be less interested in the objectives on which online campaigns tend to focus, like direct sales and lead generation. But it's also because the execution in interactive work is much more media-focused.

A successful online media campaign necessarily includes a stated objective that allows for strategies to be executed in such a way that the agency can determine the levels of success for each buy. The media people need to be able to focus on a "blessed" number. It might be the ultimate cost per sale for a campaign looking to make money or perhaps the clickthrough rate for a campaign designed to drive traffic to a media site. Blessing a number allows for a specific, iterative process, whereby the agency can continue to improve the results of the advertising as the campaign progresses.

Without this feedback information, we would only know that the money was spent—not the effect it had. If online media were less expensive than TV or print, this wouldn't be such a problem. But given the reality that online media tends to be more expensive on a CPM basis than other media, merely spending the money will not make this online part of the campaign appear competitively spent relative to the other parts of the overall campaign.

There are exceptions to this rule. An advertiser that requires a very specific target audience, more easily reached online, might choose to buy impressions in a campaign that lacks accountable measurement—provided they cost less. But unless the online portion of the overall campaign takes advantage of this or another unique advantage of the online medium, the budget will later appear ill-spent.

Most failed online campaigns today suffer from ill-defined objectives. Most also suffer from strategies that might make sense in the offline world, while not necessarily providing for executable or measurable tactics in the online environment.

A frequent cause of unmeasured online media campaigns can be traced to attempts to make the traditional media objectives of a campaign perfectly match the online objectives. Most online media buyers have worked with clients who attempt to make their online media purchases complement the offline campaign's creative. Most often, these campaigns wind up providing very little feedback in terms of tangible results, merely adding to the number of impressions the overall campaign achieved. While branding is an achievable objective with online media, strategies need to be developed specially for the medium to best take advantage of the buy. Merely pasting the brand name on banners to compliment an offline campaign is likely an inefficient use of media dollars. Other media are often less expensive for bulk impression purchases.

Our priority should be ensuring that the online objective and strategies contribute to the overall objectives of a larger campaign, while making sure we fully exploit the value of the online opportunities for those parts of the budget dedicated to online.

Most online campaign objectives can be broken down into two categories: response objectives and branding objectives. These need not be exclusive of one another, but they are best described independently.

Response objectives tend to play to the online medium's strengths. Better than most other media, we can measure in a variety of ways how viewers respond to seeing ads. These objectives may include seeking more information from the advertiser, purchasing something, and giving information to an advertiser. Testing the success of such a campaign frequently involves looking at three different sets of data:

- The agency's list of negotiated media rates and buys (to count the costs)
- The sites' subsequent impression levels and clickthrough rates (to count the exposure)
- And the subsequent user behavior as measured on the advertiser's site (to see if the exposure had the desired effect)

A quick warning on clickthrough as a measurement of success: Many online buyers fall back to the clickthrough measurement as the metric to determine success merely because it's the last measurement in the chain that's easily obtained. Sites send their impression and clickthrough numbers back to the agencies, and it becomes tempting to rely on these numbers as the determination of performance.

Clickthrough can, indeed, indicate that a user is responding to a particular offer, but this depends on the creative used. If a banner reads, "Click here to get find out where you can buy Brand X dog food," you will likely get a decent measure of purchase interest. But if the creative involves a celebrity endorsement of the dog food, you will likely be getting a strange mix of measurements, including the popularity of the celebrity. Each piece of creative needs to be judged as to how useful it will render the clickthrough metric.

Some folks in the industry advocate throwing out clickthrough rates altogether, since it's so frequently abused as a metric. But understanding its limitations, and the individuality of its nature, will allow for some useful performance measurement.

Most companies find branding objectives very difficult to measure. Sometimes an advertiser will invest in a branding study, polling viewers to determine the effectiveness of a campaign. More often, media buyers will merely use the comparison of how efficiently a specific target is reached online to help determine the relative efficiency of employing online media in a branding campaign relative to the traditional media. Because of a great number of corroborating studies, media planners assume that—given the proper creative—online impressions are about as effective as offline impressions for branding purposes.

A testing regimen should be established well before the site selection process begins, letting the people who choose the media vehicles know the criteria against which their decisions will be judged.

Audience

The first decision marketers need to make regarding the target audience of an online campaign is whether or not to allow the online part of the campaign to specialize relative to the broader campaign. Oftentimes, target audiences for large media campaigns are defined in terms that make sense for print and television—like audience demographics. Depending on the product category and desired audience, it often makes sense for the online component of media budgets to be spent against a smaller segment of this target—like a portion of that larger group, or the ones who happen to exhibit a particular type of behavior we can measure online.

Online media provides many ways to get to a company's audience. We can go ahead and apply demographic relationships, trying to purchase those sites that attract the proper segment. We can target a psychographic, much like traditional media. But interactive media also allows us to go directly to the *behaviors* most relevant to our marketing ends, obviating the need to deal with indirect relationships like demographics. For example, unlike in most other media, we can reach people who are *acting* like they are interested in buying a car.

The way an advertiser states its target audience frequently has a radical influence on the sites and technologies used in a campaign. While "men 34 to 48, 100K+" might lead to the choice of certain types of content sites that get such traffic, "brokerage account users" will lead to the choosing of more specific content sites. "People who have visited a brokerage site in the past 10 minutes" would give an even more specific range of people, and probably result in the use of one of the available profiling technologies.

In general, the more targeted our audience, the more expensive the media will be. So, we always have to monitor the targeting premiums versus our demonstrated increase in advertising effectiveness. It might be twice as effective to reach people with a special targeting technology offered by a site, but if that technology costs four times the rate for untargeted media, it's not worth it. Inevitably, a media buy will reach a point where additional targeting will not be worth the additional targeting costs.

To better exploit the online dollars, media buyers will sometimes want to further refine the targets already being applied in their print and television campaigns for a client. This is most often done by adding an additional behavioral measure. Instead of merely reaching men, for instance, the buyer might want to reach men who are putting the words "hair loss" into search engine queries. It is frequently this additional level of audience qualification that justifies the slightly higher CPMs in online advertising.

The Briefs

The objectives and strategies of a campaign need to be boiled down into two important briefing documents for campaign execution. The creative brief and the media brief should be concocted so that each complements the other. This might sound obvious, but a lot of ad agencies are so compartmentalized that departments frequently have difficulty working together closely on strategy issues.

The creative brief is a document that tells the creative people exactly what they are supposed to attempt to make the target think or do. It is the basic working document that directs them to do their work. [See example in appendix.] In most traditional media campaigns, the media folks have very little to do with the creative brief. Online is different. The brief needs to include not just the online target, but also the mechanism that the media people are likely to use to find that online target. The creative will need to be radically different if the media folks are planning on using search engine keywords to reach a target, as opposed to demographic or content targeting. For example, a banner scheduled to appear on search engines with the keyword "hair tonic" will likely be different than the creative used more broadly on sites with men.

The media brief similarly spells out the tasks at hand. It defines the level of budget, the desired target, the messaging that will be involved and any other required criteria for choosing sites. [See example in appendix.]

Sometimes one brief needs to be completely designed around another. When rich media was very new, for instance, advertisers experimenting with the creative would task the media people merely with finding the few sites that could display the new, richer creative work. Likewise, creative briefs are occasionally written solely because of a special sponsorship deal negotiated by the media team, requiring special creative assets and sometimes even slightly different positioning or messaging. These processes cannot be completely divorced unless the agency intends on conducting very predictable, non-customized buys for creative that is indistinguishable from previous work.

Both creative and media components to a campaign will require that attention be paid to the measurements that will determine which elements succeed or fail. They need to know, for instance, what type of performance—and based on what metrics—a site will be dropped from the buy. This should be spelled out in the respective briefs, along with the proposed actions that depend on the results. Will the creative be revisited and modified given learnings that will inevitably happen in the first part of a campaign? These resources need to be noted from the very beginning so that the people working off the briefs can make sure they learn what they need to know for the subsequent work.

Having complete and mutually understood briefs in the creative and media departments sets the advertisers up for potential success.

PHASE 2: PREPLANNING

The preplanning stage lets the planner roughly determine what types of strategies to pursue given the set of objectives laid out in the briefs.

Planners will frequently consult several data sources, as well as their own intuition, to figure out what categories of media opportunities should be investigated. No one can sift through every site and targeting option out there for each campaign. Some winnowing down needs to be done, and the preplanning phase accomplishes this.

Agency-Side Data

The very first place to look for useful information on an upcoming campaign should be the information already collected by the client and agency. Especially if the campaign is another installment of a series of campaigns, data that the advertiser and agency collect will usually prove much more useful than any other source of data that might be found or bought. The experience collected by the particular brand, with the unique positioning and market share, the particular target audience and product gives a much more controlled set of data to use for future predictions. Experience shows that this proprietary data almost always predicts future campaign performance much better than any syndicated research source an advertiser might purchase, like Media Metrix or @plan.

Many of the assumptions advertisers make turn out to be false. There are so many details affecting the result of a customer seeing an ad, it's impossible to predict how a particular piece of creative or a media placement will perform. It might be that one product category's competition positions itself in such a manner as to render certain types of creative more or less effective. In another product category, the relative media weights of the larger and smaller players may have a great effect on the burn-out rates of certain buys. The point is, there are literally tens of dimensions and hundreds of factors that affect the effectiveness of any placement. Using client-side or agency data that already "control" for these factors remains the best way to control the chaos.

To illustrate the complexity of the relationships, it might serve to think of a phrase that might be used in many different conversations. If we took one phrase and inserted it rather randomly into 100 different conversations at random points, we'd get a wide variety of responses from the listeners. Most times, our phrase would seem like a completely irrelevant interjection. Sometimes it would happen to appear appropriate, and perhaps even witty. Other times it might give offense, depending on the context. That isn't much different from showing a piece of creative in different places at different times to different people doing various things. Anyone who thinks they can gauge the reaction with a great deal of precision or consistency is in for some disappointment.

We've found, however, when we began to track these creative placements on different sites, that our previous buys and campaigns turn out to be the most predictive about our future performance. If we were to continue with the conversation analogy, it would be as if we decided to drop this random phrase only into certain types of conversations—where the product category and brand elements were all the same. When we do this, we stand a greater chance of being able to predict the reaction.

Those syndicated research companies that sell data on web site traffic and user demographics can provide interesting directional information, but they don't come close to being able to provide information as relevant as our own past campaign data.

The Internet has given us the power to increase the scrutiny we put on our past decisions. One of the more frustrating aspects of an accountable medium like the Internet has been the tendency for it to repeatedly prove our predictions wrong. The ad industry values a certain character trait among its executives—this elusive quality sometimes called "ad gut." And, in traditional media, it's difficult to show that someone's gut feel about a piece of creative or a media placement turned out to be wrong. The interactive folks have no such luxury. Automated reporting servers email our mistakes on spreadsheets to us each morning at 9 a.m. But that very learning can be accrued and that experience used later with the next campaign—so long as it is carefully collected and preserved in a useful form.

The most typical, and the least sophisticated, way for agencies to keep this information is in the spreadsheets used for planning and post-buy performance reporting. These are useful for quick reference in a subsequent campaign, but they quickly become unmanageable when, seven campaigns later, a planner sits in a cubicle with eight post-buy reports, trying to make sense of all of them all at once.

The better method is to track everything in an agency-side database, enabling planner to ask the database important questions, like what happened over the last year of campaigns across a particular type of client, on a special type of site, with a specific type of creative. This type of sophisticated analysis can't be gleaned across multiple spreadsheets.

Unfortunately, very few agencies have the capability to keep all their post-buy performance in one database. The advent of banner serving (more on this in a future chapter) has meant that the agencies have been limited to the compartmentalized reports available to those systems and limited to the relatively poor data consistency they provide.

Agencies face another problem with their performance data databases, when they can't always capture the many variables needed to determine why something succeeded or failed. The better ones take into account different variables about the creative used, the type of copy, the campaign objective, the number of times the banner was shown to an individual and other types of factors that might materially affect the viewer's reaction. This way, when a media planner returns to the database to make a query, she can factor out all of these types of variables. This is called "norming" the data. A planner might, for instance, ask the database which sites proved to deliver the lowest effective cost per click, but factor out campaigns bought with the objective of branding in mind. Without this type of information recorded, performance reports might prove very misleading. Of course, certain types of simple queries don't require much norming. Querying the database about effective CPMs and comparative results within campaigns requires the scrutiny of fewer variables.

The easiest information for advertisers and agencies to collect comes from the sites in the form of post-buy reports. But this data that is collected for the purpose of determining whether or not a site met its media obligations is insufficient for many of these querying purposes. Merely collecting impressions and clickthroughs will not sufficiently "instrument" the data with all the variables needed to get at the more complex interactions happening between your ads and your audience. Only those agencies that deliberately insert this additional information into their database will be able to later query it with a great deal of precision.

For instance, when my Microsoft client's Corporate division asked us what the average CPMs were for a series of sites, we knew that they were looking for the data relative to the types of buys they would conduct for themselves—generally large CPM buys across broad targets. But much of our Microsoft data came from very expensive, highly-targeted special buys. Because we were able to winnow one from the other, we were able to give them a reasonable approximation of what the effective CPM rates were for the sites based on "branding" buys, as opposed to high-end, business-to-business direct marketing efforts.

3340-TILL

Client-Side Data

Clients will sometimes collect useful data from their sites, especially the data involving the transactions and traffic patterns resulting from previous online media campaigns. If available, this must be consulted. It will provide informative insights. Perhaps more to the point, though, the client is unlikely to approve any media plan that seems to contravene conclusions drawn from this well of their own experience.

The subtleties, problems and uses of client-side data will appear later in the context of evaluating media performance.

Syndicated Data

Syndicated research data available to online buyers falls into three rough categories:

- Panel-measured data on site traffic and demographics
- Competitive spending information
- Behavioral information linked to media viewing

When a campaign uses demographic targeting or behaviorals that happen to be measured by an online panel company, these sources become very valuable. Companies like Media Metrix and @Plan can provide ready sources of site lists based off of the tens of thousands of panel members they watch and measure.

A warning should be heeded at this point. Because these companies can spin out report upon report of information about the major sites, it's tempting to rely on them as a quantitative comparison among sites. This should be avoided. The type of information the panel companies publish relies on categories of users (demographics and certain self-reported behavioral measures) that frequently are only indirectly responsible for user behavior online. In other words, the fact that X percent of one site happen to be above 54 years old and that 40 percent prefer Pepsi might have very little to do with the media from the site delivered to a specific advertiser. Any one advertiser's buys will most often come from a narrow portion of the site, and likely take advantage of further targeting as well. Once we add these factors to the buy, the syndicated data becomes less and less likely to predict the results our own campaigns will receive.

A general interest site might have its visitors broken out by gender 50 percent males, 50 percent females. But you can be fairly certain that if you purchase the "Fashion" section sponsorship, your results will vary.

This panel-derived information should be treated merely as directionally helpful. For instance, when a planner sees that a certain type of site performed well on a previous campaign, they might look to see what type of demographic and behavioral measures seem to line up with the well-performing sites. This could suggest other, similar, sites that might be tried out in a future campaign. Another example would be looking for sites with a high composition of a particular type of viewer to match up with an offline media campaign targeted to the same category.

Some of these syndicated research tools provide applications to determine the reach versus frequency an advertiser might experience when buying a certain combination of sites. A tool like Media Metrix might tell us that purchasing 100 impressions on Yahoo.com and 100 impressions on Google.com might give us a reach of 180 individuals, with an average frequency rate of 1.1. This would signify that 20 of those 180 people saw the ad on both sites, accounting for the "missing" 20 impressions.

But, again, this all presumes that there is no targeting involved in the two media buys. If, for instance, the Yahoo.com media buy involved purchasing the "Dave Mathews Band" keyword and the Google.com media buy also involved the purchase of the same keyword, we could expect a much higher rate of overlap. The frequency would jump upward, and the number of individuals seeing the ad would plummet.

Sales Rep Information

Many times, the objectives of a campaign, coupled with the advertiser and the product category, will suggest a certain set of obvious sites. If your advertiser is launching a new computer programming tool, you will likely be seeking awareness from the audiences of a group of programming-oriented sites. Planners will benefit from approaching some reps from these sites, even before the planning process begins. Some reps will be able to give some good ideas as to what types of inventory, targeting opportunities and special deals might be available. Some will even provide special research that they've done on certain product categories and types of online advertising performance. You can be sure it will all be flattering to their own site.

In the least, the information should prove helpful in constructing some intelligent questions to put on the requests for proposal (RFP's) that will later be sent out to likely sites.

Typically, a planner will develop some personal relationships with the reps who turn out to be the most useful for this purpose. The reps don't guarantee themselves a place on the final buy, but they do their companies great credit by being so informative.

The RFP

The request for proposal provides two major functions for the planner. At the outset, it puts the planner in a good negotiating position because the answering site is effectively put into a blind auction. They have to bid (lowest price wins) to earn the right to provide media. Once all the proposals are collected by the agency, it provides a common set of criteria against which the sites can be compared.

The other main function of the RFP is to generate special media opportunities from the answering sites. Depending on the nature of the questions included in the RFP, sites may respond with special sponsorship programs, cost per performance deals, or perhaps complex packages of targeting and extra creative capabilities.

Sites do not treat all agencies' RFP's equally, however. They've learned over the months and years that some agencies put a great deal of thought and analysis into their RFP process, and other agencies merely use it as a part of a rote process. Site reps commonly believe that a majority of agencies use the RFP only as a negotiating tool for price—not to inspire new and creative media packaging from the reps. Those agencies will receive plain responses. Agencies that are known for reading the responses carefully and rewarding sites when they prove especially useful or creative, find themselves receiving more and more useful and creative ideas from the reps.

Here are some points of advice to encourage the best responses from sites:

- Ask different questions each time you send out an RFP, and make sure that these questions tie in to the campaign objectives.
- Send out RFP's to as many sites as you can reasonably respond to. If you send out RFP's to too many sites, you will not be able to respond to each one, and sites will perceive you are wasting their time.
- Make sure that you maintain basic fairness between the sites. All sites should receive the same information in roughly the same timeframe, allowing for comparable responses. Sites perceiving they are disadvantaged will return only plain vanilla responses.
- Once a site is known to not meet your criteria for the campaign, let them know. You waste their time as well as your own if they continue to respond.
- You can expect the quality of the answers to vary with the amount of time you give the sites to respond. A fair amount of time is at least four or five business days.

- Only send out RFP's if the campaign's budget warrants it. Reps will sometimes feel antagonized if they are requested to write up proposals for very small amounts of money. A typical RFP might look something like this:

> Dear Mr. Joe Rep,
>
> My client, the Leaky Boat Corporation, will be spending $100,000 in the next quarter on a campaign to introduce its new line of disposable watercraft.
>
> Our objective will be to reach a majority of disposable boat consumers on the Web, with as low a frequency rate as possible. Using estimates from @Plan and other sources, we think the universe of disposable boaters is about one million people, but the number seems to be shrinking every day.
>
> Under no circumstances will the client allow more than 15 percent of the budget to go to any one site, unless it can be reliably shown that there will be no threat that a high frequency rate will result.
>
> To be considered among the sites we purchase in the campaign, please answer the following questions by the close of business on Friday:
>
> - Do you have any information to indicate a specific number or proportion of disposable boaters on your site?
> - Can these boaters be specially targeted via any content area or technology?
> - What would be a desired CPM rate for a purchase of 1MM impressions, both targeted and untargeted.
> - How often do you allow the creative to be switched out?

- Upon failing to perform above the average of the other sites in the campaign, what penalty must the client pay to revoke the remainder of the buy after the first month?
- Do you allow for third party tracking?
- Will your site agree to the terms laid out in the standard AAAA/IAB terms and conditions? [See appendix.]
- What types of banner sizes are available on the site?
- Are there any rich media formats supported?

Thank you in advance for your considered responses.

Sincerely,
A. Beyer

Notice a certain trick played here in these questions. The RFP states quite clearly that the client will not pay more than $15,000 under most circumstances, yet it asks for a price for 1MM impressions. This suggests that right off the bat, the agency is demanding a price cap of a $15 CPM. At the $15 CPM, the 1MM impressions cost precisely $15,000. This is just one reason among many why RFP's should be carefully crafted, and even more carefully read.

The style of the RFP varies radically from agency to agency. One shop in the Northwest always insists on asking a "creativity" question, like "If you were a tree, what type would you be?" Most stick to the details.

Once these answers are all collected, the planning phase takes over, and the final winnowing process begins.

13340-TILL

PHASE 3: PLANNING

If all of the previous phases have been done properly, the planning process should be a relatively smooth one. We should be receiving responses back from the RFP's, and we should already have a set of criteria against which we are prepared to judge them. The planning process starts to use the strategies developed from the media brief to apply to the data being returned from the sites in the preplanning phase.

Of course, in the real world, it seldom works out quite so neatly. Often, the sites will answer the questions in ways designed to engender additional conversation. They will want a larger portion of the media budget. They will offer special deals and extra special types of packaging. This is not a bad thing. In that jumble of media offers are often some of the most efficient media buys.

In the media buying business, there exist two schools of thought on these additional conversations with reps during the planning process. One school holds that the less information the rep has, the more powerful the negotiating position of the buyer. The other school holds that the more information the rep has, the more tailored the responses will likely to be, resulting in an even more efficient campaign. The adherence to one school over another depends primarily on the buyer's opinion of the usefulness of the reps.

My own experience shows me that the first school of thought can be short sighted. I've found that the more the sites know, the more innovative they've allowed us to be in exploiting their media opportunities. However, in the bustle of the real world, agencies frequently don't have the time to deal with all sorts of customized deals based off of detailed briefings. In other words, if the buyers don't have the time to take advantage of complex deals and new, innovative ways of advertising, they might be better off keeping the information presented to the site relatively simple.

Underlying the dealings with the sites should be the principle of fairness. The buyers have an ethical responsibility to allow all the considered sites a similar amount of information and opportunity. To do less would be to shirk the agency's financial responsibilities to its client. No matter how many expensive lunches and baseball games the buyers get from the reps, each site should be treated equally when it comes to the facts and figures.

That said, there is a legitimate argument for factoring in certain types of agency-rep relationships into the decision-making process. When reps are responsive, honest, experienced and knowledgeable enough to make advertising on their site much easier than on someone else's, this is a good reason to choose their site over another one, perhaps even one with a slightly lower effective cost. Those site-to-agency communication issues will have a great deal of an effect on how quickly the media plan gets updated, revised, and improved. A site that has poor communication or organization can be a nightmare to deal with, making agencies regret the selection of a low bidder.

From the RFP's, the agency will select a reasonable list of sites that, combined, deliver the right target audience in the correct proportions, with the right estimated level of frequency, and any other criteria that might have been mentioned back in the media brief.

With this list, the agency creates a suggested level of weightings among the sites, using the rates given on the RFP's. This list is often drawn up as an official document by the agency for client signature at this point, signifying approval and authorization to negotiate the final prices.

The agency should, by this time, have all of the pertinent information about these site finalists. If the site has made it this far into the process, it is likely necessary to forward its banner size requirements and other technical data on to the department that will create the actual ads and traffic them out to the appropriate site people. This might be the creative department or the production department of an agency. Sometimes agencies will have their own special traffic departments for just this purpose. A data checklist would include the following:

- Banner sizes required
- Looping requirements
- Any rich media specifications, if applicable
- Alt Text requirements
- Linking URLs
- Ad serving information formats and 3rd party tracking compatibility
- Lead times required for insertion

If they fail to receive this vital information, the campaign will be delayed at best. Often, these departments will require this technical data several weeks in advance.

Phase 3: Planning—Dealing with Reps

Media representatives have their ups and downs. It can be amusing to make fun of the stereotypes and extremes (don't you think for a minute that they don't make fun of us buyers, and deservedly so). But they do serve some useful purposes.

Of course, the first thing you think of is getting those Cubs tickets or a lunch at Hyde Street Bistro. In dirty politics we'd call that "payola," but in the media industry it seems to be acceptable. But this isn't why reps are useful.

We agency folks have different objectives for every client and for every campaign. The site people have all sorts of different media, sliceable in all sorts of ways. To pretend like there's one right way to buy or sell this media—for instance, by CPM—is lunacy. These different needs require different types of media packages. And these different types of media should be packaged to meet those needs by reps. We could no more say a rep is unnecessary than to say a media planner is unnecessary.

Reps should be bringing us creative ideas to solve our particular objectives. But here's the rub: this requires that we tell them what our objectives are and that the reps sit down and spend the time to truly put together something more useful than their generic packages.

Here we find two major problems. First, on our side, we're often queasy about telling reps too much about our campaigns. We often operate on a need-to-know basis, thinking that they more information we have, the more powerful a negotiating position we put ourselves in. Worse still, it requires us to invest a great deal of time talking with many reps.

On the other side, not very many reps bother to venture off their rate card or their site's special-of-the-month. Too many requests for proposals come back with cookie cutter answers.

To really do the job right, you need a buyer and a seller who can trust one another to put in the due diligence. Otherwise, neither is going to want to bother going through the motions. This might be the only rationalization as to why it might be a good thing that reps spend all that money taking buyers out for drinks. To the degree that these personal relationships develop, that trust can allow the two to invest the time to be creative.

Until, of course, the buyer quits the agency a month later to turns up somewhere else. The turnover rate at agencies makes it difficult for reps to develop long-term, trusting relationships.

Problems with Reps

Buyers can criticize reps all they want about their being slick and sleazy and all the other words typically thrown at a sales department, but those are mere personality issues. Here's my list of the most substantive problems my buyers have faced with sellers.

- The Needy Rep: This is the person who calls on a schedule. It's not that they have anything truly new to tell you, but they're afraid their bosses will get mad if they can't say that they've spoken to you in the past four weeks. Buyers don't need these calls taking up their time, and they can smell tickler files through the phone line.
- The Guilt Tripper: Usually as a direct result of not returning the calls of the "needy rep," this fellow becomes a guilt tripper. Buyers really don't want to talk to someone who whines into their dwindling voicemail megabytes complaints about how they never call him or her. This works about as well as it did in high school, trying to keep that star-crossed relationship alive.
- The Loud Mouth: Sometimes reps will lean forward, they will look from one side to the other, and then they tell you some juicy bit of intel about the competition. This isn't doing their site any favors. Buyers are generally smart enough to know that dealing with this person will likely put their own clients' information on the market.
- The Company Man: Reps who refuse to budge from rate card structures to consider more creative media packages can be written off. If the function of the rep is merely to wine, dine and then negotiate a CPM, then we can do it by email and save a lot of time.

Rep Management

I think sellers frequently don't realize that our biggest issue is our time management. It's a game to most sellers, where they play against one another to see who can claim more of our time, thinking that this will lead to a corresponding share of budgets. We simply have to be honest about what we're looking for. Here are the four things buyers must do to make their relationships with reps more sane and useful:

- Select a relevant group of reps and make sure they are well briefed as to your upcoming campaign objectives and needs. Be proactive about this, rather than choosing to tell those who happen to call in a given week.
- Say no to reps, and don't take any guilt trips. If you don't think a calling rep is going to give you what you want, tell him or her to send you an email with details and promise to read it. And then actually read it. And maybe even respond with a quick email thank you so they know they can trust you. If a rep persists too much in trying to get your time, tell the rep explicitly that their best odds of making a future buy entail leaving you alone.
- Send out detailed RFP's to a manageable number of sites, encouraging them to bring you creative packages. Make sure all of these receive review and response. If you find yourself filing these RFP's without much consideration, you need to reduce the number of requests you send.
- When you grant meetings to reps, schedule them precisely. I advise folks to make these meetings no longer than half an hour, if it's not the first meeting with this site. 20 minutes is optimal. Otherwise, the remaining 40 minutes will often be filled with banter and irrelevant site promotion. These meetings should be a priority, once scheduled.
- Make sure that reps from a site that fails to make the buy understand why they were left off. This stimulus-response cycle can train reps to give you better and better offers over time. Without the response, they are often left assuming the lost for whimsical or invalid reasons.
- Always be courteous. Not only is this an important business practice, the rep you brusquely brush aside is certain to become your client or boss sometime in the next five years.

Once reps sense that they can trust you to be on time, to give them a fair shake and to give them the right information, they will serve you better than they serve everyone else. In addition to saving a great deal of time, it can be a great competitive advantage to you and your agency.

PHASE 4: NEGOTIATING

Media agencies distinguish themselves in the long-term based on the degree to which they make deals that are more efficient with media vendors. Negotiating, then, becomes the most important part of their jobs. The negotiating stage occurs between the time the agency receives the responses to the RFP's from the preplanning process and the point at which the agency brings the final site list to the client for approval. It usually takes a week or two to go through the one or two rounds of negotiation discussions with all the sites.

Setting the Right Attitude

Buyers have the duty to get the best price for the client. Sometimes sales reps will try to make it seem as though buyers have an obligation to include their sites on a buy or to keep them at a certain proportion of a repeated campaign. It might be because the reps have a very long-term relationship with the buyer, or perhaps that they've spent a great deal of time trying to convince them to buy their media. The buyers owe them no money. The buyers do owe them the courtesy of prompt responses and professional dealings, but they owe them no money.

When the salespeople move the discussion from the rational points of media needs and the supply versus current demand, the client generally starts losing money. Discussions of price should be kept in the realm of practical realities, client needs and competitive bidding.

New media buyers often dread their first few media negotiations. Often they are fresh out of college, and they're not used to business dealings where they have to refuse offers and make ultimatums to people who are being very polite to them. They worry about seeming too much like a pushover at the same time they worry about being too rude to these very friendly reps.

New buyers can take comfort in the fact that everyone starts to feel comfortable after the first few times. Most find this part of the job the most fun and exciting part.

The first thing a buyer should do before picking up the phone with the first rep is to quietly remind herself of two things. She has a responsibility to the client to get the best price (in other words, it's not her fault that she needs to demand a better deal), and saying "no" is a completely expected and accepted behavior.

Buyers should obviously not be abusive to reps, or even give the perception that they enjoy refusing offers, but nor should they feel ashamed for having said no.

Negotiation Tactics

Buyers and sellers negotiate on the premise that both sides marshal up rational arguments supporting either a higher or lower price. Information therefor becomes the tool by which price moves. And that information can be about any aspect of the buy.

For instance, the buyer might bring up concerns about a high CPM. He might tell the site that it made one of the worst offers in terms of effective CPM. The site might counter by pointing out its more flexible "outability" terms, giving the advertiser little excuse for trying out the site out for an initial period of time. The buyer/seller interaction involves bringing to the table informed arguments to justify price positions.

The buyers should assume that everything is negotiable. If the sales rep claims that she cannot possibly agree to one term, the buyer finds himself in a much stronger position on other terms. The drawback to this type of negotiation—and one that shouldn't be underestimated—is that when each deal's terms wind up very customized, it becomes very complicated to make sure all the sites met all their requirements.

Some agencies create relatively inflexible contracts to prevent this problem, but they generally wind up pushing higher costs onto their advertisers. A very large interactive agency started creating very inflexible, pre-negotiated rates for this purpose in the mid-90s, but abandoned the practice later when they found their "special" rates eventually much higher than what their competition typically received. Online media prices have consistently trended downwards over time, making "grandfathered" rates unfavorable.

Types of Arguments

Several categories of information will prove handy to the buyers in creating arguments for lower prices.

- **Previous performance data** will come in especially useful. When a site is confronted with past performance, it's tough to explain away performance problems. Agencies can frequently serve one client by employing this type of data from the performance of another client's campaign.
- **Establishing the appropriateness of the media** will prove a common point of argument. Reps will maintain the ad buy being discussed is of critical importance to the client, perhaps due to target composition or some other special factor. Buyers will frequently try to maintain that the media seems to be no better than other opportunities. This will sometimes lead to dueling research reports. As a general rule in these negotiations, actual performance statistics trump audience research.
- **Competitive pricing concerns** often drive the degree to which sites will come down in pricing. Most reps remain acutely aware of the competition, particularly the competition in their own narrow category of site content. They

will often consider a buy that goes to their competition a double blow: it not only fails to enrich their own coffers, but it goes to support and prolong the life of their enemies. When a competing site looks to provide a better value, make sure the negotiating site rep knows this.

- **The determination of the actual value** of the media to the particular campaign factors into the perceived appropriate price. This will vary greatly between advertisers and campaigns. Typically, direct response campaigns that involve sales and revenue can draw up profit expectations that place a very specific perceived value on the media. These types of campaigns tend to establish high real values of the media. In contrast, branding and awareness campaigns tend to prove lower in provable value to the client. Branding—assumed to be about as effective online as offline—winds up equating the CPM value of online media to that of offline media.

This leads to an interesting difference between online and offline media. In the offline world, media is seen much more as a priced commodity, where one set of impressions on a media vehicle tends to have the same price as another set of impressions on the same vehicle. In the online world, this changes a bit. The relative level of desire a given client has for that set of impressions may have a material affect on the price. As a result, different advertisers may find themselves paying very different prices for the same media. On the Internet, identical sets of impressions tend to sell for different prices much more often, reflecting the appropriate valuation that respective clients assume that media for their particular marketing purpose.

It might be that Match.com, the computer dating service, knows it can make an average of $5,000 in profit with a set of 100M ROS impressions on Google.com. Yet Proctor & Gamble, attempting to conduct branding online, compares those impressions to its average television CPM. P&G then values those same

100M ROS impressions as being worth $500. Google.com may choose to sell one set to Match.com at a $50 CPM and an identical one to P&G for a $5 CPM.

As a result, some advertisers deliberately fail to inform sites as to the intended purpose and potential profit of direct response campaigns. This practice harkens back to the issue of the two different schools of thought in developing RFP's for sites. This practice is a staple of the school that tries to keep the sites as ill informed as possible.

Other Areas to Negotiate

When reps can't come down further in price, sometimes other factors might make the difference. Among them:

- Long-term deals warrant lower prices, especially ones with clauses that make it difficult for advertisers to later back out.
- Money forwarded upfront is often worth much more to a site than money coming in after the buy. While this can be a risky strategy sometimes (many buyers have had upfront deals blow up when a site company shuts down), with healthy sites it can greatly improve rates.
- Larger volume purchases deserve better rates due to the efficiencies the sites enjoy and the level of commitment the advertiser makes.
- Sometimes, purchasing across brands within a larger client company will win price breaks, as one brand effectively receives a finder's fee for encouraging the other brand to participate.
- Taking away the targeting options on media will make the media more generic, and therefor less expensive. ROS buys are always the cheapest. Conversely, if the price can't budge downwards, sometimes a buyer can negotiate extra targeting—such as keywords—without extra charge.

- New advertisers will sometimes receive special first-time promotional rates, although this practice is less common today than it was in the early industry days.
- Some agencies have attempted to negotiate long-term rate contracts to "grandfather" themselves into a good media rate for the future. This has seldom worked to the advantage of the buyers, as CPM rates generally have continued to fall over time. The trend, in fact, has been for agencies to negotiate for shorter and shorter-term contracts, thinking they can get better rates at a later date.
- The lubricant of the industry seems to be the "overdelivery" impressions that a site may deliver to an advertiser. While a rep's supervisor may have a hard limit to the negotiated CPM, that same rep might have a cozy relationship with the site's production department, allowing her to arrange for extra impressions to be delivered to an advertiser who would have otherwise been disappointed in the effective CPM. This under-the-table type of negotiation has its risks. Buyers cannot be guaranteed delivery of these extra impressions, and if they fail to materialize, they cannot demand them later as part of the makegood. This is an arrangement sometimes agreed to only tacitly, and almost always only between buyers and reps who have very trusting relationships.
- When sites cannot give better rates, they can sometimes at least provide special sponsorship packages or other content-related packaging that increases the value of the advertising.

Pricing Models

The pricing model itself may be a part of the negotiations. Most sites desire to sell their inventory by the impression. This is the way they can best predict the resulting revenues, simply multiplying what they've sold by the various CPM rates they've negotiated.

Agencies will frequently want to purchase media based on more sophisticated measures, involving actual performance. The most common is the Cost Per Clickthrough (CPC) method. Even better for agencies is the Cost Per Action pricing model (CPA). Buyers might also find this measure referred to as Cost Per Transaction, or CPX.

The action-oriented methods allow the agency to more readily discern which media buys and which creatives perform better than the others. Rather than having to guess based on the numbers of people exposed and the relative qualifications of those audiences, the agency can judge a campaign by a quick look at which site or creative performed better in terms of sales or leads.

The site, though, finds it very difficult to predict what level of revenue will be generated by such a campaign. It will only know in hindsight, and sales force managers loathe this type of uncertainty. Clever buyers, hoping to get more sites to sell by performance metrics, will add contract terms such as guaranteed payments schedules and minimum amounts. Money advanced before the entire campaign ends shows goodwill that many sites find difficult to refuse. This does away with some of that uncertainty problem.

A common compromise is to conduct a "hybrid" deal, where part of the money gets dedicated to a CPM deal and the other part to a performance metric. More and more deals are seen in the industry where there is a low CPM, plus a small bounty for a clickthrough, and a larger bounty for a subsequent action. Of all the deals conducted today, hybrid deals outnumber both straight CPM deals and CPA deals.

For instance, if a buyer had made a deal for a $9 CPM against 1MM impressions, plus a $10 per transaction bounty, the site would be able to at least guarantee the $9,000 part of the deal for the impressions. They would expect some additional revenue from the subsequent transactions, but they wouldn't be as worried about the deal as they would have been with a purely performance-based contract.

On the other side of the deal, the advertiser would know it was liable for the $9,000, but wouldn't know what the ultimate out-of-pocket expense would be. The remaining expense would be known only when the ads had run and the transactions could be counted. If the ads garnered a 1percent clickthrough and of those folks who visited the site, 5 percent chose to purchase an item, this would result in 500 sales. At $10 per transaction, that would mean the client would have to pay the site an additional $5,000. The total out-of-pocket expense to the site would be $14,000, for an effective CPM rate of $14.

This hybrid deal type is perfect for the times when a rep maintains that the site has a special benefit for a specific client, yet the buyer remains skeptical. If the site salesperson truly believes the deal will perform well for the client, they should have little problem in constructing a per-performance deal. If the salesperson is wrong, the client is compensated by an effectively lowered CPM.

Site reps sometimes don't fully appreciate the degree to which agencies rely on this type of direct measurement and comparison for media performance purposes. The direct performance measures tell us not who saw an ad, but what types of behavior resulted from people seeing the ad. And that information is really what the client cares about. How many widgets were sold? How much profit was made relative to the media costs? This information can be used to directly compare the efficiency rates of sites.

In the end, it doesn't matter that media is priced by CPA or CPM because the advertiser continues to purchase media only on those sites that show a good return per action. In effect, even though some sites sell only by CPM, they are bought as a result of their CPA performance. If they don't perform well, they won't find themselves on the buy next month. This irrefutable market force will make the significant difference between CPA and CPM prices lower over time, eventually making the issue mute. As the media market is still very young, a temporary situation exists today in the market where CPA deals tend to have much lower equivalent CPM prices. This won't last long, as the CPM deal prices will continue to decline.

Agencies, when they try to guess at the relative efficiency of sites with merely the impression and click data, don't stand much of a chance. They're stuck back in the days of traditional media, without any direct connections to draw to performance. The click data will suggest performance only in those few cases where the campaign objective was to drive traffic to a site. In that one instance, the click suffices as the performance measure, but will otherwise prove misleading.

The best way to frame these options is to put them in terms of the equation clients use to judge their profits. It looks like this: the equation to get at the visits is Impressions * Click Rate = Visits. To get the sales figures, we use the equation: Visits * Transaction Rate = Sales. Finally, we come up with the client's profit figures with the following: Profit = Margin * Sales.

The information for the first equation—the one to calculate visits—we get from the sites. The additional information needed for the next two steps, we get from the client. The client needs to provide both the transaction rate (since these transactions generally occur on their sites) and the profit margin.

This means that the trail from impression to sale is a constantly diminishing figure. We might receive 1,000 impressions, 10 visits and 1 sale (which suggests we have a clickthrough rate of 1 percent and a transaction rate of 10 percent). If we can get figures from our media buys all the way down to sales, a lot of our job is done for us. But if we can only get impression numbers or visits, then we have to make some assumptions about click rates and transaction rates in order to guess at the relative efficiency of sites. This is much less precise.

Performance-based deals tend to lead to lower effective CPM's. Two major factors play into this trend. When a site sees that a client is selling a product relatively well from its website in a performance-based deal, it tends to get a little greedy and try to increase the level of media dedicated to the deal. This saturation increases the revenues, normally without incurring any additional expense for the site because they tend to use unsold media for this purpose. The end result, however, is a recognition by the client that it received a great deal of media for a relatively low price. That client will be a difficult sale in the future for the relatively expensive CPM deal.

The other reason the effective CPM's tend to decline in performance-based deals is that CPM rates are frequently arbitrarily high to start. The performance-based metrics allow the media to find its natural value among advertisers, based on their real needs. Since rate cards tend to show CPM's ranging from $15 to $40, it's not surprising to see performance-based media deals offered much lower effective rates. In order for the deal to be profitable to the client, the effective CPM's frequently need to reach a level on par with traditional media—approaching $2 to $5 CPMs.

Both agencies and sites find it at least slightly more difficult to execute performance-based deals because of the extra data involved. The performance data from the client's site must be linked in a very specific way to the data from the media site, and sometimes as well to the data in the agency's own banner server. This makes the conducting of these deals cumbersome for all involved.

Optimally, the data would be linked all the way from impression to sale, allowing for the client to determine who bought what from which site and with what piece of creative. More often, however, the client's systems don't allow this. The common quick fix is for the client to set up separate and parallel web pages for each site participating in the performance-based deal. This allows the client to at least determine the gross number of transactions coming from any given site, and allows them to pay the sites properly.

The Break-Even Analysis

The algebra employed to help us figure out the right performance-based rates, gives us a final equation called the break-even analysis. We essentially reverse the math to figure out what the media cost point is where we stop making money, and we start losing money. This is a great figure to have in mind when negotiating.

We start by making some guesses—hopefully some educated guesses from past performance data—regarding the click rate and transaction rate of a particular audience against a specific product. Once we have those rough estimates, we can plug them into a slightly re-arranged version of the above equation: Break Even CPM Rate = Margin * Transaction Rate * Click Rate * 1,000. (The extra 1,000 at the end of the equation accounts for the fact that CPM stands for Cost Per Thousand.)

So if we had a product involving a Margin of $12.50 per sale, a Transaction Rate of 5 percent and a Clickthrough Rate of 1 percent, our Break Even CPM Rate would be $12.50*.05*.01*1,000, or $6.25. Providing your sole purpose was to make money from selling goods, you wouldn't want to negotiate any media deals with CPM's over $6.25. Things get a little more complicated when you are also seeking to increase awareness or perform other objectives as well. The performance of those objectives must be added—much more subjectively—to the equation.

A simplified version of this equation allows us to find the break-even point for cost-per-click deals. We just eliminate the part involving the transaction rates and the extra 1,000 factor at the end. We wind up with this equation: Break Even CPC = Margin * Transaction Rate. With our recent example, our break-even point would be $12.50 * .05, or $0.625. That means we wouldn't want to pay more than 62 cents for each click, if our sole purpose was to profit from online sales.

A warning should be mentioned here. Sales never happen in a vacuum. Even if you do not intend on doing branding while you are attempting to sell goods online, you are nevertheless affecting everyone's impression of that brand. My agency failed to realize this early on in the industry. We had a client that sold very high-end jewelry, and we developed a direct response campaign online. As the campaign was refined week after week, we started rewarding the creative that performed better with more and more of the impressions allotted for the next week. We would up with more and more creative that was very "salesy," or as one assistant account executive called it: "Blue Light Special cheesy." The campaign performed better and better according to our sales metrics, but after we did some focus groups, we discovered that we were doing great and irreparable harm to the sense of the brand.

Online advertisers are fond of saying that it's not just the sale, but that there's also a lot of branding going on online. This is true, and it works both ways.

PHASE 5: THE BUYING PROCESS

The buying process is a lonely one. The preplanning research is done. The sites you chose to send RFPs have responded, and you've negotiated the final prices with each of them. Now you have to make the final choices as to who will make the list of sites on the buy. You will have to take into account all of the quantitative data you've amassed, as well as a lot of the subjective arguments proposed by either you or the individual sites. Harkening back to the media brief, you will want to make sure you follow the stated criteria to choose the winners.

Once you've done this, a document is created for the client to sign. Theoretically, the client has been informed along the way of the planner's progress, so there should be few major surprises on the list. This document is very important because it allows the agency to represent to the sites that it has the legal authority to bind its client to media deals. If the agency doesn't get this document signed, and something goes wrong, the agency could be left liable for the cost of the media. This has happened at almost every agency, and buyers will find the finance department appropriately nervous.

When clients get this final site list, they frequently want to go over the conclusions, and sometimes even make some modifications. Once it is finalized, a contract called an insertion order is drawn up for each of the sites, and the trafficking process—discussed in detail in the next chapter—takes over to start the execution of the campaign.

Finally, once you decide on the sites that make the final list, remember to tell the ones who fell off along the way just why they failed to make the buy. This will help you greatly in future campaigns, both because of the common courtesy extended, and also as future negotiating clout. In the absence of a reason why they were left off the buy, salespeople will often assume it was arbitrary. If you can point to statistical factors as to why they were left out, they will remember that very clearly next time they answer your RFP.

What's a Good Rate?

An appropriate rate will depend on a few things. The type of audience reached, and the narrowness of that audience will have a large effect on the price. The degree to which additional targeting is employed will further up the cost. Generally, media bought by the impression has dropped in price from a $25 CPM in 1999 to a $20 CPM in 2000 to a $10 CPM in 2001. But this is just the average. It's not unreasonable to see a CPM of $150 on the same campaign as one for $3. One might be a very sought-after niche site audience coupled with a targeting technology, and the other could be run-of-site (ROS) media on a large network.

The Value of Big Sites

Throughout the history of media buying, the sellers have naturally tried to increase the value of the inventory they sell. They've used arguments regarding demographics, time slots and other factors that can mathematically work out to a buyer's advantage. But they also—frequently—appeal to this ethereal thing called "brand." This warrants some analysis, as there are, indeed, times when the brand of the media matters to a campaign. And there are many times when it does not.

Here are the arguments salespeople will employ to try to get online buyers to pay relatively high prices for media on very large sites.

- We get very large traffic figures
- We have a greater reach
- Everyone else is doing it
- Our content is branded, giving a patina of credibility to those advertising with us
- Someday, in a clutch, you will need us, and you had better be good to us today

I venture to guess that in most situations, most of these arguments are specious—they simply don't add any value to the advertiser. Any one of them could potentially be valid, but only in particular circumstances.

The first one, the large traffic figures, is the most useless factor. In traditional media, like TV or print, this matters. There, the more viewers you have, the more impressions the advertiser receives. Not online. Online, all the traffic is divvied up into precise lots that are given out only to folks who've paid for the particular impressions. There is a rare exception where traffic figures prove useful, however: if the advertiser requires a very large buy to be executed over an extremely short period of time, a high traffic figure will allow this to happen. Don't be fooled into thinking that this means you're reaching more people. You'll very likely be reaching the same people over and over again, but I have seen instances where this was compatible with campaign objectives maybe once or twice.

Having a very large reach at a site is helpful only to those advertisers who are making buys so large that they are purchasing a relatively high percentage of the entire sites inventory—something that is rarely possible or desirable on very large sites. When you purchase small lots of media on large sites, you can most times expect to reach a lot of individuals. It's only when you're buying one out of three impressions that you begin to worry about the site's reach versus gross traffic figures.

The "brand" argument is the toughest to figure out, largely because it's almost completely subjective. Brand does exist. Brand is useful in advertising. But does branded media give a greater value to advertising on its pages? Most times, no. It direly matters who you reach, at what time, in what functional context, etc . . . It, most times, does not matter whether you reach that person in the deepest depths of BigSite.com versus NicheSite.com. I know of exceptions to this. Sometimes, with particularly new or shady advertisers, they like to give themselves a patina of credibility by showing up on a respected site. This can be useful, but I've seen most of those very advertisers gradually move their media buys to more specialized sites as they refine their targeting and as they react to the efficiency of their buys.

So why is it that the vast majority of advertising is done on these relatively expensive sites? The simple answer is that it's easier for the agency to do it this way. It's a lot easier to start off with a list of the largest 50 sites and narrow it down than to start off with the list of 3,000 sites and try to find many more buys that add up to the same amount of media. Expensive as it already is to manage these buys and campaigns, ad agencies aren't eager to increase their internal costs that they can't pass on to the clients. This is one of the fundamental conflicts of interest between agencies and clients that seldom gets discussed openly.

The large sites get larger as the inconvenience factors work in their favor. This is not something they should get heady about. A lot of automation products are developing out there that may turn this situation around in the coming months and years. Also, buyers are getting much more educated about what really matters in media and in brand. They've begun to figure out that the site's brand matters a lot less than the advertiser's brand, and that buying one doesn't necessarily mean building the other.

A Good CPM

The average CPM, as negotiated and presented to the client is around $11. But getting hung up on this average number would be dangerous. Very few of your buys should be for $11 CPMs, as many should be less expensive, and many should be more targeted and much more expensive.

Several research companies publish figures of average CPM, but they tend to be more deceptive than helpful. They tend to use rate card rates, not the actual negotiated prices paid. I don't think the folks touting the higher numbers out there are being dishonest. I just think the information they're giving out isn't very useful given the means they've employed in its collection.

In my estimate of $11 CPM, I'm not including barter and "house ads," as a financial analyst would in assessing a site's revenues. Those added confusing factors (driving the true average much lower) are irrelevant to buyers. My methodology, admittedly, isn't iron-clad. It consists of consulting my anecdotal experience across tens of millions of dollars of online media spending and a greater deal of experience dealing with the management and motivations of media buyers. As a control to my methodology I asked some friends of mine who run large online buying agencies. None were too eager to offer their own figures, but throwing the $11 out seemed to garner more nods than head shakes. Some thought it was $9, some thought it was $12. Amusingly, all were convinced that they were getting much lower rates than everyone else.

Even with a CPM average of about $11, you can quite happily pay $150 CPM and know that you are getting a good value. It all depends on two factors: demand and targeting opportunities.

Targeted Media

We can target in many, many ways today. We can hit regions, demographics, behavioral profiles, content adjacencies. All of these will add a premium to the price. And, most times, it's worth putting some intelligent targeting on a buy. While a straight 1,000 impressions on a site might cost 10 or 15 dollars, buying that same amount of media in a specific zip code and limiting it to people who have recently used their American Express card will

13340-TILL

cost you 75. If you have good rationale for choosing these criteria, though, you should feel proud defending that price to a client.

High-Demand Media

Some media just can't be bought. There's just not enough media out there for some product categories, like a lot of the vertical and B-to-B markets, which drives the price through the roof. This isn't new, as the trade print for these very same industries generally enjoy CPMs greater than $100. Likewise, some regions, some targets and some behavioral profiles are simply too sought-after to be value priced. Again, if you have a good rational and link to your client's objectives, you can proudly put some of these very expensive buys on your plan.

I remember one extreme instance when the Internet Explorer division of our Microsoft client at the old Anderson & Lembke (now McCann/San Francisco) demanded that a site dump another existing advertiser that had bought up a piece of targeted media the Explorer Division decided it should possess. They needed the highly targeted and very rare audience. The Explorer people were willing to pay a high premium for it. When we called the site in question, it turned out that another division of Microsoft—what was then called the Desktop Applications Division had already purchased it out from under another advertiser. Microsoft was bidding itself up higher and higher.

There's a great deal of pressure for an agency to appear to be giving clients deals they couldn't get at another agency. This leads sometimes to "bottom feeding," where a lot of media is purchased for little money, but perhaps with little result as well. A typical trick agencies employ to get their campaigns' average CPMs lower is to fudge the weight levels around. They'll take 90 percent of the weight out of the $30 CPM buy and throw it into the already-huge $4 CPM buy. This way, they're able to show the premium site on the list, yet show a greater perceived value on the bottom line. This can be short-sighted, especially when the long-term evaluation of media performance will be measured by sales or leads or some other direct criterion.

Today's Prices May Be Too High

Back in the old days, we used to have to make up online media rates out of thin air. We'd take a stab at what we thought was fair (just north of print rates, generally). It turns out, we overestimated. The numbers turned out to be too high not because the media isn't worth that much—it is—but rather because the supply has become very great.

A lot of media out there goes unsold. It gets soaked up with barter between sites and with internal "house ads," but any neutral estimate has to hold that even the most successful sites rarely sell out. My personal guess is that about 40 percent of media gets used by a paying customer on a good month on a good site.

The other sites—the middle-market ones that still have great brand names—are probably selling only 25 percent of inventory or less.

Sellers speak of "rate card integrity" as a moral principle, wishing to deviate only slightly from stated rates during the negotiating process. But this might prove shortsighted on their part. When a site decides to sell only 20 percent of its media at a very high price, its revenue may be identical to selling 100 percent of its media at a very low price. In fact, it gets to use those 80 percent of the extra impressions for its own marketing and barter purposes. At first, this seems like a good strategy for the site. But it gives the same revenue to the site at the expense of indicating to advertisers that the online media are more expensive—and thereby less efficient in many cases—to traditional media.

Instead of busting through the price points of other media—making obvious the superiority of online media to print and direct mail, we find ourselves wandering around similar price points to traditional media. Were the industry to take a more high-volume sales strategy, the other media would have great difficulty comparing favorably.

As an industry, we once had the opportunity to blow past the media budgets of the older media, we now are stuck nickling and diming around the industry share levels of outdoor advertising and radio. We haven't yet begun to threaten print.

This suggests buyers should not be rewarding the larger sites with media dollars at the $10 to $20 CPMs. It's not important enough to include big search engine names on a media list just for the sake of client recognition. More efficient buyers should be rewarding the sites who are employing all their media—at much lower rates.

PHASE 6: TRAFFICKING

Once everyone agrees that the campaign is approved—with signed documents from the corresponding authorities at the advertiser, agency and media sites—the traffic department moves into action. Its job is to make sure the campaign materials get to the right people and that the media begins running the right ads at the right times.

The traffic department has been around only for a few decades. Back when the TV media markets began to get a little more complex with the addition of spot, cable and syndication markets, ad agencies began to find it harder to keep track of which ad was supposed to go to which TV station. It was a whole lot simpler back in the days when network television was the only option.

Many ad agencies now turn to that same group to help get the many different forms of creative to the still-more-diverse media vendors in the interactive field. Agencies that don't have their own separate traffic department will often add the responsibilities onto the role of the buyers. It's a bear of a job, and most companies severely underestimate the amount of time, resources and scrutiny it takes when they first start conducting online media campaigns.

Responsibilities for trafficking staff in an interactive group may include:

- Ensuring insertion orders are sent and signed
- Entering information from insertion orders into accounting systems

13340-TILL

- Making sure the production and creative departments produce all of the right ads in the right formats and sizes for each site
- Creating lists of which creatives are to be run on which site when
- Producing the testing matrixes that will allow different creatives to run against one another fairly, in controlled circumstances for creative tests
- Sending the right pieces of creative to the right sites at the right time
- If applicable, managing the client or agency's own ad server
- Ensuring that the right ads appear in the right places and times on the sites
- Collecting the raw performance reports from sites
- Determining if any of the sites failed to live up to any guarantees given in the insertion orders
- Resolving those discrepancies if media department involvement proves unnecessary

When we first started spending tens of millions of dollars in online media at my agency in San Francisco, we started to wonder where all of our staff time went. In frustration, I finally made everyone audit their time for a month, down to the quarter hour. We were shocked to see that the trafficking was sucking productive time from people in every department. Since clients liked to have their campaigns start running on a Monday, we even had art directors and account planners helping the media people handle the Friday night glut of trafficking tasks. With a staff of about 100 interactive people, we were spending the equivalent of 15 people's time handling trafficking. Worse still, we didn't even have any full-time traffic employees at the time.

Only by streamlining some of those trafficking tasks, introducing some automation, and making our clients pay for specialized staff time, did we finally contain that problem.

Trafficking, Step By Step

This section goes through each of the trafficking steps in order.

Insertion orders

In the early days of online media, both the buyers and the sellers wanted the transaction to be handled through their own insertion order terms. Buyers would send their insertion orders to the sites, and the sites would send another contract over to the agency. Sometimes there was an argument before one side signed the other's contract. Sometimes neither document got signed. Now we finally have a better way of working, since the two largest trade groups that represent sites and agencies have finally agreed on some standard terms [see standard insertion order terms in the appendix.] Trafficking staff need to make sure that each media buy has a corresponding signed contract. Without this document, the agency might not be able to enforce makegood terms, and might even be liable to the advertiser for any media value lost.

Accounting System Set-up

Many agencies have accounting systems that require that each media deal be entered into its database before the campaign runs. This allows the system to generate its own form of insertion order and provide a tracking system to discover any discrepancies between media bought and received. They also facilitate reliable billing to the advertiser. Unfortunately, this often involves an extra step for the trafficking person.

Traffickers in agencies that use the very large and expensive accounting packages, like the Donovan system, find themselves having to revisit the system four or five times through the media buy.

Production Requirements

Early in the buying process, the media people will forward a list of the sites that will likely appear on the final buy. This will allow the traffic department to create a master list of creative requirements. Any piece of creative for this campaign will need to be produced in all the sizes and requirements for each of the sites. The list can get very complex if the creative format is to be a form of rich media, as each site will have special needs and requirements for each creative format.

Prior to having to send the creative out to the sites, the traffic department will verify that each required iteration exists.

Scheduling

Most campaigns will produce several different creative executions. Often it's the job of the traffic people to determine the correct rotation schedule for each of these creatives. They will make a list of the different executions that should be switched in at different times, with any eye toward preventing burnout as well as making sure that they can get good data to compare one execution's performance versus another.

In order to get such a comparison, the traffic people will make sure that each creative gets a similar rotation schedule in terms of time-of-day, media weight, targeting and any other significant factor that might otherwise impact one execution's performance over another's. The rotation list that accounts for the control of all these factors is sometimes call a "testing matrix."

While the traffic people might hand over all the proper executions over to the respective sites in the beginning of a campaign, they will continue to revisit the site to make sure that they continue to switch out the executions on time.

Sending Assets

The actual dispatch of the creative assets to the various sites is called "trafficking the ads." This is the action for which the department is named and remains the primary responsibility of the traffic department employee.

In most cases, this involves sending the creative executions to a specified traffic assistant at the appropriate site and then following up by phone. Sometimes, though, it signifies an act of uploading creative executions to a banner server at the agency or advertiser. When employing third party ad servers, the traffic department keeps the creative assets on that server and merely sends an HTML reference link to the various traffic assistants at the sites. That link will then insert the right creatives into the purchased pages from the server when required.

Using such a system proves a great advantage when traffickers can use the ad server to generate informative reports as to which sites have initiated a campaign properly. The ad server can tell when the sites begin to pull the creative executions from its database, and it can tell which specific pages and areas of the site are demanding the executions. This lets the traffic department know very soon if a site has failed to start delivering the media.

Verifying

In the absence of such a banner serving system, the traffic people must visit each place on each site where the ad is supposed to appear to verify compliance. They must see the right ad at the right time and make sure that the graphic points to the desired web address as well.

Since many sites put banners into random rotations, this process can involve sitting in front of a site for many minutes, pressing the "reload" button tens of times to see if an ad appears.

Collecting Performance Reports

If employing an agency banner server, agencies can get good apples-to-apples data. But regardless of access to this type of data, the traffic people will need to collect the performance reports from the sites themselves. Almost without exception, the sites require that the insertion order contract be executed against the site numbers, not a third party banner server's numbers. This means that while the agency might get a more accurate set of figures from employing the banner server, it will still need to collect the site numbers to finish the discrepancy resolution process.

This process is the biggest single labor-sucking part of the process. Of all the inefficient parts of the process for an online agency, this section stands out as the most egregious waste of time. The profitability of an online unit will often be tied to the degree that agencies can automate the post-buy information collection and analysis.

Some sites will fax reports on banner performance periodically. Some require that agency staff visit special web sites with passwords set up specifically for the purpose of checking performance. These numbers must be collected into one form—usually a spreadsheet—for later comparisons with expected impression, click and sometimes action levels to resolve discrepancies.

Discrepancy Resolution

An odd situation develops sometimes because the agency collects two different sets of numbers. When employing a banner server, the agency is tempted to use the automated reports from that ad server to resolve discrepancies, taking a shortcut by avoiding the collection of the site numbers. Agencies will sometimes presume that sites are meeting their obligations unless their own banner server indicates a very large discrepancy. Typically these agencies try to follow up on discrepancies greater than 10 percent of the media owed, although the inconsistency of banner ad server logs frequently makes this practice more practical when they allow a "fudge factor" of 20 percent or more.

Clients sometimes disallow agencies from using this practice because it means that many real discrepancies that simply fall below the 20 percent minimum never get resolved. This can exact a great cost from the client. In most cases, the agency discloses the fudge factor to the client.

When the discrepancy resolution process is well delineated in the insertion order, the traffic department will frequently handle the process. If, for instance, any discrepancies will automatically result in a "makegood" media buy plus a 20 percent media penalty, the traffic people will send out the special insertion order with the proper amount of media listed (discrepancy plus 20 percent) and start the other elements of the trafficking process to make sure the media gets exploited correctly.

Sometimes, though, the discrepancy resolution process is more subjective. Some insertion orders leave the issue more open so that the buyer and seller can negotiate the issue only in the case it comes up. In such cases, the media buyers tend to handle the discrepancies.

Database Population

Some agencies have their traffic people commit the raw data—whether received from the sites or through a third party ad server—into a special agency database. This allows the planners and buyers to later query the database to predict future campaign results and efficiency implications of various targeting and strategy variations.

Sometimes these databases will require the traffic people to "instrument" the data with additional information. An example of that extra instrumentation might include:

- Product type
- Creative used
- Special targeting employed
- Campaign objective
- Type of creative (Teaser vs. Direct Response Appeal, etc . . .)
- Call to action message (Click here vs. Buy now, etc . . .)
- Makegood status

This extra information will prove very helpful in the future for determining why a piece of creative or a type of media performed in a certain way.

PHASE 7: CAMPAIGN MANAGEMENT

Once the campaign is up and running, the traditional media folks might stop here, but in the online world, the important work just begins. Where putting up a print campaign might be likened to boarding a train for a long journey, conducting an online campaign is much more like driving a car. If the interactive media people go to sleep, they'll crash into various obstacles of great inefficiency.

Inevitably, despite our great intelligence, innumerable past experiences, impressive talents and handsome good looks, we make a lot of mistakes in setting up a media campaign. It is patently unavoidable. The online media industry is a great humbler, proving over and over again that no matter how many online campaigns we generate, the complexity of all the variables working together allows for all sorts of necessary modifications once a campaign starts.

Creative we think will work with certitude turns out to fail miserably. Targeting we believe will multiply response rates will sometimes do the reverse. The good news remains that since we collect so much performance data that we can diagnose and fix these problems early on, before the brunt of the media spending happens.

This suggests an interesting theory about the traditional media markets. I have every confidence that this propensity for getting a few campaign elements wrong cannot be localized to just the online media. I believe it's merely detectable in the online media. This suggests that a great portion of the work we do in

13340-TILL

traditional media might be less effective than we hope. Most agencies and advertiser marketing departments attempt to represent their past and ongoing campaigns in the best possible light, but that might not be the way to improve their collective efficiency.

Monitoring Campaigns

Media buys need to be consistently monitored in two major capacities: media performance and creative performance. These are often mixed up together sufficiently that it might be hard to independently act on one side without effecting the performance of the other. For that reason and others, we need to see this monitoring process as a constant and necessary task. For instance, if a piece of creative begins to experience burnout, that might necessitate changes not only to the creative, but also to the media. We cannot assume that once a campaign's performance seems to be leveling out to constant rates that we can stop looking at the ongoing efficiency rates.

Creative Monitoring

On the creative side, buyers will monitor the relative performance of the banners, the banners that seem to do better or worse at various types of sites or with various types of targeting, and rates at which different banners seem to reduce their effectiveness over time and exposure. It should be noted that a banner might not need a great number of exposures to lose effectiveness. Time alone might out-date banners.

In 1997, my agency ran a banner ad that had a man dancing the Macarena. Surprising most of us, it performed magnificently. It got about 15 to 20 percent of people to click on it and a very high percentage of those people to start buying services from the client. Over the course of the next few months, the response rate dwindled to a small fraction of the initial performance, even though we weren't buying enough media to get many people to see the ad multiple times. Our client was experiencing not burn-out, but increasing creative irrelevance. The Macarena became passé, and the banner grew stale along with it. Interestingly, Al Gore, reinvigorated the Macarena by doing a little dance at the Democratic National Convention the next summer. On a lark, we put that old banner back into rotation after Gore made the song and dance popular again for a brief while. The performance shot back up to its original rate and declined slowly, just like it had in the first placements.

Obviously, if the vagaries of cultural trends and popular media phenomena have such a great effect on our performance, we have to monitor the ads consistently over time.

Data coming back from a site might look like the chart below. For the sake of simplicity we'll assume that all ads ran on the same site at the same time with the same targeting. Only under these circumstances can we accurately compare the performance of one buy to another.

Week #1

Creative	Imp.	Clicks	C Rate	CPC
Setter Ad	1000	10	1%	$1
Brittany Ad	1000	15	1.5%	$0.66
Pointer Ad	1000	20	2%	$0.50

The data that we first get back from the sites will show us the impressions shown for each banner and the number of clicks they attracted. At first appearances, we might suppose that the pointer version of the creative performs the best. That ad maintained a cost per click of $0.50, the most efficient of the three. But after we add in the data taken from the advertiser's site, our picture of the actual performance will become more sophisticated. In the chart below, we add the subsequent actions taken by the people who clicked on the various ads:

Week #1

Creative	Imp	Clicks	C Rate	Action	A Rate	CPC	CPA
Setter Ad	1000	10	1%	1	10%	$1	$10
Brittany Ad	1000	15	1.5%	3	20%	$0.66	$3.33
Pointer Ad	1000	20	2%	2	10%	$0.50	$5

After adding in the actual sales garnered by each placement, we can see that the brittany ad performed better. It didn't get quite as much clickthrough, but it did get more qualified clicks because, as we can see by the superior cost per action of $3.33.

This is a very common pattern. Carat Freeman Interactive, the large Boston shop, found that after hundreds of campaigns involving thousands of pieces of creative for all sorts of clients, that the creative with the best click rate performed best on a cost per action basis only 14 percent of the time. This would seem to indicate that the click rate is a counter indicator of actual performance, but that is overly simplistic. Some things to keep in mind when evaluating relative creative performance:

- The cost per action metric is most useful for direct response campaigns. Branding and awareness campaigns aren't geared to cause specific actions.
- When the copy shown on a banner indicates very specifically the nature of the product and the offer being made, the click rate will likely be an accurate measure of performance.
- When the copy does not mention the product (as in teaser ads), uses celebrities or offers promotions, contests or discounts, the click rate is likely to be a very poor measure of relative efficiency

Media Monitoring

Just as we measure the creative, we employ almost identical methods to evaluate the different media buys. Continuing our example from above, we will list data from two sites. In one site (Cats.com), we tried out a targeting technology, so we will separate out that portion of the buy to compare it independently.

Week #1

Site:	Imp	Clicks	C Rate	Action	A Rate	CPC	CPA
Dogs.com $10 CPM 3000							
Setter Ad	1000	10	1%	1	10%	$1	$10
Brittany Ad	1000	15	1.5%	3	20%	$0.66	$3.33
Pointer Ad	1000	20	2%	2	10%	$0.50	$5
Cats.com $10 CPM 3000							
Setter Ad	1000	2	0.2%	0	0%	$5	$NA
Brittany Ad	1000	3	0.3%	1	33%	$3.33	$10
Pointer Ad	1000	4	0.4%	0	0%	$2.50	$NA
Cats.com $20 CPM 3000 (with special targeting)							
Setter Ad	1000	10	1%	1	10%	$2	$20
Brittany Ad	1000	15	1.5%	3	20%	$1.32	$6.66
Pointer Ad	1000	20	2%	2	10%	$1	$10

Here we are able to determine that Cats.com doesn't compare very favorably to Dogs.com, at least when purchasing ROS media. When we used the targeted version of Cats.com, it gave us performance identical to that of Dogs.com, but the efficiency still under-performs due to the additional costs of targeting the media (in this example, the costs were presumed to have doubled for targeted media).

The example above uses round numbers and tends to simplify many variables that, in real-world situations, often create much more subtle trends. For example, in our table above, the relative performance of the different pieces of creative were presumed to have held constant over all of the different media placements.

Tracking After the Click

The above tables also over-simplify the difficulty of acquiring and marrying the different data sets needed to conduct the analysis. While the sites will give us impression and click figures, we need to marry those numbers to the performance figures from the advertiser's site. And this needs to be done independently for each piece of creative on each part of the media buy.

Generally this advertiser site-side data can be collected by pursuing two strategies:

- Creating separate, yet identical, landing pages for each iteration of creative and media site (subsequently giving us separate pools of results we can relate to specific buys)
- Putting an invisible, tiny graphic—usually one pixel in size—on these pages and on into the other pages of the advertisers site (which may then be counted each time it appears as a result of advertising)

The presence of those single pixels allows us to use the server logs to track how far viewers delve into the site from each media vehicle and each creative execution, provided a database is set up beforehand and the pixels are individually tagged.

Once that information gets collected, it can be combined with the data from the sites to give us tables like the ones above. This whole process can be partially automated through the use of a single ad server at the advertiser or agency. That prevents the buyers from having to manually collect all the performance information and collate it into complicated spreadsheets.

A Valid Comparison Involves Apples VS. Apples

The most common failing in this testing and iteration process is the assumption that the data we get from one source can be compared to and used with data from another source. Many media buyers takes the click-through rate of one site and compare it to the click-through rate of another site to determine the quality of audience relative to creative. Unless those two sites happen to be reporting via the same technology and methodology, however, the numbers will prove deceiving.

But media buyers are an optimistic lot. They tend to know that the numbers they throw together into their Excel spreadsheets aren't exactly apples and apples. Maybe there are a few pears and peaches thrown in, perhaps even some carrots. But it'll all work out in the wash, won't it? Well, not really. You have to remember that the differences we seek in the numbers are quite small. We're looking for a 5 percent difference in media performance, for instance. This requires a great deal of data harmony to not set off our data detectors at completely inappropriate times.

There's a graphical way to show this that readers can do on their own. The resulting charts prove very useful in helping show clients and others the importance of data integrity.

- Put together your own Microsoft Excel spreadsheet with three columns of numbers. Make them obvious patterns, like 1, 2, 3, etc. . . .
- Make a fourth column that multiplies them all together in some sort of an equation; like column A times column B divided by column C to the 7th power.
- Now, chart that last column, and you'll see some sort of pattern. Perhaps a sine wave or a trending curve.
- If, however, you deliberately introduce some deviation in each of the numbers (easily done by employing Excel's deviation function), the graphical results quickly go awry.
- Use the deviation Excel function to change the first three columns of numbers by 15 percent. Essentially, this allows you to take that original list of patterned numbers and have every one of them changed within a specified range. After doing that, look at your graph. It gets rather ugly.

- In fact, the each time you recalculate spreadsheet, you wind up seeing different "patterns" in the graph. It goes up one way one time, and down the other way the next. This is the moral equivalent of employing different site numbers from different sources and attempting to draw conclusions about your campaign. Phantom patterns surface frequently, and real patterns get hidden among all the data noise.

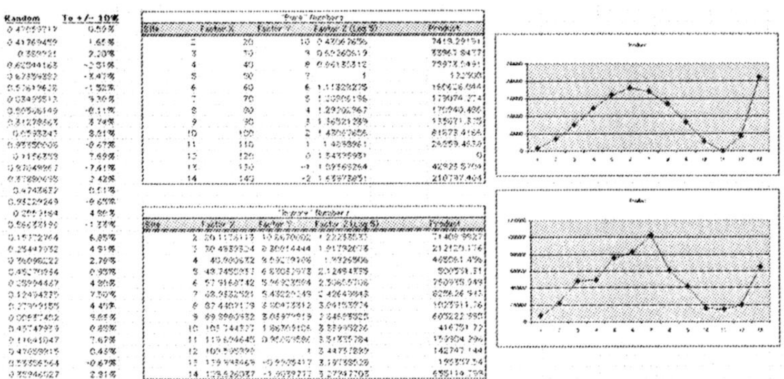

The data from this spreadsheet can be seen as a smooth pattern in the top chart, a trend difficult to determine with the deviated data chart just below it.

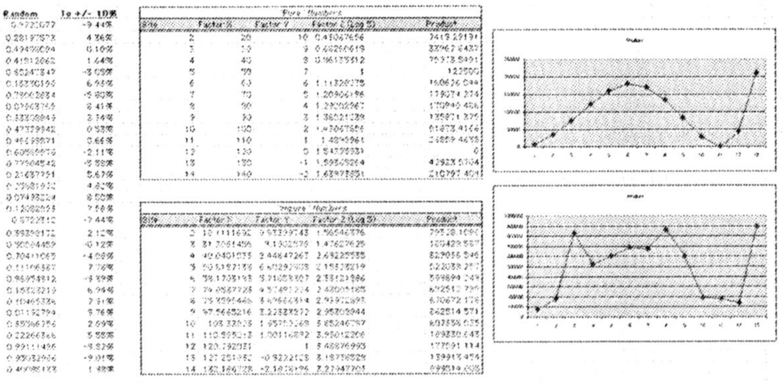

Every time the deviation is recalculated—even at the same percentage of deviation, the bottom chart will take on still another pattern.

Anecdotal versus planned tests

This brings us to the "any jerk" factor. Any jerk can look at a set of numbers and see some sort of pattern. Many of us have experienced this while playing pool with friends. There's usually some person who whacks the heck out of the white ball, which then wings around the table hitting all the others several times creating havoc. When one of his balls goes into a pocket, he smiles as though this were the intended result. This, any jerk can do. We know the validity of the trend or of the player's ability only when the player "calls" his shots.

Online testing can be just like the random billiards break. Anybody can look at a post-buy report and draw all sorts of conclusions about which creative and which sites are doing better and why. The hard part is predicting the next month's performance based on these. To gain this sort of predictive rigor, we have to set up the tests first, deliberately testing a particular hypothesis against known controls.

Controls

When we test a given hypothesis (for instance, that creative A will perform better than creative B on sites that have users of type X), we have to eliminate all those random factors that would otherwise mislead us. We must make sure we have identical counting mechanisms (usually banner servers) to get apples-to-apples data. And then we have to set up the test to make sure that other errant variables won't spoil the mix. We do this by purchasing media in identical, smaller batches. We then test only one variable at a time, to make sure that the particular time of day or particular site we purchased or some other factor doesn't give us a false read. For instance, we take two identical little media packages and put the two different creative pieces on at the very same time, with all other factors presumably "controlled." Predictions made from results are much more likely to reflect reality.

Accumulated Knowledge

If we do our media buying with these deliberate tests in mind, we can accumulate an enormous amount of data from our clients' purchases. Over time, this becomes an incredible resource for the agency. After buying millions of dollars of media, we can even begin to run predictive "phantom" media runs, where we query the database to tell us what a particular type of creative would likely do for a particular product on particular sites. And, if enough good data is in there, we can get some fairly good predictions.

This assumes that we collect all our data via an accurate mechanism, that we use the same technology for all these media buys, and that we keep pretty good records as to what creative runs where and just what type of creative that is. Some agencies—some of the best ones—take the time to categorize the creative in their media database. This way, they can later query the database, "What are the best sites in terms of transactional performance with direct marketing creative in this product category?" Useful stuff.

PHASE 8: THE POST-BUY ANALYSIS

After the campaign finishes running—and in the case of longer campaigns, perhaps in the midst of a running campaign—the buyer will need to collate all the performance reports into a final analysis. Agencies normally put these together into a formal presentation and document that they provide the advertising client.

Depending on the objectives of a campaign, the analysis will focus on different parts. At least four elements of the campaign results need to be detailed: learnings will be summarized for the different creative executions, the types of targeting that worked best, the sites that outperformed the average, and the types of media transactions that proved most efficient.

Instead of just presenting the spreadsheet numbers showing comparative performance, the documents need to take into account all of the various circumstances that might have interfered with the results. A good post-buy document will not only show which creative or site did better, but also suggest theories as to why. This is the learning from which the advertiser hopes to improve the results of the next campaign.

A final section of the post-buy document should summarize the key learnings and the results these should have on subsequent campaigns. If possible, specific media and creative tests should be roughly outlined and suggested for inclusion in the next campaign to help prove the theories in a controlled manner.

A post-buy document will sometimes combine the results of multiple media, encouraging the comparison of media results via objective measurements. If the campaign objective is to sell products, this can be a simple comparison of the costs per sale.

When other objectives exist—especially different objectives among the different media—the buyer must determine the relative accomplishments of all media in all objective categories. For instance, the buyer would be responsible for not only determining the sales resulting from online media placements, but also the relative awareness and branding accomplishments.

A final performance comparison among media might show sales of $10,000 and an exposure value (whether awareness or branding) of an additional $5,000. The exposure value is most often calculated by estimating the value of the number of targeted impressions that would otherwise have been bought in print.

Effects of Data Sources on Integrity of Analysis

Although the standard data source for much of our industry's post-buy analysis remains the banner server logs, this type of data is seldom very accurate. To describe the reasons why some data are better than other data, we need to get a little technical. We'll start by chronicling the wild adventures of a single impression.

Logs

Our impression starts off innocently enough. Somewhere, a user clicks on a link to a web page. That site calls together content from two servers: a content server and an ad server. Most times, both return their desired HTML results and they get displayed on the user's browser on the same page. Both servers log the request and the fact that they made an attempt to serve what was requested.

Already, some uncertainty rears its head. At the end of the campaign, a site might base its performance numbers off of the banner server's numbers or the content server's numbers. It might choose to count the requests that came in for banners, or the number of banners that it sent out. Believe it or not, these numbers differ significantly. These log files were not initially designed to measure real-world performance. They were originally intended to measure server loads and efficiency in serving requests—computer stuff, not human stuff.

Alas, when the advertising industry "standardized" the definition of an impression a couple years ago, the process was run mostly by the sites. Partly as a result, the current definition is so broad that a site can use about any methodology it chooses and still come up with "standard" impressions. When my grandmother sneezes, that probably costs some online advertiser somewhere 10 cents. But before we start talking about how to reign in this disorder, we have to follow our impression further along its adventure.

Caching

Caching—the act of saving a page in a temporary file so your computer can quickly re-render it without pulling it back down from the Internet again—adds another set of problems. Some sites employ one of a variety of "cache busting" techniques that force your computer to go back to the Internet to make sure that a page viewed again gets counted as another impression. That different servers do this in different ways only adds to the confusion when comparing numbers from one source to another. Worse still, there exist many types of caching. Your browser has a cache. Your ISP might employ a type of cache. Perhaps your employer has yet another cache for its network. One cache busting technique may or may not get around some of these.

Server Chains

Several additional servers may also be inserted along the way, further removing the reported performance from reality. Sometimes ad agencies want the site's banner server to call their own agency server so that they can measure the event first hand. If the creative employs a richer form of media, like streaming media, it might require yet another specialized server for that purpose. Any given media buy will involve three to five servers. Each link added into this chain will introduce statistically significant noise to the results data.

Our industry definition of an impression doesn't help us much. It remains silent on all of these issues. There are even some sites that still count the impressions served to the "bots" that search engines use to scour the Internet to index content. When a banner has a feature called an image map, some of these bots even go ahead and click on every single pixel on the banners (for those of you paying by the click, that's tens of thousands of times, depending on the banner dimensions). Many users unnecessarily double-click on links, which actually sends two requests to the servers, sometimes double-counting performance.

Since the last server on the server chain is the closest to the user, that last server almost always has the numbers that most closely reflect the reality of how many visitors saw an ad. In the case where a site's ad server calls upon a third party ad server, the third party ad server—usually an agency's server—generally has the more accurate numbers (tests show about 85 percent accurate).

Are Clients Being Cheated?

Yes and no. The fact that the sites' numbers tend to be untruthfully high, strangely, does not do any harm to the client. Ultimately, the forces of supply and demand will pay the right sites the right fraction of the media dollars out there (assuming they all use equally corrupted numbers).

The clients do get cheated out of a different kind of value: the value that agency folks promise them when the agency gets them into interactive in the first place. Interactive agencies brag about how accountable the medium is—how we can see real-time performance and react with changes to creative and media choices. But, in point of fact, our numbers are so noisy in the end that we can't really draw very good conclusions about a lot of our data.

The value lost isn't the fictional impressions and clicks that we tell our clients they received. The lost value is the lack of our ability to use this fictitious data in a useful way.

Server Fights

A big issue of late has been the battle between sites and agencies to determine whose numbers should be "blessed" in the end. The battle seems to be about which numbers are superior, but to be honest there's a bigger issue going on here. If a site is going to automate its internal workings, such as ad trafficking, it must serve its own ads so as to make the numbers automatically flow through their database systems. Likewise, if the agency is going to get close to profitable with its interactive operations, it requires similar automation. Thus, both sides insist that their numbers should be employed as the gold standard at the end of a campaign to resolve delivery discrepancies. Neither wants to be stuck entering 100 faxes into an Excel spreadsheet just to determine potential discrepancies. They want a server of their own to track these numbers, and to do so, they have to make sure their own numbers are the official ones. In a perfect world, ad servers would return similar enough numbers for this issue to be insignificant, but as it is, servers tend to report numbers from 10 to 40 percent different from one another.

So far, the sites have largely won this battle, forcing agencies to bear the brunt of collecting different numbers via different methods from different sites, then compiling it all for the client's post-buy presentation where everything is fudged together to pretend it's all apples-to-apples. And just to add some sand in the face, the sites' numbers tend to be exaggerated relative to the agencies' numbers, mostly because the sites' servers reside at the beginning of that server chain.

What Next?

If we limit our ambitions to merely watching obvious trends, like rough correlations between our banner ads and concurrent online sales, then these banner serving systems we use now might be just the ticket. But if we aspire to bring online marketing to the level of a true discipline, we must become much more critical of our data. Even if we want to deliver the value that traditional direct marketing firms give to their clients, we need some great improvement.

When we conduct media deals based on performance, like sales figures, the intervening impression and click figures matter less.

In the cases where you wish to conduct proper analysis, you have to directly measure customer behavior. This generally means using what is called "client side tracking" to measure ad performance. A little Java or Javascript applet is placed on the banner itself—or the transaction locations on the advertiser's site—and reports directly to the agency database. Only this type of data will give us the accuracy of results needed to make the more subtle interpretations.

Ultimately, I'd like to see a re-opening of the site-versus-agency debate about the definition of an impression and the standard mechanism by which one is reported. There's no reason why we can't all agree on a metric that reflects marketing reality. There's even less reason why we can't put this information in a standardized format that would allow one banner server to export the information into another company's systems.

Until then, I'm going to continue to use the banner servers with the rough stuff, and use client side reporting on the important stuff.

Levels of Site Performance Data

Different campaign objectives will dictate that we use different types of metrics to evaluate the performance of our media buys. We spoke of the different types of objectives and the corresponding metrics in previous chapters. These different types will fall into three major categories:

- Basic impression data (e.g., numbers of impressions delivered)
- Simple performance measurement data (e.g., numbers of sales generated)
- And individually-tracked performance measurement data (e.g., sales generated by individual viewer of a particular ad)

Level I: Basic Impression Data

Despite our ambitions to be more clever about our buys and to exploit more complex data, a majority of media buys are conducted via CPM deals or hybrid deals. Both of these types of deals use basic impression data to measure compliance. This is the measurement of how many times an ad is shown. And this metric comes most frequently from the site's banner server.

Level II: Simple Performance Measurement Data

Even with simple CPM deals, which require impression data to ensure compliance, advertisers frequently desire additional information to better determine which ads and which placements have the most effect on performance measures like clickthroughs and sales. Buyers will frequently want to see things like:

- The number of clickthroughs generated
- The number of submissions or entries caused by a placement
- The number of transactions inspired by a placement

This information can then be used to judge individual pieces of creative or the individual web sites carrying the ads. Frequently we find that a site that gives us greater efficiency in terms of cost per impressions will not give us as much efficiency by other measures, like cost per transaction, or cost per dollar of profit generated.

Importantly, these "simple" performance measurements are limited to gross numbers of certain performance metrics. We are not measuring the behavior of individual customers; instead, we are looking at the gross number of certain types of transactions, like clicks or purchases. We can't say any one ad on a specific site caused a particular person to purchase a certain amount of merchandise.

Level III: Individually-Tracked Performance Measurement Data

We get more personalized with the next level of data because we begin to track performance measurements to individuals. This becomes important when we want to see if individuals become more or less likely to purchase products well after they see an ad. Some companies can go back to their database following a customer purchase to see which ads that individual has seen over the course of a recent period of time. This helps the advertiser figure out which ads are having the desired effects, however latent. This becomes a fairly important ability in certain product categories, like those that involve very high-cost items or other goods that require a great deal of consideration and comparison.

This third level of measurement also comes into play when trying to determine which types of ads or media placements are most effective for different types of people. By collecting information about these individuals, companies can help narrow down the targeting and creative that will make those individuals most susceptible to ad messages.

Of course, keeping track of this data becomes very involved. We need to keep unwieldy databases of individuals, get the web sites we purchase to allow us to employ cookie information, set up data tracking mechanisms on the client site. We also have to make sure not to run afoul of privacy standards—still an imprecise and squishy set of standards.

Putting these systems in place, managing them and interpreting the results is an expensive, time-consuming process. Because it involves the client's site and the unique types of information that the client desires, there aren't off-the-shelf products to conduct this type of measurement. Each company that puts this together creates their own custom solution—one that requires a great deal of re-writing whenever a site gets redesigned or otherwise modified.

When is it worth setting up Level III data collection?

All the factors have to be controlled very carefully. If any one of the factors in this measurement scheme becomes divorced from an individual's file in the database, then the rest of the data becomes useless.

A common disconnect in systems that fail to deliver this continuity of data happens on the client side. The internal information technology department at a company may not prove open to the idea, or perhaps nimble enough, to provide the customer data from the company web site. Sometimes they can't put it in the right format. If that happens, then all the cookie information and other effort conducted with the web sites is rendered useless. If the client can only give aggregated sales data, or data on individuals who cannot be directly linked to specific cookies, then the data becomes too dirty to draw conclusions about creative or media choices.

Keeping the data clean enough to draw useful conclusions is like trying to keep a large house warm in a New Hampshire winter. You need to have every door and every window closed.

With just one open, you might as well save money and turn off the heat. If, for instance, you can't get a web site to send users seeing different pieces of creative to different client URLs, it might not be worth the cost setting up tracking of individuals from certain ads and media buys.

Getting Data

Not surprisingly, different sources will give us different levels of data. The most common source for performance data remains the sites themselves, the ones who sell the media packages. They need to track the performance to make sure they give the right number of impressions or other measures to the paying advertisers. But this can pose a conflict of interest. Some agencies like to monitor the sites by employing alternative counting sources. Other sources include third party banner servers, "client-side" reporting mechanisms and information tracked from the advertiser's web site.

This is a potentially baffling topic, and the terminology involved certainly doesn't help. Hopefully going through the four categories one at a time will dispel the confusion.

Site-Reported Data

Almost all web sites will provide post-buy reports that show their servers' figures for how many impressions of the advertiser's ad were shown. In most cases, this is the number against which the insertion order will be resolved.

Some sites will give additional performance information over and above mere impression and click figures, hoping to provide a competitive advantage over the other sites. Sometimes buyers will be given break-outs of performance based on user segmentations. A site might break out the data by demographic data, or more likely simply by the section in which the ad appeared. This data can be useful to help determine the most effective placements for that site, but is most often not comparable to similar data on other sites.

Third Party Banner Servers

Employing banner servers as counting mechanisms will probably look, in retrospect, like a poor industry decision, given the uncertainty they contribute to performance figures. But they've proven a necessary evil. Since sites use different definitions and different metrics to count impressions and other media data, we need some sort of consistent reporting mechanism. Early on, it became tempting to use banner servers for this purpose, and now we're pretty much stuck with them.

Rather than going through the hassle of forcing sites to adopt a common definition of performance and to be able to automatically get that data into an agency database, buyers instead used banner servers to get the quick, rough idea of how the sites performed relative to one another. To most agencies, that alone was worth the additional 10 percent of media expenditures it cost to use a banner server.

Buyers employ banner servers in one of three primary ways.

- Sometimes, though rarely, a client company will mandate that a particular banner server be used. Sometimes this allows large companies with multiple agencies to norm all their data in one place, giving greater potential leverage. When clients do this, agencies frequently find it problematic when the client's banner serving system proves incompatible—either process-wise or data-wise—with the agency's existing serving system.
- More often, an agency develops a contract with one of the off-the-shelf banner servers, passing the costs on to the client. This is most typical in agencies that conduct a lot of online advertising.

- For those companies or agencies that do not conduct a great deal of online advertising, most banner serving companies offer campaign-by-campaign pricing. Some agencies choose to have the banners served only for some campaigns or for some clients.

It should be noted that some agencies have a problem allowing some of the banner serving companies to become infrastructure partners. Many of these technological infrastructure providers have been bought up by web sites and web site networks, creating a conflict of interest. Where a few years ago, agencies would have dropped those media vendors as potential media sources, today most agencies hold that straddling both sides of the fence is acceptable.

Client-Side Technologies

In the cases where buyers wish to conduct very accurate analyses, they have to directly measure customer behavior. This generally means using what is called "client side tracking" to measure ad performance. In this instance, we're using the word "client" in the technical sense—not as a representation of an advertiser who hires an agency. A client, in computer terms, is an application that sits on the end-user's computer and reports information back to a central server.

A little Java or Javascript applet is placed on the banner itself and, once downloaded onto a site visitor's computer, reports directly to the agency database. This type of data will give us the figures very close to the truth needed to make the more subtle data interpretations.

Advertising products like the ActiveAd technology, offered as an added feature by some of the major networks, provides this client-side data. Bluestreak, the company that recently purchased AdKnowledge from Engage, has still another offering.

The Server Fight for the "Blessed" Numbers

A big issue since the advent of the industry has been the battle between sites and agencies to determine whose numbers should be "blessed," or employed in the official discrepancy resolution process. The battle seems at first to be about which numbers are superior, but there's a bigger issue here. If a site is going to automate its internal workings, like ad trafficking, it must be serving its own ads so as to make the numbers automatically flow through their database systems. Likewise, if the agency is going to get close to profitable with its interactive operations, it requires similar automation—and similar reliance on its own ad server figures. Thus, both sides insist that their numbers should be employed as the gold standard at the end of a campaign. Neither wants to be stuck entering 100 faxes into an Excel spreadsheet just to determine potential discrepancies.

Discrepancy Issues

Sometimes, while running a campaign for a client that tracks its own data on its own site, the site numbers an agency receives will wind up causing discrepancy problems. Since the sites use different reporting methods and servers further up the server chain, their numbers can be as much as several times those of the agency. For instance, clickthrough figures can be doubled, as reported by the sites themselves.

This problem goes beyond the mere impression discrepancy issue that everyone faces. Even after the agency and site agree on the media delivered, the client now has a different set of data (the number of people who landed on their site) that may prove both agency and site incorrect.

Three reasons might explain why these numbers don't match up:

- Some people click on the banner at the media site, but stop the page or click elsewhere before the client's page can load. This has to account for a very small portion of the discrepancy. It is behaviorally rare and technically unlikely, unless your client's site runs quite slowly. However, I do hear this as the most common excuse cited by sites. And well they might, as it suggests that the discrepancy is a valid one and that their medium is delivering all the contracted impressions and clicks.
- The user double-clicks on banners, and the media site is either dumb enough or dishonest enough to count both clicks. This is extremely common behavior for users, particularly new ones, and I'm not aware of what the common counting policy is at sites. I assume the worst. I have to suspect that most of the discrepancy comes from these simple counting methodology issues. Others would include counting search engine robot traffic (which can mean many, many added clicks) and traffic from the site, client and agency. Some sites—particularly the ones that offer "optimization" packages, where they observe performance to winnow down to the optimal banner or media placement—tend not to include all this superfluous traffic because it hinders their accuracy in optimization.
- The site is baldly defrauding buyers. This, fortunately, is the least likely scenario. I've come across it in the distant past, back before the West was won, but not at all recently.

So, what's a media buyer to do? In purchasing media, buyers will want to hold the sites' feet to the flames. Performance-based media works to incent them to give buyers quality media, but the real performance is determined by traffic seen at the client's site, not the media site. This means buyers should try to make the performance criteria based on their client's numbers. Unfortunately, many sites are unwilling to do this. Such truculence should be taken as a warning sign.

Eventually, enough buyers will be savvy enough to reward the sites with the greater true performance, and all sites will use better reporting methodologies. But, for now, we live in a media environment in which we buyers are along for the ride in a race to the bottom of reporting methodology. No matter the method, the higher numbers win. As part of diligent buying, buy-side people need to voice their disapproval and insist that proper measurements be used for their advertisers. The most accurate figures will be the last step in the chain of servers: often the user visiting the client's site.

13340-TILL

TARGETING: FINDING THE RIGHT SITES

The online media have all the same types of tools traditional media buyers employ to choose from among traditional media vehicles. We have ratings-based metrics, demographic matching and categories of sites that roughly match those found in print or the daypart categories of television.

But the online media also allow for several additional evaluative tools that often prove even more effective in choosing the best sites. Internet media planners enjoy the use of special proprietary performance databases, high-tech targeting mechanisms within sites, and often applications within sites that allow advertisers access to viewers in a very particular mode of behavior. Online planners seldom employ just one type of targeting tool. Often they will find themselves using all of them.

One of the most unique qualities of the Internet—its interactivity—provides planners with much better targeting opportunities. It allows planners to better use their common sense to help winnow down the media choices. Because people interact with sites, rather than simply view them, we can often purchase parts of sites that contain particular applications. Instead of merely putting our ad next to a type of published information, we can get our ad into a process, like searching for a home in a particular neighborhood or looking up the phone number for a certain type of business. These application-oriented opportunities allow planners to put themselves in their customers' shoes to help figure out where to find someone with a propensity to buy the advertised product.

In traditional media, we might make some gross assumptions to guess that cosmetics buyers watch Ally McBeal and read Parade Magazine. Online, we can purchase ad space right where people are working to determine which cosmetics best suit them. Often, we can even buy ad space where people are buying cosmetics. The applications-focus of the Internet gives us much better, mostly behaviorally oriented, targeting options.

All targeting tools and data should be considered up front to figure out the order in which sites can be winnowed down for the buy. They include:

- Proprietary Agency Data
- Proprietary Advertiser Data
- Sales Reps
- Common Sense Consideration of User Behavior
- Site Categories
- Demography and other Syndicated Research
- Competitive Tools
- Customized Research

In the chapter on planning, the agency and advertiser databases were taken into account. We also discussed much of what sales reps can add to the process in the negotiating chapter. The other areas need to be further explained.

Common Sense Considerations

It would be irresponsible not to make a list of the different types of sites an advertiser's target audience would likely visit. We can safely assume that car buyers will visit several of the automotive brand sites as well as some of the general car buying sites. We can also assume that many of them will go to search engines and type in keywords related to cars.

Business to business (B2B) clients will often correctly assume their corporate buyers go to vertical industry sites to get more information on what are generally products that are more complicated.

These are the types of assumptions that will initially direct our media lists. If we can't see a prospective buyer visiting a certain type of site, we can cross off the entire category. If we can see a prospective buyer visiting a type of site, we want to choose the particular vendors that make the most sense relative to the product category and the particular brand.

Most media planners happen not to be in the target audience of any given client. This puts them at a disadvantage. They might not be accustomed to visiting car sites or, most certainly, the vertical industry sites concerning their clients.

This is exactly why they must go through the exercise of pretending they are a customer. Much like method acting, the planners must put themselves in the role of a buyer, with all the attending demographic, psychographic and behavioral assumptions. They need to walk the walk:

- Reading discussions on the products on the Usenet or other bulletin boards
- Subscribing to relevant email newsletters
- Finding and exploring all the relevant vertical portals
- Going to the major search engines and typing in related keywords, exploring the highest-listed sites

If they do all this for long enough, they will begin to get a sense of how the industry considers the relative merits of the individual sites, and the advertising seen on those sites.

Site Categories

The different types of sites deliver different types of exposure and deliver ads to viewers in different modes of thinking. People go to vertical portal sites for a different reason than the one they have in mind when visiting a search engine. As a result, sometimes a product category or a particular campaign objective will suggest that some categories will be more appropriate than others. Different agencies and planners might categorize sites differently, depending on their types of clients, but this is an acceptable generic categorization:

- **Portals**

By definition, these sites are the ones that pop up on some users' browsers when they first launch the application. They are the starting points for people when they first get on the Web.

They might be Internet directories like Yahoo!, or special interest sites that have particular appeal to the viewer and offer the right links to get them where they generally wish to go. Sometimes a search engine site suffices as a user's portal.

Portals tend to get high levels of traffic and from a broad audience, unless it is one of the interest-oriented portals. The traffic generated from portals tends to have a wonderful quality to it: the people who see ads on a portal are necessarily looking for a new place to go on the Web. That generally means that an ad that attempts to get them to click over to a new site often stands a better chance of success.

A traditional media analog might be the cable TV station that displays the programming guide. People advertising on a portal to get people to visit a website would be similar to TV networks advertising on the TV programming guide.

- **Vertical Portals, or "Vortals"**

These are portals that concentrate on a specific, vertical industry. There are vortals for the food service industry, aerospace, and everything in between. They often have their own editorial content as well as links to important industry sites. Sometimes they are affiliated with existing print trade publications.

They benefit from the same type of pliant traffic as portals, except they tend to have very highly-qualified audiences. The costs tend to be very high as a result.

• **Search Engines**

Search engines are those sites that let viewers type in keywords in order to find a list of sites that tends to have relevance to the meaning of those words. Again, like with portal sites, the ad traffic from these sites benefits from the fact that users already expect to move off the search engine. Ads tempting users away to an advertiser's site tend to have better clickthrough rates than found at other types of sites.

The keywords also provide special targeting opportunities absent from other site categories. This will be discussed in greater detail in the chapter on search engines.

• **Broad Content Sites**

These sites are akin to the general interest magazines in print. They seek broad audiences, hoping to segment them by content sections and sometimes the use of targeting technologies, like profiling. Sometimes they will promote themselves as portals, deliberately encouraging their readers to make the site their browser's preferred homepage.

Because broad content sites organize their audience in such a wide range of ways, the media opportunities are difficult to generalize. They have to be considered each individually to determine which way the audience is most likely to behave: like a portal audience, like viewers visiting targeted media, or like random viewers with no focused purpose.

• **Narrowly-Focused Content Sites**

These niche sites cater to very specific—generally small—audiences interested in a very specific and narrow range of topics. The media tends to be very expensive because of the high level of topic targeting, and anything but the smallest of media buys tends to garner a great deal of frequency.

These sites offer the most exclusivity deals, as many advertisers find it useful to deny their competition the right to promote their products to the niche audience.

• **Regional Sites**

These sites focus on specific cities or other localities. They tend to have broad content related to the region, and they are often affiliated with traditional media vehicles, such as newspapers or local TV stations.

The prices for this media vary radically, depending on the region. Some markets have difficulty selling media for single-digit CPMs, and others—like New York City or Chicago—regularly sell out media at many times that.

This regionally-oriented media category is one that often benefits from new technologies. Since some regions have such a premium on the media, companies have developed all sorts of location-based technologies to reach people interactively. My favorite example is the Adaptmedia.net company in New York City. They married a global positioning system with the electronic billboards you sometimes see on taxicabs. This allows them to switch to appropriate advertisements for each and every different street corner. They might run a Starbucks ad on one end of the block and a McDonald's ad on the other.

Local media tends to run into similar low unique user counts as do the niche sites. Medium- or large-sized media buys will often get a few users seeing an ad many, many times.

• **Commerce Sites**

Sometimes the best media results come from placements on other advertiser's sites. A media buy need not always be on a site that presents itself as a publication. Sometimes buys can be arranged on sites that do business, much like the advertiser. Barnes & Noble, for instance, allows several commerce businesses to advertise on the "thank you" page that appears after customers purchase books.

Companies who've used these types of sites typically see better than normal response rates because the audience they find there happens to already exhibit purchasing and other relevant response behaviors.

These opportunities can be hard to find sometimes, as there is comparatively little media in the commerce part of the media market. Often the brands that do appear on one commerce site do so as a result of an affiliate program, barter exchange, business development deal or other type of contract that is likely structured differently than a pure media buy.

• **Site Networks**

Rep firms, Ad networks and media exchanges of various types can all offer placements on many sites with a single contract. This media is often very generic, not only running in unpredictable places, but often times in such a fashion that advertisers are unable to receive reports as to where their ads ran at the end of a campaign.

Some networks will allow some advertisers to hand pick the site mix, eliminating this problem.

These services tend to offer cheaper media (the largest few ad networks, like DoubleClick, being notable exceptions) and the benefit of dealing with one transaction for many sites.

Syndicated Research

Several companies offer panel-based research on the largest websites. These companies recruit thousands, or even tens of thousands of Internet users to allow the companies to monitor their web usage. Some companies use behind-the-scenes computer programs to do this monitoring and others merely allow the panel members to report what they remember viewing. Once they get these usage figures from the panel, they then extrapolate on them to guess what the average relative traffic levels might be on the sites that get enough panel usage to become statistically significant.

This allows the companies to publish lists of the top sites, trends in web usage and many finer reports on individual sites indicating the number of unique users, average time spent on the site and the number of pages viewed.

Since the watched behavior comes from a controlled panel, the companies can know a great deal about the individuals who tend to view specific sites. Most of the research companies know the basic demographics of their panel members, and they increasingly collect psychographic information as well as behavioral information, especially as it affects use of certain products and brands.

The companies sell their services to large agencies and advertisers (most are priced in the tens of thousands of dollars), but they offer some general market-wide data for free from their websites.

Each company employs a slightly different methodology, different sizes of panels and different types of knowledge about the panel members. Even when they report the very same type of information—like the number of users of a particular media site—they very seldom agree with one another. Subscribers to the services commonly find differences of 10 to 20 percent between different versions of the numbers.

Different types of advertisers are likely to prefer one research company over another, but I cannot make a gross generalization about their relative merits. Factors helping decide for one over another in a given situation include:

- The degree to which the panel covers both home and work audiences
- Panel size
- Amount of information known about panel members
- Reporting capabilities provided by the services (usually through subscriber web sites)
- Coverage of local and regional sites
- Ability to determine average reach and frequency figures

- Capability of estimating the average overlap of users among sites
- Whether or not the panel is monitored by computer or self-reported survey (self-reported surveys in traditional media are notorious for sketchy results)

The major syndicated research companies include Nielsen/Netratings, Media Metrix and @Plan (recently made into a subdivision of DoubleClick). The Nielsen/Netratings offering and the Media Metrix product both employ automated panel tracking programs, while @Plan uses self-reported data. The @plan application, however, offers much more information about user behavior relative to product categories and brands.

Whenever one panel company produces a new type of data, the others seem to quickly catch up. To choose which makes most sense for a particular client, visit the websites of each to make a determination.

In any case, the syndicated research can only tell buyers fairly general information. Experience shows that each individual brand and campaign involves enough complexity and intervening factors to make this research less than predictive. Actual campaign performance and the relative performance among sites will best be determined with the advertiser's and agency's own data.

Competitive Data

Companies like CMRInteractive and AdRelevance can help an advertiser see where the competition concentrates their marketing efforts online. They can estimate how much they are spending, where, and frequently with which creative.

The panel research companies also offer some competitive information, like the Netratings BannerTrack service.

This information can provide very good ideas for different types of sites that might perform well for a product category.

Proprietary Research

Very often, the information an advertiser requires simply isn't tracked by any of the syndicated sources. Occasionally, the advertiser can provide a research budget to acquire the most immediately relevant information.

Hundreds of research firms—many with roots in traditional market research—can help design surveys and studies for existing advertiser site visitors.

Some companies can also help determine the effect advertising has on the people viewing it. MBInteractive and Marketing Evolution, for instance, have a great deal of experience conducting pre- and post-buy controlled studies to determine the effect of ads on hard-to-measure metrics like the increase of awareness, relative brand preference and brand recall.

The studies that the people running these two companies conducted early in the industry's development helped to scientifically establish the online media as legitimate options for branding purposes.

The Case Against Online Audits

In traditional media, an ad placement goes out to everyone who received the publication or saw the TV show. So knowing about everyone who saw that publication or show was pretty important, if only to show how much wastage resulted. This made a product called a "circulation audit" fairly important for publications.

The equivalent product in the online space—the site audit—has less value, however, for the same purpose.

On the net, people buy discrete batches of media. A buyer might purchase 50,000 impressions from EfficientSite.com, targeted at folks who visit the job search section. The buyer doesn't care that the site experienced 500,000 impressions that week, or that they happened to come from Shriners in San Francisco or born-agains in Tuscaloosa.

The buyer is concerned with a very particular set of impressions and the characteristics of those very particular viewers. Audits do not give this information. In fact, often the only useful source of information on these folks tends to be the behavior the viewers exhibit after seeing the ad—something trackable on the client site.

Audits of site popularity and viewer characteristics do not, therefor, give useful information to buyers in most cases. There are a few instances where the audit numbers might come in handy—like calculating the average frequency of exposure a given user might experience with a certain weight level—but for the most part, this is esoteric stuff.

Two major problems exist with existing audits:

- They track the whole site, and not individual media buys
- And the methodologies they employ can be quite drastically different from site to site

There does, indeed, exist a screaming need for audits in the online world. In particular, people buying impressions from web sites need to know that they are, in fact, getting the right amount of media for their ads, and at the correct times and locations. Currently, they have to trust the site's numbers, sometimes with the rough verification of their own agency-side banner servers. The audits, instead of giving relevant buy information, give them the gross numbers of all buys, plus all the media the site didn't even sell.

In an example of bad going to worse, some auditing companies have come up with the solution of "certifying" sites. This means they look to make sure that the site's measurement policies are followed, allowing the ad reporting information they give agencies to be endorsed by the auditing company.

But the audit companies allow standards to change from instance to instance, at the arbitrary behest of their individual site customers. This worked alright in the world of financial audits because the IRS forced companies to obey a common set of principles: GAAP. But there's no equivalent to GAAP in the online advertising world.

If a site decides to have an ad reporting process of 1—Lying 2—Cheating 3—Stealing 4—Inventing numbers arbitrarily to cover it up, then the audit company comes in to ensure that this process gets obeyed. The site will fail the audit in this case only if it mistakenly perpetrates honest behavior.

I was an early witness to the devolution in the online audit business. As an agency person, I watched in the mid-90s the competitors in the audit industry strive to gain market share. The pressure forced all the companies to adopt the most appealing policies to their customers: the sites. The agency people just weren't sophisticated at the time to see the wool coming down over their eyes. There was a great deal of pressure to make sure the reported numbers looked large, and no countering pressure to make sure the numbers reflected reality.

SEARCH ENGINE SITES & THEIR SUBTLETIES

A search engine is a site that allows users to type "keywords" into a text box to get the site to give back a list of relevant sites by comparing the keyword query against a pre-compiled index of the Web. Someone typing in "pointing dogs" is likely to see a results screen pop up with listings of sites having to do with brittanys, setters and English pointers. AltaVista is an example of this type of query search engine. Typically, these sites show ten results at a time, allowing users to choose to see another screenfull of results if the first ones don't meet their taste.

Another type of search engine is the "directory" site. This site, like the popular Yahoo! site, will make a catalog of many web sites and organize them into convenient categories. To get to the brittany pages you might have to first click Family, then Pets, then Dogs, then Pointing Breeds, and finally Brittanies to get to your desired pages. For our purposes in this chapter the generic term search engine will suffice for both.

Search engines deserve their own chapter because of their importance to several facets of online advertising. They provide an important—in fact, the most common—form of targeting on the web. They tend to attract viewers who happen to be in a net-roaming mode of behavior. And the majority of most advertisers' site traffic comes from referrals from search engines

Behind email, search engines remain the most commonly used application on the Internet. Several studies have shown that about 5 out of 6 web users deliberately employ search engines to find out about things they buy. This makes them hot real estate for media buyers.

There are two main ways to take advantage of search engines as media opportunities. Like other sites, you can purchase media on the sites. Marketers especially like to purchase impressions associated with very specific keywords. My old client, Match.com, for instance used to look for opportunities to purchase media associated with the keyword "dating." The other way to exploit search engines is to make sure the client is listed in the site's index of the Web, so that when people query the database, the client site pops up among the other results. Both methods deserve some explanation.

Listings

The cheapest and often the best way take advantage of search engines is to simply get listed. The search engines operate much like the Yellow Pages, listing all sites they know about—for free. They catalog information about each site automatically by searching the web with special servers alternately called worms, crawlers or "'bots." But the Internet remains a pretty big place. As of this writing, none of the search engines were able to catalog more than 16 percent of the Web.

The search engine will then apply a formula to determine what types of categories should be most relevant to each site. This algorithm varies from site to site. In the early days of the industry, people would try to increase the number of categories in which they were listed by inserting all sorts of tricks into the HTML code of their client's site. One such common trick involved putting long lists of words at the ends of web pages coded to appear invisibly in the identical color as the background. Users wouldn't see them, but the search engines would chew through these words to help place the site either higher up in one category or into many more categories.

Very quickly, word spread of these practices, forcing the search engine companies to continually adapt their algorithms. An arms race of sorts developed, where some determined web site developers continued to try to trick the systems. That arms race continues today, with entire companies dedicated to raising the prominence of clients' sites through the use of various strategies and tricks.

A major problem facing these companies and their clients is the fact that what might make one search engine list the client as the very first listing for a category, might make another search engine ignore it completely. As the search engine algorithms evolved away from one another, it became increasingly difficult to trick one engine successfully without messing up the listing on another.

A strategy called server farming effective avoids this problem. Server farming replicates the first few pages of a site on separate servers for each search engine. This allows web developers to create sites slightly customized for each engine. Companies like Web Site Publicity.com manage this labor-intensive process for many clients. At the end of the day, most clients find more traffic coming from these listings on search engines than from any amount of banner advertising. And, aside from management fees, it's free.

Each search engine posts the process by which a site can get listed within its content. Doing this with the most prominent 20 or 30 search engines should be the first priority of any search engine strategy.

After that, clients might consider hiring a firm expert in the vagaries of search engine algorithms. Most ad agencies find that they do not have enough clients to warrant the hiring of special experts in this field. As a result, few are known to be very good at keeping clients high among the listings.

Periodically, one search engine or another decides to start a program whereby they will charge sites listed on the index for higher placements. In the past, these business models haven't done very well, as users tend to shift away from using services that bias the results toward paying customers. The user experience tends to be less relevant when the search engine foists client sites upon the people typing in specific queries. Most sites that tried it years ago abandoned the practice for fear of losing site traffic. Another spate of this has occurred recently, however, as the ad revenue pressures have increased.

A great resource for determining your site's position relative to its competition is http://www.positionagent.com/. This site, now owned by Microsoft's bCentral site, produces a chart showing a site's position in the search engine rankings, both by page number and by listing number. This basic service is free, and extended services can be purchased on a subscription basis.

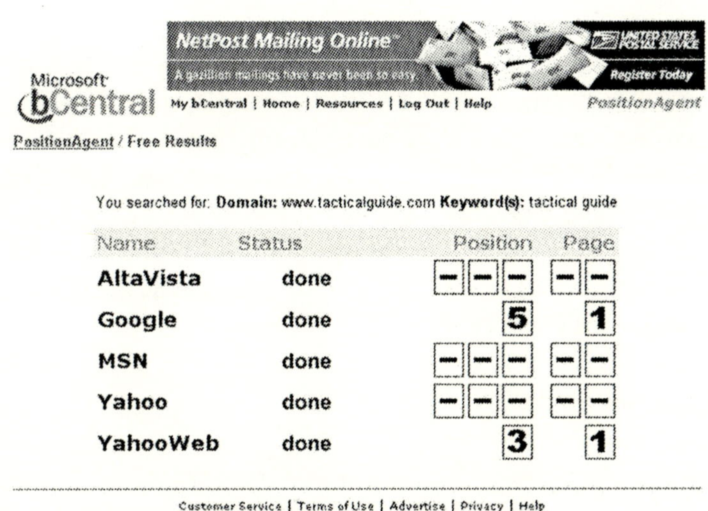

Name	Status	Position	Page
AltaVista	done	- - -	- -
Google	done	5	1
MSN	done	- - -	- -
Yahoo	done	- - -	- -
YahooWeb	done	3	1

Industry experts regard Searchenginewatch.com as a good source of updated information on the ongoing algorithm wars and the relevant services.

Paid-For Listings

Recently, many of the major search engines have started to institute fees for listing within the engine's editorial content. In the beginning of the industry, this was tried and abandoned because users didn't like the idea that those sites were giving them references based more on pay than on relevance to their search criteria.

The new fees-for-services might take the form of "expedited" services, where they can get a new site listed in a few days, instead of the normal weeks or months. This allows web sites to cut through line and get listed faster. Some staff at some sites worry that this is a precursor to search engines charging for listings, or charging for the higher placements in the listings.

Just before this book went to the printers, a Ralph Nader group called Commercial Alert filed a complaint with the Federal Trade Commission about the placement practices. Specifically named in the complaint were MSN, Netscape, Directhit, HotBot, Lycos, Altavista, LookSmart, and iWon. The group alleged that posing paid listings as content is the moral equivalent of infomercials that are not adequately labeled as advertising—a practice the FTC has challenged in the past.

Placements

Only after that low fruit is plucked from the marketing tree by taking advantage of free listings on the search engines will advertisers want to promote their services with paid placements.

Not only do the placements give them prominence where their listing fails to show up, but it also gives a sense of industry leadership. Users employing keywords often understand that the ad placed above the results page is a purchased spot, indicating that company's initiative relative to the specific product category. In the mind of the viewer, the brand that appears above the results page earns an association with the topic searched. This can be used for repositioning and rebranding efforts, such as taking a company with a stodgy reputation and imparting a cutting-edge impression.

Planners will concern themselves with answering the following questions to determine the right search engine advertising opportunities:

- Search engine audience trends
- Keyword availability
- Service levels and contract flexibility
- Ability to use customized creative to keywords

Audience Trends

The audiences for each search engine differ significantly. Mostly because the search engines do a great deal of offline and online promotion, the very branding that they adopt attracts different types of users who exhibit different behaviors. For instance, AOL, Yahoo!, and Excite tend to attract more "newby" web users, while Altavista, Google and HotBot tend to attract very advanced users.

These trends can be seen when demographic and behavioral reports are run on the syndicated research services, such as the panel companies. Reports from Media Metrix and Nielsen/Netratings will show distinct trends in audiences, at least in the broadest strokes.

There are many hundreds of different types of search engines out there. The top 10 search engines tend to be the very broadest in concentration—not focusing on any particular industry niche. They tend to get the vast majority of the search engine dollars. Many others warrant a look, though, especially in niche categories relevant to clients.

The best source of data, though, will come after an agency does a few placements with clients. The performance data that comes back from specific campaigns with the client's peculiar type of branding and special use of keywords will suggest more accurate trends in behavior than those any panel company could provide.

Planners should take note that panel company comparisons of search engines often prove misleading, once the influence of keywords gets taken into account. Panel companies sometimes offer a feature referred to as a reach overlap determination. This allows planners to type in the media weight levels they propose on various sites and have the panel database return information on the likely overlap that will occur from site to site. A big buy of 1MM impressions on two different sites, even with a frequency cap of 1 impression per person, will result in some overlap of some people seeing the same ad once on both sites. These panel data companies make the assumption, however, that all people visiting a site are as likely to see one ad as they are another ad. But, with search engines, an individual user is likely to use the same keywords on multiple sites. Presuming that many advertisers buy the same keywords across multiple sites, this means that the overlap factor among search engines will be much higher than reported by the panel companies.

Purchasing Search Engine Media

The cost of impressions on a search engine is quite low for untargeted media. CPMs frequently extend below $10, and depending on the size and structure of the deal, even below $2 CPM. For targeted media, particularly keyword-associated media, the CPMs can be quite high. Keywords are seldom bought for less than $15 CPM, and sometimes can exceed $100 CPM for special words in high-demand categories. Most sites sell keywords one word at a time, allowing market demand to help determine price.

Some advertisers like to lock up their keywords with exclusive deals. For extra fees, they can get search engines to contract away their right to sell certain words to competitors. Often this means the advertiser must buy all of the media that results from those keywords, but with other types of deals where the advertiser purchases only a set quantity of those keyword impressions. The rest of the resulting media gets thrown into the ROS inventory pool.

Many planners fall into the trap of misunderstanding the difference between sites that can use only words as keywords and sites that can employ full phrases as keywords. I learned this the hard way when some planners of mine thought they were buying the phrase "phone card" for my Sprint client at J. Walter Thompson in San Francisco. Some of the search engines interpreted as giving them the right to give us all the media that resulted from queries on the words "phone" and "card" as well as "phone card." Others took the more strict definition and gave us only the media from the queries with the full phrase. The difference was dramatic. While we received (and had to pay for) tens of times more media from the first set, the quality of the responses from users was tens of times higher from the second set. As a matter of course, planners should always confirm the site's intent with keyword purchases.

Because search engine sites deal with so many advertisers—a seemingly unmanageable quantity of agencies, advertisers and campaigns—they often will set monthly minimums for advertising. Few of the large search engines will want to do business with companies wishing to spend fewer than $5,000 per month on one site. Many won't even return phone messages regarding smaller deals.

The proportions of the budget between ROS buys and keyword buys should vary by campaign and site. The more targeted the buy, the higher the price. As a result, planners and buyers have to monitor whether or not that extra media premium proves to be worthwhile. Frequently, search engines seek such high premiums for the targeted media that a lot of brands find it more efficient to buy the media in bulk, without the extra targeting. Brands featuring broad audiences and product categories that involve confusing keywords often find that keywords aren't worth the extra expense.

A contract clause that allows for the shifting of media in or out of the keyword structure should protect buyers from most problems. Often, buyers will find a compliant salesperson when they guarantee a gross amount of dollars spent, but leave open the option to exploit low-CPM ROS media in the case that the keyword performance fails.

Choosing Keywords

Often, a campaign's objectives will determine the type of keywords appropriate to the client. For instance, if a planner works on a skin cleansing pad account, and the campaign seeks to break out into the teen market, the planner might choose words such as "zit," "pimple" and "acne." That same product, in a campaign to cosmetics users might use keywords such as "astringent," "wrinkles" and "facial."

The best keyword campaigns typically have creative designed for the specific words. Because of the very early planning involved, and the high cost of production, this isn't done in most cases, but planners find that customized creative tends to multiply both clickthrough rates and response rates. This makes sense when different keywords imply different types of people viewing the ad, or people in different modes of behavior. A piece of creative designed to address the teen acne market might well ensure that an older woman seeking astringents never purchases the product.

All those companies that have the word "solutions" in their product name find this a bear of a problem. Someone who types in the words "telecommunication solutions" into a search engine might want to buy a phone, long distance service, a PBX call center, hire a messaging service or change their internal Ethernet wiring to fiberoptic cable. Purchasing such a keyword phrase often leads to a lot of bum site traffic, despite the sometimes attractive-looking clickthrough rates.

Putting yourself in the user's shoes remains the best way to find keywords. Basic due diligence needs to be done before coming up with an initial list:

- First, make a list of all the words you intuitively know will be used to locate your client's type of products. Eliminate from that list the words that people might use to look for other types of categories too.
- Try to find your client's site through the major search engines using the most obvious keywords, and note which ones fail to show the client site prominently.
- Pretend you are a potential purchaser of your client's products, and go to the sites you suspect such a person would visit to find useful information. Note what words and themes tend to be used.
- Use a search engine like Goto.com that will give you a list of "related searches" after querying for some of the obvious keywords. This information comes from looking at what real users tend to search for after having typed in the same thing you did.
- Write down the names of competing brands and related products.
- And, finally, take down a list of all the publications you find that focus on these types of products.

From this long list, buyers will need to cull down to the better keywords, but first they must determine the availability of these keywords on the considered sites.

Keyword Availability

Keyword media is both a finite resource and a fundamentally unpredictable one. No one really knows how much media will be produced in a given month from a specific keyword. Sites can just go by past precedents and trends.

Often, fewer impressions occur than expected. Buyers should also beware the potential of too many impressions happening, especially if they've negotiated a deal that involves buying up the keyword's entire inventory.

As part of the RFP process, buyers will ask reps for the availability numbers of the words they hope to purchase. Depending on what type of traffic the given site generates and how much of that media has already been sold, the sites will come back with greatly varying numbers. When just a few hundred queries are performed on a given word in a month, it's usually not worth the trouble to buy them, and buyers frequently find themselves surprised by which words prove unpopular.

Search Engine Issues

Since the search engines deal with so many advertisers, and with many special conditions, such as keyword targeting and impression caps, they tend to have a harder time keeping track of deals. Experience shows that the search engines tend to have a higher error rate in basic trafficking issues, like putting up the correct linking URLs and alt text. Discrepancy resolution tends to become nightmarish, especially when many keywords are used with different guaranteed levels, caps and prices.

Buyers can avoid some of these problems by ensuring that they don't enter into more deals or more complex deals than their existing resources will be able to track and manage. Do not count on the sites to handle this quality control by themselves.

Be sure to confirm, before placing an order, that performance data will be returned in the right format and with the right frequency. For instance, some search engines have surprised buyers by providing them with generalized performance data, summing up the figures from all the different keywords purchased.

Also, banner burnout may happen faster with search engine

keyword buys, as most search engine users employ more than one search engine and often use the same keyword multiple times at multiple sites. This leads to a very high frequency average and a lower reach figure than many expect.

OTHER TARGETING

If I have a criticism of media departments at both clients and agencies, it's that they like numbers too much. I'm a quantitative person myself, but sometimes I see that we begin to rely on numbers less for the reality they represent, and more for the comfort they give us. In the media world, we've come to put trust in numbers that turn out to be rather meaningless online.

Problems with Demographics

Back in the 1880's, James Walter Thompson invented a system of making generalizations about people by classifying them by age, gender and other factors and applying this to media choices. This "demography" that resulted launched his company into one of the vaunted top positions among ad agencies. Some say that he even invented the ad agency because of these applied insights.

And this demography worked—or at least it worked better than anything else around. It was true that women of a certain age tended to hold beliefs and subscribe to differing publications than older or younger women. Creative could be geared to them. Media choices could be adapted to them.

But all along, the connection was an indirect one. There is always the imperfect assumption that what you are and where you come from defines what you believe and buy. True enough to be useful, but not correct enough to be completely true.

We in the media departments of the world have come to assume that demographics are a science that can't be ignored. I frequently get asked why we did not include demographic information in targeting briefs or media rationales. And here's why.

The Ghost of a Ghost

In the online environment, we don't have very good demographic information. Sure, you can get generalizations about who's appearing on one site versus another by looking at various sampling studies done by companies like Nielsen/Netratings and Media Metrix.

But these are indirect means of measuring. In other words, we are getting only a decent guess at the information that gives us a decent guess of what a person is likely to think or do. When you add these two levels of indirectness into the equations, we're on very shaky ground.

Let's say that demography gives us a 60 percent chance of being right about an individual's behavior online, and that some study will give you a 60 percent chance of knowing the correct demography of that individual. Mathematically, we have to multiply the .6 likelihood against the other .6 likelihood to receive a very inaccurate 36 percent chance of being correct.

When I've asked people who set up the sales departments of web sites, they've told me the reason they provide demographic data is merely because a lot of the larger, traditional agencies ask for them—not because they prove useful in subsequent targeting.

Another common problem with demographics is that they change radically from section to section within a given site. Buyers cannot assume that they are getting a particular kind of viewer, despite syndicated research and figures provided by sites.

So, What Are Our Alternatives?

Fortunately, the online world presents a great diversity of targeting to substitute for the wanting of demographics. In particular, online is great at directly measuring behavior. When buyers rely on such information, they don't have to guess at who the customer is in order to further make a guess at what that type of person might do. They can, instead, directly see what the customer is doing online.

Media folks sometimes try too hard to make the online media look just like the offline media by forcing themselves to use the same metrics. This is needless because they now have new metrics, like figures that show us who is buying what and visiting where. Many of the profiling companies, like Engage, provide media based on these more behavioral measures.

While online media's metrics aren't as familiar to buyers as traditional media's demographics, they can be more useful. To take advantage of them, buyers need to have more of the philosophy found in the creative departments of ad agencies. There, people use "ad gut" to divine new ideas. Online media buying is now more about experimenting with creative suppositions of where clients' customers are most likely to be and which technologies and behavior information are most likely to lead to them.

Targeting Types

This industry's first efforts at targeting online merely emulated all the traditional types of targeting. In the Internet world, we now have demographic targeting, focusing on gross generalizations about our clients' markets. We've done plenty of content association targeting, getting our advertising merely adjacent to content that is similar to the product being proffered. This last type comprises the vast majority of online advertising targeting to date.

We've also tested out all sorts of other types of targeting mechanisms, like profiling, topographical associative targeting, and other types of behavioral targeting. These technologies allow us not to get at particular types of people, but people who have done particular types of things. It is here that the Internet provides unique media opportunities. The medium is uniquely suited to behavioral targeting precisely because it is so measurable. We will go over each of these types in detail.

Behavioral Modes

I've found much better results by purchasing media online that delivers people who either have done or are doing a desired behavior. The most desirable behavior is often the purchase a product similar to the one my client's selling. Buyers can divvy up the viewers out there into different types of behavioral types—a targeting type called "modes."

We can generalize the entire Internet universe into a system of modes for each client. Depending on their product categories and brand nuances, a client might want to employ a different type of segmentation. One brand might divide the universe into the behavior modes of buyers, procrastinators, information seekers, and interest groupies. Another might group the inventory available into the categories: self-directed, looking for guidance, random surfers. Over time, agencies and clients can tweak their segmentations to reflect how well they are able to show statistically significant performance benefits over non-targeted media. And each product category and brand may develop its own custom segmentation to fit its needs.

We execute behavioral media campaigns in five steps:

- Propose a modal segmentation for the advertiser
- Choose a targeting system that will provide behavioral data to suit your modes
- Determine media available that can meet the behavioral requirements to qualify for the relevant mode
- Purchase the media while tracking its performance against untargeted media buys

- Analyze the benefit gained through modal targeting and assess cost-worthiness

When purchasing highly targeted media, we frequently must re-assess how much the extra cost of the targeting helps the campaign. Depending on how effective your targeting proves, it may well be more efficient to purchase untargeted media. This is particularly true with product categories involving very broad categories of people and very common behaviors.

One of the benefits of modal targeting is that it doesn't always lump certain people in one category, no matter their propensity to purchase a product. Any one individual may be a member of one mode at one moment, and then evolve into a member of another mode the next moment. It all depends on what they're viewing on the web at that instant and—more importantly—what they're doing with that content. Your client should be concerned merely with the temporary group of people who, at that moment, happen to be in the particular mode that makes them most vulnerable to their marketing message.

Profiling

Profiling does this in its own fashion, providing the company doing the profiling collects the right, relevant data and is able to keep it fresh and instantly accessible.

The easiest way to exploit behavioral targeting via profiling is to employ an existing technology company, like Engage or DoubleClick. They have systems already in place to provide a great deal of media based on user behavior.

The Engage system, for example, follows users from page to page on its network of sites. Using cookie technology and a very a large database, Engage can tell which users are—at this very moment—in a particular type of mind frame. The company discerns this by directly observing which pages the user travels to and what the user does on those pages.

Engage has developed its own set of modes, keeping track of each individual's current likelihood of being relevant to about 170 categories of behavior.

If the user goes to the Volkswagen site, the car purchasing mode ratio will shoot up. If the user goes to several competing auto web sites, the ratio will go up still further. If time passes since those visits, the ratio will go down. Users like this are precisely the ones that automotive companies want to see, and they pay an extra 200 to 300 percent on the CPM to get such targeting.

You can rough out a modal media buy, however, on your own, and you can frequently do it without paying exorbitant CPMs for working with a major network and employing extra targeting technologies.

Site reps will frequently work with you to determine the particular types of desired behavior you require for your client, and figure out ways of packaging their media to fit. If you're purchasing media for an online commerce company, like a bookstore, you might want to put an ad on the "thank you for your purchase" page of another e-commerce site. I think Barnes and Noble does this quite nicely, when they show you five or six other commerce sites on that thank you page. By doing so, they are able to sell an audience that is shopping, with credit cards out and with confidence in online security.

Setting Expectations

First, determine the behavioral modes that might be relevant to your client. For each client, a different segmentation might be appropriate. Then, figure out the right combination of your existing marketing messages (or have new ones created) with these new modal targets. You will likely be wrong the first time or two. But, with a few campaigns under your belt, a client's brand will begin to fit into the data picture with greater clarity.

When employing modal methods of targeting, be sure to set

your client's expectations as to how long it may take to strike upon the right modes and the right media opportunities. Marketers rarely figure out the exact segmentation, message and media choices the first time out. This can be very frustrating to clients, especially if the agency sells them on the benefits of behavioral and modal targeting without warning of the highly iterative nature of the process.

Topographical Targeting

In the past few years, several companies have come out with some complicated, high-tech targeting mechanisms called topographical associative targeting (more recently referred to as collaborative filtering). This is the rocket science of online marketing. The premise of it operates on the theory that by watching closely what one group of people prefers, a marketer can predict what another person will like based on very little behavioral information.

For instance, if my brother Mark purchases a couple Dire Straits CD's, some Sting and The Complete Works of Mark Knoepfler, the system will loosely associate these selections. When I come around to buy a Dire Straits CD, the system suspects that I'd be a sucker for the other two as well, so it presents me with an advertisement for the latest albums of Sting and Knoepfler.

These systems develop complicated profiles of different types of people. The problem has been that they just haven't worked very well so far. The example I used looks pretty good, but the information that a site collects is often much more complicated. In reality, my brother buys a CD for my dad for his birthday (Carly Simon), then he goes and buys term life insurance on his way to buying that Dire Straits CD. And that's why the Allstate insurance company feels burned when they wind up paying a premium to get in front of Carly Simon buyers. It's difficult to truly divine the predictable preferences of humans with so few inputs.

The good news is that these types of systems are getting smarter, and the information that feeds them is getting more integrated as time goes on.

There are some great implementations of this technology on a few commerce sites, like Amazon.com. Whenever I visit Amazon, they have a list of books waiting to spring on me. And I usually want to buy a bunch of them. They've gotten to know me pretty well from my past purchasing behavior. It's easier for Amazon, though, because they limit it to a single category of products at a time.

I've always been a proponent of experimenting with these new technologies. After all, this is really the future of online advertising. When Firefly came out in 1995, I was eager to get my Sprint client to spend some money on some experiments. What happened with Sprint, unfortunately, became representative of all the other subsequent tests. We ran a campaign on Firefly, controlled to gauge the effect of the targeting, and we found no great difference between the media that used the technology and the stuff we ran without it.

To be fair, the measurements available to us at the time were very rudimentary, so we could only gauge "performance" based on clickthrough. And we know from myriad studies done in the past couple years, clickthrough is a very poor indication of performance.

Also, the product category of long distance communications is so broad, that it was a very high hurdle to set for the new technology. When the system determined that one person clicked on the Sprint banner, the information known about that individual was very difficult to fit into a pattern with the others who did the same.

Some of the profiling applications available today, like that of Engage, attempt to exploit a similar technology. I asked an engineer from Engage about the efficacy of this particular part of the program, and he summed the problem up for me most succinctly.

"Some things that are intuitive to computers aren't intuitive to humans, and some things intuitive to people aren't intuitive to computers," he said. "We're trying to use computers to give us that good stuff that isn't necessarily intuitive to us by doing the topographical thing. But to get good topographical information, we need to use humans to point out the classifications and logical relationships that computers don't understand well."

In other words, it remains a fairly manual process to get good targeting information. For better or worse, we keep rediscovering that human talent remains the best capital investment for the improvement of advertising performance.

Content Type Targeting

Content targeting remains a very simple concept in the online world. We make assumptions, sometimes backed up by viewer studies, about what type of person looks at a type of content.

In the traditional media world, we typically break these people up into demographics. Women 18 to 54 watch daytime TV. Men 24-54 watch sports on Saturday afternoons. In the online world, we tend to break this up into more behavioral measures. People who golf go to Golf.com. People who play and buy games go to Gamespot.com.

Content targeting can be employed whether a campaign is based on demographic or behavioral approaches. This sometimes makes for interesting conversations with sales reps. They, of course, are going to want to sell their media based on the most expensive categorization of their users. It might be that the average CPM for targeting men is $5, and the average CPM for targeting known golfers is $25. When you speak to the Golf.com rep (a very nice guy named Tim Shannehan) about your new campaign for a hair tonic, you don't really care about golf. And you certainly don't care for that extra $20 on the CPM because these men happen to be golfers. Lacking titanium drivers and putters to sell, the behavioral element of the target isn't something for which you want to pay.

Typically, what happens in cases like this depends on the available inventory. While a golf site is unlikely to give an 80 percent discount to a golfing company, with remnant inventory unsold, the site is quite likely to offer deeper discounts to non-golf companies. They know that they are not destroying the integrity of their golf-oriented rate cards when they sell to non-golf-oriented companies.

The seller justifiably discriminates against buyers with a greater demand. This is one of several reasons why you never know what's going to happen before negotiations start. It's also another great reason to make sure that rep relationships remain cozy.

This topic will come up again when we discuss the different philosophies of sales rep engagement. One school of thought—the one I eventually came to support—holds that buyers should disclose all they can about a campaign to reps, in the hopes of getting better solutions proposed. The other holds that much information should be hidden from the rep. These folks hope to trick the people at the golf site into believing their client is looking for men rather than golfers. While sales reps sometimes complain about buyers who fail to be forthright, I have little sympathy, given their discriminatory rate structures.

"Keyword" Search Terms

Keywords were covered in greater detail in the last chapter, but we should put them into context with the other forms of targeting here.

Keyword buys on search engines perform very well, when the right words are used for the right product categories. It makes sense this would perform so well, as the users typing them in are deliberately identifying themselves as people interested in a particular topic. Additionally, since they know they are about to face a page full of links, they tend to be in the mode of web exploration. That makes them more vulnerable to interesting pitches in advertisements.

As with other forms of targeting that generally involve paying CPM premiums, buys need to be re-evaluated frequently to make sure that the benefit granted by the targeting mechanism produces efficiencies that outweigh the increased media costs.

Local and Regional Targeting

That local and regional targeting have proved to be very difficult on the Internet poses a puzzle for a lot of media buyers.

To start, the regional information that many sites provide about their users is quite inaccurate. Most sites selling regional buys employ their server logs to determine a user's location. But those server logs provide very poor information. Most times, they merely provide the addresses of the viewers' Internet service providers. That means that all 40 million people using America Online supposedly live in Vienna, Virginia. I know Vienna pretty well, and it's certainly a shame that it's become so over-crowded, but it's not *that* over-crowded.

Because of this glaringly poor methodology, many advertisers looking to purchase media locally look to other types of targeting. Content targeting is probably the most commonly used method to reach certain cities. Local newspaper sites, regional organization sites, and sites that divvy up national content into local divisions provide many good opportunities for local inventory.

Sites like Weather.com nationally provide content that is inherently local in nature. Since most users type in their zip code, they can easily target their audience with great precision.

Less commonly, regions may be targeted by topic. This takes some figuring, but examples can be found for almost any region. For instance, watermelon pickles are (thankfully!) limited to certain regions of the South. I doubt there are too many sites on the topic, but folks seeking people in that region might find other topics useful too, like Cavaliers Football or the wintering grounds of tundra swans.

This brings us to the other major problem in local targeting. By its very nature, we wind up dealing with relatively small sites and even smaller slices of inventory on those sites. This makes the costs of conducting the transactions to purchase the media very high relative to the media costs themselves. Sometimes, the sites we identify for a region are small enough or unsophisticated enough that they don't even have regular advertising programs. At this point, we need to make the decision of whether or not to bother getting relevant sites to cooperate with an advertising program, or turn back to the large networks.

Big networks like AdSmart and DoubleClick sell inventory targeted by locality. Sometimes these networks have information better than mere server log reports, and can get buyers zip code level information. The networks tend to charge high CPMs for this inventory.

Remember when conducting local buys that the administrative tasks will multiply. You will be dealing with a much higher number of sites relative to the impression counts. These sites will tend to be less sophisticated and comply with fewer standards. They will be more prone to inaccuracies of media weights, flight times, linking URLs and about anything else that can conceivably go wrong.

At Anderson & Lembke, when we launched Microsoft's new local site portals, then called Sidewalk.com, we put a staff of four people from the media department on the project for about three months. All four considered this project to be the most understaffed project on which they'd yet worked. Finding enough media to spend the budget was much harder than expected, and the scrutiny required to make sure everything went up correctly and on time turned out to be an impossible job for just four people. We sometimes even had the creatives on the project pitching in to help with the trafficking late on Friday nights.

Is This a Job for Email?

Sometimes audiences, especially those with very narrow interests, can best be found through a purchased email list. We will speak in greater detail about this process in the next chapter, but be sure to consider the direct email campaign as an alternative to local targeting with typical ad placements.

Demographics as Last Resort

Even James Walter Thompson recognized that the link between the demographic categories and the propensities to buy certain products were very over-generalized.

He marketed cookware to women and shotgun shells to men, but he knew that at any given moment, it might be the man purchasing the cookware and the woman seeking shells for the family larder. Back at the end of the 19th Century, this was due largely to the fact that we couldn't divvy up media in a more useful manner.

Fast forward 12 decades and we're pretty much doing the same thing, except we're marketing Biore face pads to women 18-34 and razors to men 24-54.

But when we employ the demographics today, it has less to do with the fact that we can't divvy up the media in certain ways—because now we can. It has more to do with the fact that some of the products we advertise remain difficult to target any less broadly than with demographics.

If Thompson were alive today, he wouldn't be targeting cookware to women. He'd be targeting it at people interested in cooking. He'd try to sell the shotgun shells not in a place that got a high percentage of men. For that product, he'd go after people who shoot competitively and recreationally.

He'd be employing demographics for the face pads and razors, though, because they remain behaviorally relevant to those particular demographics, and can't be much further targeted.

As for demographic media online, the campaigns my agencies have bought over the years have performed very much like "remnant" media, the stuff that's not targeted at all.

EMAIL MARKETING

In email marketing, the advertiser either sponsors an existing email newsletter or acquires the use of an email list to send out its own message independently. That message usually tries to lead a reader to respond to an offer of some type, either through a return email or—more often—through a web site created specially for the occasion.

More and more media buyers find themselves conducting email marketing campaigns along with their online media campaigns. The two go hand in hand, as both frequently use direct marketing tactics to inspire transactions that are then measured and analyzed for campaign optimization.

When these messages are well targeted, and perhaps even customized to individuals based on database information, they often receive great response rates. When advertisers send out bulk emails to ill-targeted groups, they tend to get very poor responses, and they fall afoul of online "spam" policies.

The campaign's responses typically finish coming in within three or four days, often making for a frenetic pace. We can break the process down into four stages:

- Target determination
- List acquisition (or creation)
- Offer determination
- Execution

Before we get into the tactical email process, we first need to ensure we don't violate the privacy expectations of the audience.

Opt-in Issues

Our early experiences in online marketing show that consumers become much more concerned about their privacy when the form of communication is an email. When banners get targeted to them based on personal information, it remains a relatively indirect connection. An email in their in-box makes them feel like someone has reached out and touched them.

On top of that, most users experience a growing flow of emails over time and become more and more sensitive to the ones that waste their time. Poorly targeted marketing emails will literally enrage some people, as they often feel that other people and organizations should not have the right to pass on their email address. These poorly targeted emails are called "spam," and there are two types:

- From the perspective of the consumer, spam is any message that was unsolicited and irrelevant
- From the marketer's perspective, spam is a message sent to an email address acquired through means other than a special process called "double opt-in"

It doesn't take a very critical eye to realize that even if you meet the criteria of the marketer's definition, you still may run afoul of the consumer's definition. This is a topic to revisit after going through the different types of opt-in standards.

Non-Opt-In Lists

Companies can harvest many email addresses off the web with relatively little effort, but the use of those emails becomes very problematic if the people behind the email addresses haven't given permission for their use.

Some shady companies will employ 'bots to search web pages for listed email addresses and churn through discussion groups like the Usenet to steal the addresses from all the people posting comments. They then sell these lists to anyone who wants to send out spam offers. (My favorite being the one where I could buy a law degree for $40. I forwarded that one to my wife during her 2nd year in law school.)

Once people find themselves on one of these lists, they frequently can never get off. When they send an email back to the sender to request to be taken off the list, they are just confirming the validity of the email address. Most of these types of list creators will make a "new" list each time they sell it to a different advertiser, so when the person takes herself off one list, she still finds herself still on every subsequent one.

In many states, this type of spamming has been made illegal, but it hasn't stopped some folks.

Opt-In Email Lists

When a company offers a person the option of joining an email list or newsletter, that suggests that the subsequent list of names will be a more voluntary affair. These email addresses are much more valuable because the opt-in process suffices as a form of pre-qualification. The people behind the email addresses are already expressly interested in some form of information, and they desire to be recontacted.

Fraud remains a major problem with opt-in lists, however, because dishonest list brokers can merely send their spam-quality lists of email addresses in to an opt-in list. It, in effect, becomes a form of list laundering, giving the old spam list a façade of credibility. There isn't any real interactive element required between the addressee and the list to verify the addressee's true intent.

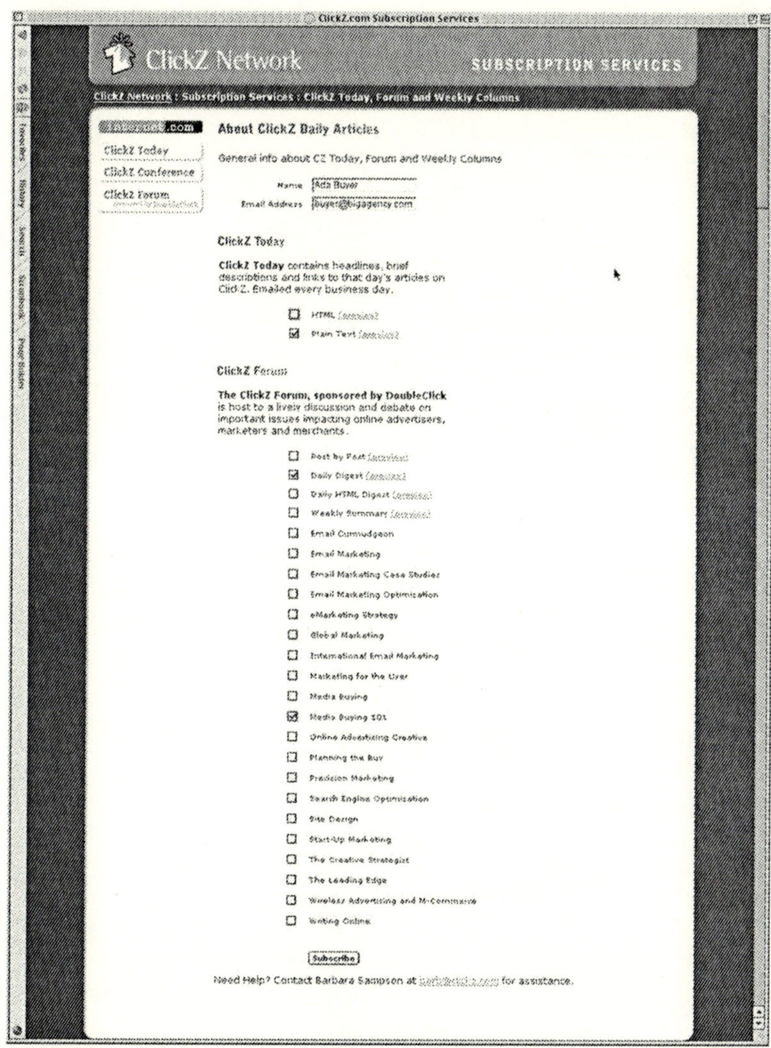

The subscriber enters in basic personal information and selects the appropriate email list

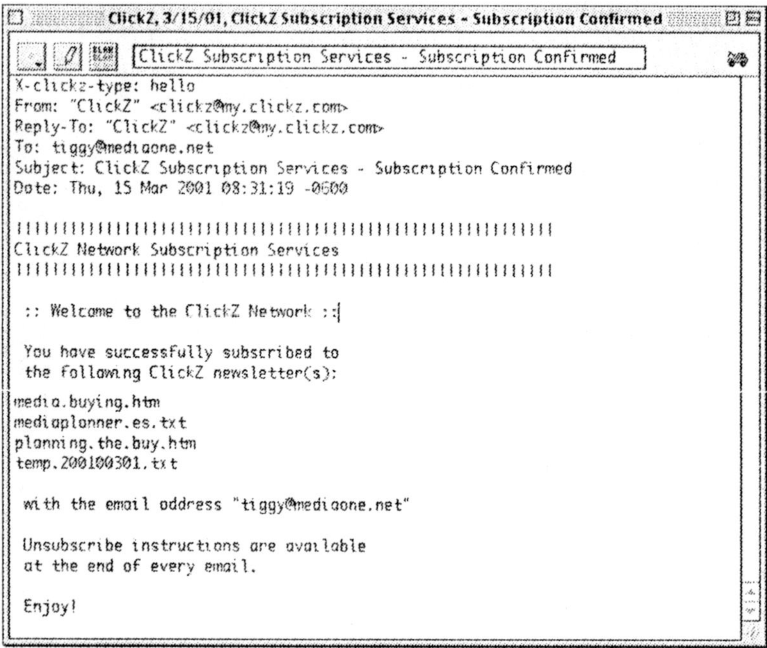

ClickZ, 3/15/01, ClickZ Subscription Services - Subscription Confirmed

ClickZ Subscription Services - Subscription Confirmed

X-clickz-type: hello
From: "ClickZ" <clickz@my.clickz.com>
Reply-To: "ClickZ" <clickz@my.clickz.com>
To: tiggy@mediaone.net
Subject: ClickZ Subscription Services - Subscription Confirmed
Date: Thu, 15 Mar 2001 08:31:19 -0600

||||||||||||||||||||||||||||||||||||||||||||||||||||||||||||
ClickZ Network Subscription Services
||||||||||||||||||||||||||||||||||||||||||||||||||||||||||||

:: Welcome to the ClickZ Network ::

You have successfully subscribed to
the following ClickZ newsletter(s):

media.buying.htm
mediaplanner.es.txt
planning.the.buy.htm
temp.200100301.txt

with the email address "tiggy@mediaone.net"

Unsubscribe instructions are available
at the end of every email.

Enjoy!

The subscriber then receives a confirmation email. Were this a double-opt-in list, the subscriber would be asked to send a response to this confirmation.

Double Opt-In Email Lists

The gold standard nowadays is to go through the opt-in process of requiring users to put in their own email addresses, and then verify their intent by using that email address to get deliberate confirmation. The process involves these steps:

- A user wants to subscribe to my weekly email column on ClickZ.com
- She clicks on the Subscribe button on top of the column's web page

- She enters in her name and email address into the form presented to her
- Moments later, she receives an email message to that same account, asking her to send a response back indicating she confirms the subscription

This process prevents many people from mistakenly or fraudulently being placed on email lists, and has become an industry standard.

The degree to which advertisers appreciate double opt-in lists over mere opt-in lists can be seen in the relative pricing. Companies that sell both types of lists find that double opt-in lists fetch five or more times the price per name as single opt-in names. A recent check of the index that Media Mart, an online media auction company, puts together weekly, showed an average price of $0.04 per opt-in record and $0.27 per double opt-in record.

The industry enforces this standard through an organization called Mail Abuse Prevention System (MAPS). It publishes a list of domain names called the Real-time Blackhole List (RBL), from which spam has come, allowing Internet service providers (ISPs) to shut down the email traffic from these domains. It works very well, as most ISPs cannot afford to have a spamming subscriber effectively shut down everyone's email functionality. It very quickly sent all the newsletter and email-list people scurrying to set up proper double-opt-in procedures.

Third Party Opt-In

Another, still higher, standard exists but is rarely used. Sometimes, especially with very sensitive audiences like children, a list compiler will wish to get not only double opt-in responses, but also permission from a third party.

Nintendo, for instance, created a video game oriented list that required children below a certain age to also have their parents give their permission as well.

List Scrutiny

Within these broad categories of different types of opt-in lists, there remain many questions that the list buyers must be sure to ask. Beyond the simple technical means by which the list was assembled, buyers will want to know:

- Why did these individuals sign up? What was very specific offer they answered, and in what context did they see it? If, for instance, they signed up for someone's technical newsletter merely because they were offered $5, the buyer might find a lot of unqualified people lurking among the email addresses.
- How recently were these names collected, and how recently was the list "cleaned"? Sometimes buyers can select a subset of the list by recency. This will be highly desirable if the list has not been thoroughly cleaned up by eliminating multiple entries and the like.
- How often and how recently has this list been used, and for what messages? Of course, no buyer wishes to be the 10th advertiser to send some poor soul an email advertisement in the same morning.

List Shenanigans

Anyone conducting email marketing needs to verify the policies set out by the list owner. The best way to do this is to borrow the old direct mail "seeding" method from the traditional media folks. Put yourself on all the lists you wish to investigate. This will allow you to see who uses the list, how frequently, and even give some good competitive intelligence sometimes on competitive efforts.

But don't stop there. Try to take yourself off the list, and see if it's as easy as the list broker represents it should be. After this, put your name on the list a couple extra times, just to see if the data cleaning process works correctly.

Do not do all this with your primary email account. The industry is rife with enough honest mistakes and downright shady list companies, that any email address used for this purpose will quickly become a vortex of spam.

Finding Lists

Many online media buyers don't initially know where to start. The three main options, from the simplest to the most complex are:

- Sponsoring a newsletter list
- Renting an existing list from a publication or list broker
- Building your own list

Newsletter Sponsorship

The newsletter sponsorships work much like any other type of online media buy. These typically involve both a text message within the newsletter, and—for the HTML version of the newsletter—a banner-like graphic as well.

Newsletters can be found online for almost every imaginable topic. They vary in frequency from daily to weekly, to the downright intermittent.

They sell by the CPM, just like other online media, although sometimes newsletter publishers will allow for performance-based deals as well.

List Renting

Existing lists can be found and rented out for a specific use. These are typically sold in a slight variant to the CPM basis. Sometimes, instead of the cost per thousand, the lists are priced as the "cost per." That means that an email list priced at $0.20

isn't the great deal it initially appears. Translating that figure into a CPM gives us a $200 price.

Often the best way to find an appropriate list is to look to the web sites that planners would otherwise purchase in a banner buy. These same web site companies often compile email lists of readers who seek more information on specific topics.

Email-specific companies also go about compiling addresses associated to interests. These include YesMail, 24/7, TargitMail, PostmasterDirect and Netcreations.

List Creation

The best long-term solution for clients often turns out to be creating a special, proprietary email list, either through the advertiser's own site or through online media marketing.

Many companies have offline, snailmail information on a lot of their existing customers, which can also be used in a direct mail campaign to get companies to start interactive via email. This works exceptionally well as a tool to link email addresses to already-known information in a client database about the users. By sending a direct mail piece out to such a user, their email response will effectively link your online database about that user with the offline database.

Some agencies specialize in certain industry segments, making it profitable to create their own agency-oriented lists that they can then rent out to their clients. This proved popular with many business-to-business online ad agencies, as they become central clearing houses for media opportunity information on very narrow industry categories.

Deal Structure, Pricing and Negotiating

Perhaps even more so than in the online banner market, email list brokers seem to have an aversion to cost per action (CPA) buys. While buyers might not find themselves able to change some list brokers' minds, they might still find the arguments for CPA deals effective in helping them negotiate CPM prices.

The typical after-negotiation CPM rate for a one-time-use list rental ranges from about $100 to $300, depending on the category and quality of audience. Cost per action deals range even more widely, extending as low as $1 CPA to as high as $30 CPA.

List brokers will want to know a great deal about the typical response rate an advertiser gets before they will become comfortable offering a CPA deal. Those factors will be the primary determinants of their own revenue in such a deal.

In general, any media site or list broker that makes a claim of appropriateness to your desired audience opens themselves up to a challenge from the buyer: if they remain confident in their appropriateness, then why would they shy away from a CPA deal? This rhetorical question is a great place to start a negotiation. It leads to several typical arguments forwarded by the seller:

- CPA deals encourage over-use of lists by the brokers to squeeze out the last drop of performance
- They encourage list owners to throw in less-than-targeted addresses as well, just on the off chance they might find a willing purchaser
- The performance of the deal remains controlled by the advertiser's actions, and the seller shouldn't be held responsible for the buyer's creative, offer and transaction system

The first two arguments can be put to rest very quickly. If a CPA deal would force the seller to abuse the lists, then the lists do not offer the degree of targeting the seller promised in the first place. That would only encourage a responsible buyer to insist on a performance-based deal.

The third argument is a bit more complicated. While it is true that the advertiser's creative, offer and web site will have material effects on the results, these are things that the site needs to take into account in its pricing of a CPA deal. If, for instance, an advertiser provides ads that do a great deal of branding and very little direct selling, the list broker would be justified in suggesting a higher price on the CPA. This doesn't constitute an excuse as to why CPA should be undesirable—or, worse, that the list broker should have some control over the creative—but rather constitutes a valid factor against which the broker can negotiate.

Sellers of email lists and of online media in general sometimes fail to realize that even if they are purchased based on the CPM, they are almost always judged based on a later analysis of the effective CPA. When advertisers come back to the vendor another time, it is only because the efficiency of their media proved superior to that of others. As a result, forcing deals into a CPM structure does little good to the seller. It can only serve to confuse the real results. The more list brokers feel confidence in the quality of their product, the more likely they are to desire CPA deals.

Email Clients

People use different types of software programs to download their email. These are called clients. Some just use a web browser to get their email off a site like email.com. Others use special email programs, like Eudora or Microsoft Outlook. This becomes significant when some clients can see certain types of advertisements while others cannot. Two major distinctions exist: those that can or cannot display HTML (web-like) messages, and those that can or cannot display rich media messages.

To date, the rich media ads have performed very poorly, as very few email users' clients can support the formats. HTML ads have more of a following online.

The HTML ads, when they can be seen, generally prove more effective. The extra dimensions provided by the graphical format allow for more compelling creative. There will always be, however, people who also need to see a text version of an email ad. About 15 percent of email users currently fail to see HTML messages, with a good many of them coming from the pool of AOL users who are forced to use a relatively unsophisticated email client. The best of both worlds involves producing both types of creative and using a list that divvies itself up based on the addressee's specified preferences.

HTML ads also have the advantage of allowing for better tracking. Since the images that come with the email generally get served off of a banner server, we can determine what elements the addressees wind up interacting with. The disadvantage remains that these graphic files must remain up on the server for a long period of time. If a person saves an email to be read later, and the graphics have been taken down off the server, that person may never see the message.

Calculating the Proper Offer

Sometimes media people are asked to help the advertiser develop the proper offer to elicit a response from email marketing. If the client doesn't offer a good value proposition in the email, no one will respond. But if the client offers too much, the campaign won't be profitable. The media folks are certainly in the position to give the best feedback in terms of user response, helping refine offers as campaigns go on.

Before delving into the math part of the equation, the planner needs to look at some of the more subjective information to help determine a good offer. These pieces of information should be put together, if available:

- To what offer has this type of audience responded in the past? (the reps selling the lists should be able to answer this question)
- What do we know about cross-selling products within the client's existing customer base?
- What assumptions may we draw about demographic, lifestyle and behavioral information for this target?

- How price sensitive has the audience appeared in past direct response campaigns?
- Does the client's brand image allow for price discounting?

Often, the best offers are ones that employ related products and services, rather than a price cut, coupon or discount. But, that said, some of the best response rates with email campaigns come from pricing offers.

The math looks simple at first: the maximum profitable discount offer (MPDO) equals the profit margin of one transaction minus the CPA. Things get slightly more complex as we flesh that equation out. It turns out that the effective CPA in a media deal based on CPM is dependent upon the offer. The better the offer, the lower the effective CPA because more people will respond. Conducting CPA-based media deals eliminates this confusion.

The MPDO, however, is merely the maximum discount an advertiser can offer and still make money. It's never the best offer for the advertiser.

In other words, the better the price you advertise, the more people will respond to your offer, effectively generating additional transactions for the same media cost. Employing simple algebra won't get us very far because it sets up a chicken-and-the-egg issue of trying to determine the offer by using a variable that depends on the offer. Were we to attempt to figure this out mathematically, we would have to roll out integrals from calculus. But, even aside from scaring off the majority of readers, this isn't very practical. In the real world, our variables are so uncertain the answers the calculus equations give us are not very definitive. Variables like the price sensitivity of specific target groups just aren't precise enough to make the calculus equations worthwhile. (Whew.)

The best way to figure out the optimal offer is to employ the first equation in a couple pre-campaign tests. Here's an example:

- The Belfast Doghouse Company (BDC) sends emails to known dog owners offering a $50 discount off of the $400 doghouse they produce for a cost of $325 each. For each doghouse they sell with this offer, they make a gross margin of $25 after the discount. They spend $50,000 to reach 5,000,000 people by email ($100 CPM). This offer generates 1,750 sales (a sales rate of 0.35 percent), which earns them gross profits of $43,750. Their net profit, however proves to be a loss of $6,250 after they take into account the $50,000 cost of media.
- The BDC has faith that email can do better, though, and decides to conduct two additional experiments to see if there is a combination of offers that might turn a profit.
- The first try to give a much-reduced offer to customers, hoping to increase their margins sufficiently to make up for decreased sales. With a price discount of only $5, they discover that they sell 500 doghouses (a sales rate of 0.1 percent). This nets them a profit of $2,500.
- Their next test tries out the market at a $10 discount. There they find 1,000 buy doghouses, earning a net profit of $15,000.

Belfast Doghouse Company Offer Calculations

Media Spent	CPM	Sales Rate	Houses Sold	Price	COGS	Discount	Gross Margin	Profit
$50,000	$100	0.35%	1750	$400	$325	$50	$25	-$6,250
$50,000	$100	0.25%	1250	$400	$325	$25	$50	$12,500
$50,000	$100	0.20%	1000	$400	$325	$10	$65	$15,000
$50,000	$100	0.15%	750	$400	$325	$5	$70	$2,500
$50,000	$100	0.10%	500	$400	$325	$3	$73	-$13,750

This type of experimentation with offers will be necessary. And the offers will frequently find different degrees of receptivity depending on the very particular email list that's used, so it

13340-TILL

may proved difficult to get good, apples-to-apples data to compare the different types of deals.

And, once again, email marketers must remember not to throw the branding baby out with the direct response bath water. Remember that every time someone sees one of these offers, a brand impression is registered. This can be good or bad, depending on how faithful the creative employed sticks to the client's desired brand attributes.

Most email campaigns will find a transaction rate of about 4 percent, plus or minus a couple percent. It will depend heavily on the product category, the existing brand, the message, the offer and, of course, the quality of the email list acquired.

In-House Versus Outsourcing

All of this analysis can be quite daunting, especially if it's done across many different smaller lists with media deals that differ significantly. Some agencies and advertisers choose to conduct these campaigns and this type of analysis within their own walls. There's certainly a good argument for doing this, as the iterative process itself teaches the company about its market, brand and pricing structures.

But it can be very overwhelming to staffs already dedicated to other marketing tasks. Companies seeking a little help with the data organization and campaign execution can purchase software and services from companies like Lsoft, EmailFactory.com, MessageMedia, MailKing, Roving and Responsys Jumpstart.

Advertisers and agencies seeking more scalable help and additional staff resources can deal with companies like FloNetwork, Accucast, Digital Impact, e2Communications, Post Communications/Netcentives, MessageMedia, and UnityMail.

RICH MEDIA INTRODUCTION

There are those among us in the online advertising industry who believe that the banner ad can only be a temporary waypoint on the path to something greater. These proponents of "rich media" hope that through a combination of better production values and greater interactivity, the medium will experience a jump in effectiveness.

In point of fact, most studies show that rich media does lead to more effective advertising campaigns, but I don't yet consider myself an RM convert.

Definitions of RM

Rich media remains a fuzzy classification of advertising. Some people throw everything that's not a banner into the RM category, including everything from email ads to special advertorial placements. Most people, however, interpret the "rich" in rich media to mean that it involves a more fancy type of creative, often one that takes a great deal of bandwidth to download.

For our purposes, we'll adopt this definition: rich media involves a creative format that includes either a complex interactive experience and/or high production values for video and sound components. This effectively splits rich media into two camps: those trying to affect viewers through a TV-like medium, and those trying to affect viewers through a highly interactive experience.

Some companies will claim that they employ a technology that allows for special targeting or the ability to place a message in a unique place—like on a user's cursor, or on top of a New

York City taxicab. We'll cover that sort of stuff elsewhere, as these media do not gain quite the degree of viewer involvement that sets out our definition of rich media.

Short Shrifting RM

Each December, for the past five years, the trade press calls around to prominent advertising executives to get their comments on a year-end story titled something along the lines of "the death of the banner." In it, the reporter musters the arguments why the banner is a piddly creative device that has misdirected many people's energies away from where they rightly should focus: the rich media. And each January, all the ad executives nod their heads, and continue to purchase $2 billion worth of banners, then $4 billion, then $8 billion, etc . . .

Rich media gets scraps. In relative terms, rich media spending might even be decreasing over time. Part of this stems from a series of daunting challenges most rich media campaigns face. Part of it is caused by the fact that our current forms of rich media still do not rival the production values of some other media. Part of it stems from the fact that the people who need to be involved in creating the richer forms of creative at an ad agency, especially the TV people, tend to be just the ones who care little for the Internet.

I think, though, that there is a greater reason why rich media has failed to gain wide acceptance. In the grand scheme of things, people excited about advertising on the Internet place their hopes in one of two broad categories of value: either rich returns of data that lead to great performance, or rich returns of impactful creative that cause great performance.

Rich media suffers from two factors making it difficult for online marketers to jump from pursuing the data riches to pursuing the creative riches. First, rich media isn't quite rich enough with our current bandwidth and technology to create the desired level of creative experience (remember those McDonald's and

Hallmark ads that made people cry?) Second, because of all sorts of technical reasons, the data we get back from these rich media campaigns isn't quite as telling in many cases as the data we get back from simpler campaigns based on sound media targeting strategies.

When we conduct rich media campaigns, we frequently reach only a subset of the audience—those that have the technology and bandwidth to see an ad—and this self-selection process skews the data for many types of analysis.

That said, rich media needs to be part of an online marketer's repertoire. While it isn't yet a desirable tactic for most campaigns, it is the best for some. There are a slew of specific advantages and problems involved with conducting rich media campaigns. An equation can be applied to any campaign to figure out when rich media becomes the appropriate option. Rich media makes sense when the incremental cost of media and production is less than the product of the increment of creative performance and the level of exposure the campaign causes. We'll come back to this algorithm later.

The Pros and Cons to Rich Media

Rich media can have the sizzle that many ad executives complain the typical Internet creative lacks. If an agency can marshal its creative forces together, it has the potential of creating advertising more powerful than exists in any other media. But there's more to that marshalling than first meets the eye.

To make them explicit, the major pros of rich media are:

- Getting viewer's attention
- Delivering a more nuanced message
- Employing emotional appeals difficult to execute in a two-dimensional medium
- Allowing for interactive experiences, like games, or commerce applications

- Giving the impression of leadership in the Internet space for the advertiser's product category

But there is a great cost to these benefits:

- Bandwidth requirements tend to be much greater for rich media, by a factor of 10 to 100. This prevents many viewers from seeing the ad
- Often the rich media formats require viewers to have a certain browser or plug-in technology. This can prevent a good proportion of an audience from getting the rich message.
- Production costs on rich creative tend to be about as high as television spots. That can range greatly, but with smaller media buys on the Internet, the relative efficiency can be hard to swallow.
- Some rich media technologies do not yet have fully developed measurement capabilities, allowing us to get performance information on par with other online advertising. (Some, particularly those based on Flash or Java, do.)
- The process involves more individual parties. Between the site, the agency, the client, the production house, the technology vendor, and oftentimes a special rich media ad server, there is a lot of room for miscommunication.
- The trafficking process for rich media can be a bear, as each technology involves very different creative assets, and each site in a campaign tends to treat them differently. As a result, an advertiser faces a custom process for every part of the buy, requiring a lot of manual labor and a great deal of oversight. It's so complex that entire businesses—like my former company, Solbright—exist to automate these processes.
- Finally, a problem endemic with a lot of rich media advertising comes from its very novelty. Many advertisers fail to start off a rich media campaign with useful and

measurable performance metrics in mind. Often, the only real objective is just to run a rich media campaign so that the advertiser can say it's done so. This leads to a lot of effort put into a campaign with few visible results, and these campaigns are often orphaned after the first run.

Factoring the Pros and Cons into Our Equation

With these lists in mind, we need to first figure out if rich media makes sense for our campaign. Assuming that our campaign objective can be helped along with some of the pros in our list—like getting people's attention and giving us a more powerful, emotional medium to deliver a message—we need to factor in some values to weigh against the costs we'll find in the list of cons.

We'll hew to our original equation: rich media makes sense when the incremental cost of media and production is less than the product of the increment of creative performance and the level of exposure. To make matters simple, lets call the incremental cost of media IM, the incremental cost of production IP, the incremental creative performance rate ICP and our level of exposure E. Our algebra now looks like this: rich media makes sense if $IM+IP < ICP*E$.

Let's assume—the first iteration of the campaign can be tested to confirm—that a rich media version of a message is twice as effective as a normal banner ad. That gives us an ICP of 1 (one times again as effective as without rich media). We can pick an arbitrary exposure level (E) of, say $100,000 worth of media.

For the cost side, we'll assume that the media cost is augmented for two reasons. The sites tack on an additional charge to deal with rich media of another 25 percent, and we find that 35 percent of the sites' audience won't be able to see the rich media adds due to technical limitations. That gives us an IM of 60 percent of E.

Finally, our IP can be arbitrarily set at a reasonable production cost of $35,000. Putting all the variables together we find our equation working out to (0.6*$100,000)+$35,000 < 1*$100,000. This lead to the statement $90,000 < $100,000. Most people would agree that this is a true statement, implying that rich media makes sense in this case. If our media budget were only half that, however, it wouldn't make much sense at all. ($59,000 is *not* < $50,000.)

Why Many Ad Agencies Have Difficulty With Rich Media

Back in the early 90s, many media people looked to the large brands and agencies to see innovation in what we used to call the "interactive television" market. I feel kind of silly admitting that now, knowing what we now know.

Two major factors led to inevitable failure if "ITV." On the medium side, the technology of the time was little better than television. And on the agency side, as we've now come to expect with new creative forms, the large agencies' autoimmune reactions to new things successfully rejected rich media.

On the media side, things have changes significantly. We now have all sorts of rich media forms that not only get significant exposure on the Web, but are also simpler to develop. The obstacle that hasn't changed, though, is the presence of the autoimmune reaction within agencies, particularly large ones.

A Good Part of It Is Cultural

Creative folks in the big agencies believe that there is a hierarchy of media, and as they advanced through their careers, they would climb the ladder of promotions to outdoor on their way to print which would precede radio, and eventually, the vaunted television. This became a self-fulfilling culture. The best creatives always wanted to do what they thought was most respected.

The agencies also begin to reveal some hidden financial conflicts of interest with their clients. Agencies make a much better margin spending money on network television—when you factor in all the labor costs associated—than any other media. It's not surprising that with a staff that wishes to be seen involved in TV work and a corporate management that requires the margins seen in television advertising, our agency view of the world becomes skewed toward the large-budget broadcast media.

Another factor moving rich media innovation away from the big agencies and toward the interactive firms and creative boutiques: client size. Back in the glory days of TV and continuing today, the large budgets sought large audiences. But the rich media audiences are highly targeted. This makes them more valuable, but to a different set of advertisers. Purchasing rich media, we find a lot of business-to-business clients and others who pay great premiums for audience selectivity. These aren't the typical clientele of large agencies.

The types of clients that large agencies have often sell "boring" products that require a medium that will force viewers to watch an ad.

Time-based advertising, like TV and radio relies on an implicit contract with the audience: "You tolerate some forced ad time, and we'll deliver free content." This model breaks down online, where the users have much more control. The new implicit social contract is more like "You go find what you want, and we'll put some adjacent advertising/content nearby."

This makes rich media a difficult proposition for a large consumer goods company, for instance. How relevant to the user can you make cheese products or shampoo online, even with a rich form of creative? I know this problem intimately, as I've been assigned to do both. Seldom are agencies able to get the brunt of viewers to voluntarily sit through 30 seconds of Flash animation about cheese slices, especially when the viewers originally arrived on that page for a completely different purpose.

The Results

All this boils down to a rich media environment full of smaller clients, more business-oriented clients and a different set of agencies than the Madison Avenue crowd.

We also see, on the consumer goods side of the fence, a lot of online promotions, contests, and other "below-the-line" types of marketing that—again—tend to be avoided by the large agencies. There are plenty of places for rich media adherents to work and do interesting, creative work. These places just tend to be different types of shops from the more traditional ad agencies and advertisers.

Is Wireless Media Rich Media?

Advertisers have a tough time fitting wireless advertising into a category. Many stick it in with rich media, although most versions of wireless ads are hardly rich in content.

Wireless ads are those that get downloaded to people via some sort of a wireless network, like a cell phone or roaming Internet service. The most common conception of wireless ads today remains the messages that appear on some folk's cell phones when they try to use their handsets to get things like stock quotes and address directions. In this form, they can hardly be called richer than your average banner ad.

The value of wireless comes from two assumptions. The first is that the ad gets to the person at a time when she's likely to purchase something. For instance, if a cell phone user employs the handset to get directions to a mall, presumably she's in a shopping frame of mind. The other assumption is that these people can be reached at a uniquely useful place. For instance, when that same user gets the map to Lord & Taylor, she might find an ad for the Starbucks that happens to be on the next corner.

Without such targeting, wireless ads become, what we call in email marketing, spam. Many wireless companies have been conducting user tests to figure out what types of advertising might be found acceptable. Some have rigged up stores so that ads spontaneously buzz people on their phones when they pass by certain product counters. Others have rigged up whole towns so that people get ads when walking down a block with a certain store on it.

So far, the results have been predictable and not very positive. Wireless ads broadcast from stores are worse than spam—they actually make people cross streets to avoid certain stores and their attending messages. Wireless ads broadcast inside stores are also perceived as spam. Wireless ads broadcast inside stores, but customized to the individual's profile of preferences and purchases, have revealed some potential for further development.

The Real Wireless Ad Value

There are indeed instances in which the wireless platform becomes useful in advertising. We'll always have the banner-ad-equivalent of some text sponsorship appearing on the phone adjacent to messages, pages, web, etc . . . But this isn't really all that much more useful than, say, banner ads. Valuable, but not sexy, and certainly not something to warrant several more rounds of VC funding into your floundering wireless ad start-up.

The real value comes from the ability of a wireless device to be pinpointed with enough precision to know exactly where the user is. This could, theoretically, offer that same user a customized message based both on where he or she is and a profile of that user's preferences and previous behaviors.

This is not what happens when Starbucks spams your phone with coupons every time you walk by a store (the very prospect, a friend of mine said, would be certainly make him throw his cell phone under the next passing truck).

The scenario, instead, would run something like this: Tom arrives inside the Starbucks. His phone vibrates unobtrusively,

340-TILL

notifying him that it has information about the establishment available if he wishes to consult it. Flipping open the phone out of curiosity, he is informed that Sandi, the barrista, makes the strongest espresso (she packs it down properly), but that Karl has a tendency to spit in the foam. Now here's information you can use. I employ this example not just to be funny, but to point out that the information users would actually find valuable would likely be information the establishment doesn't want them to know. If a Starbucks wanted to tell nearby people that they had a 40-cent-off special, it would be a whole lot more efficient to just put up a sign.

In fact, there is a wireless advertising company, Adaptmedia, that does something like this by causing electronic messages to change on top of New York City taxicabs based on their current GPS location. That's a creative use of the wireless medium without becoming very intrusive.

Wireless Ads Are "Below-the-Line" Marketing

This is getting into an advertising realm in which ad agencies and most clients have very little competence: place-based advertising. We are talking about "below-the-line" advertising, much like promotions. Or, as a CEO of a major ad agency network ungenerously termed it: "chicken pee."

Ad agencies tend to hate doing retail work. They don't make money at it. They aren't structured to implement the complex databases and react quickly to the shifting needs of retail consumers. In short, the ways in which we will find wireless advertising useful are the types of things agencies don't do very well, barring those few promotion agencies that have interactive units.

To properly explore the wireless markets, we have to adjust our attitudes. We have to grow a greater respect for local advertising, promotions and place-based advertising before we'll be mature enough as an industry to properly mine the value awaiting exploitation in wireless.

Valuating New Types of Media

Every so often, buyers will have people come by with something completely new: a new form of media, a new technology, a new way of targeting or some such. Media buyers often get stumped by these things they can't directly compare with the vehicles they've bought before. But to let all of these opportunities go by is a mistake. There's a great deal of value in seizing upon new types of advertising.

I remember when search engines first began to offer keywords (yes, it took more than a year before they figured out how to work the matching of media packages with keywords). A lot of agencies took a pass on that one, while some scooped up certain keywords and locked them up to this day. Try wresting the word "database" or "browser" from Microsoft, and your search engine rep will laugh out loud.

Of course, there are a lot of losers out there too. Anyone remember "push?"

But if you find a new application online that probably suits your client needs, the question arises: how much should we pay for it? What's fair? Sometimes the difficulties answering this question will keep the new opportunity off the buy, but this should be a relatively simple question to answer.

The rough algorithm looks like this: Take the exposure provided, multiply that by the value of the particular target reached and index this product with some sort of consideration for how much messaging power the medium has.

To acquire these factors numerically, typically we look to close precedents and analogs. For instance, with online banner ads, we would take the message value of print (reduced a bit due to creative limitations) and multiply it across the relevant audience reached online. This gave us a CPM (cost per thousand impressions) of about $12, depending on the probable audience. And, indeed, as the market for online advertising matured, we saw a gradual trend toward about a $12 CPM. This price would have been quite a bit higher, had the other media—like print—not been in such great supply to suffice as an alternative.

Let's take a look at an example of a new medium, one of those nutty startups with a new type of advertising. For our example, we'll use AdaptMedia.net, the New York City company that figured out how to take electronic billboards on top of taxis and hook them up to a GPS system. That allows different ads to appear in different locations around the city. I happened to have worked with one of the people now employed over there, so I was able to get enough details answered to provide a good example.

Applying this rough calculation with the AdaptMedia offering, we can find the following analogs:

- The media value is most analogous to a combination of both outdoor advertising and point-of-purchase advertising.
- The exposure received by a given cab would be analogous to the impressions garnered by a mobile billboard execution (those trucks with billboard trailers you see in front of convention centers in NYC).
- The audience is particularly valuable, as it allows for precise geo-targeting in a very sought-after market.
- Unfortunately for us advertisers, there really isn't much alternative media for targeted point-of-purchase media. Without this backup, we will be paying a premium, particularly for hot locations.

Taking into account all of these factors, we assign numbers to the variables. Starting with a conservative point-of-purchase and outdoor cost basis of a $5 CPM and multiplying it by another 25 percent to take into account the lack of alternative supply, we come to a basis price of $6.25 CPM. For perhaps 20 percent of the locations, we will have to pay an additional premium of 50 percent to account for valuable audiences otherwise difficult to reach. That averages out to a general CPM of $6.88, assuming rather liberally that the hot locations sell only as well as the general locations. The vendor would likely disagree with this notion, wishing to get a higher average, but it is where we would start our side of the negotiations.

Using the existing mobile billboards as a good device for determining the exposure of a given ad over time, we find that a taxi will be seen by about 100,000 people in a day in NYC (estimated by cutting mobile billboard companies' optimistic estimates in about half).

Were a cab to sell all of this exposure at the average rate all the time, the cab would be worth a caroming $20,500 per month. This, however, remains unlikely. The area in Manhattan most likely to be purchased (probably at a higher than average CPM, but, as greedy buyers, we'll ignore this) remains only about 20 percent of the whole. That eventual 20 percent sell-through would connote a monthly per taxi revenue of about $4,125.

As agency buyers, we wouldn't expect to pay all of this in the beginning. As charter advertisers, we'd expect a pretty good deal and an incumbency that would allow us to renew these favorable rates for some time to come. Perhaps a cheaply renewable exclusivity on certain locations. $3,000 per taxi per month would be rather tempting. Of course, we'd want to purchase only a small portion of this per month; probably near the locations of our client's retail outlets. The real price per advertiser might be a small percentage of that $3,000 sum, depending on how much geographic area we wish to buy.

Different types of clients have different relevant media analogs. Some clients use different types of print, which imply very different rates against which the new medium is compared. Your mileage may vary, but the formula remains constant.

New media companies' pricing often starts out at an arbitrary point. I can remember Rick Boyce, from Hotwired, trying to sell me on the very first-ever banner campaign in 1994. The price: $150 CPM. I asked him why $150, and his response was a big shrug, raising his palms upwards. He had to start somewhere.

Applying our formula takes the shrug out of new pricing models, creating some valid rationale for a starting point. Better still, it puts the negotiation process on a logical framework, forcing the salespeople to justify higher price points.

Incidentally, my clients back in 1994—Sony and Dewars—decided not to purchase Hotwired for that first round. The we're-on-top-of-technology crowd, like IBM and AT&T, bought most of those first offerings. This goes to prove an exception to our rule. Sometimes, the prestige value of doing something first can outweigh an unreasonable price. And, more to the point, when a lot of companies in that media market desire such opportunities, they will drive up the price.

SPONSORSHIPS

These multi-level deals can be either a blessing or a curse. Jumping into sponsorship—also referred to as "partnership" deals—can force advertisers to give disproportionate sums to a single site. Many deals done in the past few years, especially the very large ones, have been halted before the completion of their contracts due to poor performance relative to normal media buys. The matter deserves great caution.

A sponsorship can be a lot of different things. Some sites use the term to mean just a large package of several different media buys on the same site. Most, though, use the term to mean a special type of media buy that presents the content of a certain section of the site as being branded by the advertiser. Think of it like you would the old television programming that would allow just one or two sponsors. Texaco Star Theater on ABC gave viewers the impression that the Texaco brand was linked very strongly to the content of the program. Similarly, online content areas become branded by the advertiser. This is a great benefit for brands that wish to be associated with a special type of content.

Advertisers who saw their sponsorship deals fall through in the past few years very likely succumbed to one of these sponsorship dangers:

- The value of association with that particular content turned out to not be very useful to the advertiser, perhaps because the site went ahead and cluttered up the content with other ads.

- Having given a content exclusivity to the advertiser, the site saw no incentive to further develop that content area, and instead developed other areas' content for other advertisers.
- The site sold the sponsorship at a very high price, which began to look worse and worse as the normal media deal CPMs decreased over time.
- The site, to which the advertiser paid large upfront sums, went into bankruptcy.
- The site sold the deal directly to the advertiser at a time when media budgets were larger than they later became. The deal then became an albatross around the necks of the advertiser's marketing department, as budgets shrank and the sponsorship came to represent much too large a percentage of the budget.

To look at the deals very cynically, the sponsorships do indeed offer potential benefits to advertisers, but they most certainly offer greater benefits to the sites. In 1999 and 2000, many large traditional advertisers made what would later be perceived as poorly conceived sponsorship deals. The stock market was cheering on the companies that put out press releases about $10 million deals and then $40 million dollar deals, and even a few $100 million dollar multi-year deals with the very largest sites. The stock prices of those advertisers and, especially, the stock prices of those large sites, would shoot up a few percent each time the releases hit the wires. These were deals largely negotiated directly between the advertiser and site. There tended to be little competitive bidding or other agency involvement in the process to introduce some benchmark metrics of performance goals. At worst, they were made by senior management teams, with little consultation from the marketing departments.

In part, these more poorly-constructed deals came about due to the short-sightedness of some of the sellers. Frustrated with the great deal of scrutiny agencies and other competitive negotiators put on their media, some sales departments used sponsorship structures as a device to seek very expensive deals direct to the advertiser's marketing departments. These marketers would obligate themselves to buy more media at a higher price from fewer sites and with less performance data.

These were just the kinds of deals that cratered in the coming months and years. They also helped explain why the advertising market in the beginning of 2001 looked so soft among the larger sites, even as ad revenues climbed to an annualized $8.1 billion in the interactive sector.

Desirable Sponsorships

All that said, there are some babies in the sponsorship bath water, so we shouldn't throw it all out. Sponsorships can provide several things other types of media deals cannot:

- Providing a leadership role among advertisers in a sector
- Connecting the brand to the content topic
- Avoiding some of the hassles of measurement and analysis connected with looking at many different media packages on the same site
- Getting sites to offer types of media or prices of media that would otherwise be denied to normal media buying clients
- Affording the opportunity for the agency to use special creative formats that can break through clutter

Sponsorship buyers must constantly remind themselves to always compare the benefits of their sponsorship with the cost of equivalent packages under normal media deals. There is no magic to an impression that happens under the rubric of a sponsorship contract as opposed to one that occurs under a normal media insertion order. The viewer still sees the same ad most times. Buyers should attempt to quantify the media value of the sum of the sponsorship's parts, compare it to normal online media buys, and make sure that their advertising client gets the better value.

A media supervisor who worked for me in San Francisco figured out that the sponsorship deals offered by one site for one of our major clients was overpriced. The sales rep justified this by telling our agency that there was an unquantifiable value to having a visible "ownership" stake in that area of the site. This media supervisor responded by recommending the client reject the sponsorship and instead purchase all the media on that area of the site as a normal media buy. Using one of the panel data companies, he looked up how many impressions occurred on the site and used that to correctly calculate the properly proportioned media buy for about half of what the site would have otherwise charged.

Had that site offered other elements, the sponsorship might have proven the better value. If email lists had been made available, or perhaps if there were more content-oriented creative opportunities, the value would have been perceived as much higher.

Ways Sponsorships Show Greater Value

Merely packaging up large bundles of impressions will not give advertisers a better value than could be achieved with normal media buys. Most advertisers find that after five impressions, an individual viewer isn't much additionally influenced by subsequent ads. Sponsorships that involve many impressions to a small group of people can become inefficient.

And sites need to remember that there are additional costs to purchasing sponsorships. The deals tend to be governed by customized contracts. Someone—usually at an advertiser's ad agency—needs to constantly monitor the site to make sure that the contracts terms continue to be honored. These contracts tend to work differently than an advertiser or agency is set up to operate. As a result, buyers look for value that offsets these operational costs.

Sites might involve the following to make a more valuable sponsorship package:

- Leveraging Content: Sites known for having good content can offer up certain sections as discrete areas in which a brand can be seen as "owning" the content. This lends the credibility of the content to the advertising brand.
- Giving Advertiser Control Over Environment: Some sponsored sites allow the content to be designed into the look and feel of the sponsor's own advertisements. This gives the viewers the impression that the advertiser is responsible for the content, if not its creation. This is just one step shy of advertorial, where the advertiser would actually have influence over the content.
- Dominant Positioning of Creative: Sponsorship purchasers will often get a special type of creative placement that gives added prominence. Many sponsorships will involve special slots for creative above where the normal banners appear, and sometimes even in special insets in the content itself.
- Special Sponsor Applications: Some sites will seek sponsors for important applications, like free email or other types of activities that attract certain types of users. This can be seen on any of the major portals, as all the obvious applications already have sponsors. A mortgage broker will sponsor the mortgage interest rate application. An SUV manufacturer will sponsor the new car comparison application in the automotive section.
- Bundling Multiple Ad Units: Where sites offer side banners, sometimes called "sky scrapers," they might include all the ad placements on a page as though they were all a single impression. This also serves to increase the prominence of the creative, as well as connote deliberate ownership of certain types of content.
- Special, Non-standard Ad Units: Sites that do not offer the ability to run rich media creative will sometimes make

exceptions only for those advertisers sponsoring certain areas of the site. This also serves to increase the prominence of the creative.

- Exclusivity: Typically, a sponsorship will involve an exclusivity clause that prevents the site from selling media to competitive brands, at least in the sponsored section.
- Promotions: Sites will sometimes offer special promotions with their sponsors. Games, contests, sweepstakes and celebrity appearances comprise the majority of the events, though sites are constantly coming up with clever additional opportunities related to their respective content.
- Email: While sometimes sites will keep their collected email lists deliberately separate from the site media (so they can charge separate fees for them), sponsors will sometimes be able to negotiate use of the email lists. Email and site sponsorships go well together because when a site's email newsletter refers to a sponsored area, it typically drives traffic back to its own pages, rather than sending potential viewers off to an advertiser's site.
- Research: Sometimes sponsors will be offered special research packages that tell the advertiser more about the site's users and what effects the advertising had on them. Especially when sites design sponsorship packages designed for branding purposes, they like to provide pre- and post-buy studies that will show real results.
- Original Editorial Content: Sponsorships can sometimes involve the creation of completely new types of content areas. This was quite common when sponsorships first became popular, but the practice became less common when advertisers became disappointed with the performance. My own experience with this showed that once you buy all the ads on one area, the site has little incentive to continue to invest much in the editorial upkeep of that section. Worse, the site will sometimes create very similar content areas for the expressed purpose of selling similar

packages to other advertisers, diluting the value of the sponsorship.

Some things that first seem valuable might turn into liabilities. The long-term nature of a sponsorship contract might first seem efficient—precluding the need for people to run around doing those labor-intensive discrepancy resolution processes. But a long-term deal also locks in any problems. Media rates normally drop at a fairly constant rate, and a long-term sponsorship price that seems low at the beginning can seem quite high by the end.

A Sample Sponsorship

Sponsorships can be broken down into several components. This one might prove as representative as any. The Belfast Doghouse Company (BDC) contracts for a special sponsorship on the Border Collie Monthly (BCM) web site. The site offers three major areas of value:

- Media: The BDC buys 1 MM impressions per month, knowing that the pet care section of BCM receives an average of 5MM impressions per month. This should reasonably control the frequency with which any one individual sees the creative. Another option, had the site been able to offer it, would have been a "frequency cap," whereby the site would only let someone see the ad a certain number of times before automatically switching in another banner. In addition to the impressions via banners at the top of the page, BCM offered to place several text links on each of the pet care section's pages. These links are placed in the site's content and lead to the BDC web site. These are not counted against the impressions BDC purchased.

- Applications: Aside from the media and links, the BCM offered to incorporate the BDC logo onto its special Canine Habitat Happiness Application. This web application that takes into account your climate, breed of dog and other factors to determine the best options for pet housing.
- Email: The site folks balked at the BDC's request to use the BDM email list, but they compromised by giving the BDC placements in the weekly newsletter that goes out to all the dog owners who sign up. This way, the emails will have some BDM context and tend to be less intrusive to the list members.
- Other Terms: The deal will run for three months, despite the site's initial insistence that it must be a yearlong minimum sponsorship. But, for guaranteeing only three months of fees, the site won the elimination of an outability clause.

AFFILIATE MARKETING

Advertisers selling goods online can develop networks of "affiliates" that put up banners or other types of links on their own sites in return for a proportion of the commerce generated. This can lead to a lot of site traffic and sales if handled correctly, but the management tasks are intense. Many online sellers find the affiliate networks generate more traffic and business than do all the ad budgets.

The most famous example of a successful affiliate program is the Amazon.com Partner Program. Amazon provides graphics and HTML snippets to any participating web site that wants to create their own mini Amazon store on their site. The affiliates collect 15 percent of any business generated from people visiting Amazon from an affiliate site. Amazon provides automated traffic tracking tools and sends out quarterly checks. Amazon wasn't the first company to start an affiliate program, but it did manage to patent some elements of the automation process.

Most companies don't have the resources to develop their own software and tracking mechanisms, so they outsource the management of affiliate programs out to one of the many companies that specialize in such things. These companies tend to operate as application service providers (ASP's), which is fancy way of saying that they serve the ads and HTML and do all the tracking on their servers so advertisers don't have to worry about any in-house technology issues.

This is different from the typical media buy because usually no money exchanges hands prior to the affiliate coming online (aside from any set-up and maintenance fees the advertiser incurs by using a third party service). The affiliate site gets paid only when a user commits a desired behavior. The most obvious desired behavior is, of course, the purchase of a product, but affiliates sometimes also get paid based just on having sent viewers to a site. Sometimes the media department of an agency isn't even involved in any of these transactions.

Since the program is tied directly to an advertiser's sales, the agency is sometimes left out of the affiliate loop. Some agencies do get involved in the affiliate work, sometimes managing the entire program. In the least, they should be made aware of where these brand impressions are occurring, on which sites and at what comparative media weights. An agency without this information can wind up making poor media purchasing decisions, like buying large numbers of impressions on sites already giving a lot of exposure to the advertiser's brand.

Getting Started

Before jumping in and creating an affiliate program, advertisers need to make some important decisions that will be difficult to reverse later. To prevent making early mistakes, a simple list of steps should be followed:

- Determine the Affiliate Program Objective
- Identify Who Owns the Program
- Figure Out the Offer
- Decide on the Right Outsourcing Partner
- Measure the Results
- Market the Program
- Grow and Cull Your Affiliates
- Weed Out the Fraudulent Affiliates

Determine the Affiliate Program Objective

Most times, this is a certain sales level. People managing affiliate programs can get caught up in measurements like number of affiliates, site traffic generated and other types of ancillary metrics. Sometimes the objective is to acquire new customers in market segments on which the advertiser hasn't yet decided to spend many marketing dollars. Sometimes just generating site traffic is an end to itself, like certain media sites that operate by selling advertising. The objective will help determine some of the subsequent decisions.

Figure Out the Offer

Before figuring out any prices or percentages, the advertiser needs to decide what the triggering factor will be for payment. Will it be when a user on an affiliate site clicks on a link to the advertiser? Will it be when that user later makes a purchase? The offer to the affiliate will be a small charge per click if the triggering event is merely a clickthrough. If the triggering event is a purchase, the affiliate will expect a larger fee or perhaps a percentage of the goods sold.

People with much affiliate marketing experience know that it doesn't pay to set the offer at the minimum level at which affiliates will decide to join the program. Experienced managers know that the better the offer, the more exposure the affiliate will dedicate to the program. These links at the affiliate site require some care and feeding as time goes on to keep audiences responding to them. The participating sites dedicate their time and energies only to those affiliate programs that give the better payouts. By experimenting over time, different brands and different product categories have figured out the rough levels where they experience good participation without having to give away too much of the profit.

Refer-it.com, among other sites, lists all the current affiliate programs open to sites. This is useful to browse to get a good comparison of what the affiliate competition is doing.

Consumer electronic companies tend to pay closer to 5 percent of transactions. IBM and Dell pay a percent of the revenue they make on hardware purchases. Generally, the higher the ticket price and the lower the manufacturer's profit margin, the lower the affiliate offer, as a percentage of sales.

Credit card companies offer bounties of more than $20 for honest-to-goodness customers, where other financial companies pay much lower sums—maybe a nickel—for clicks over to their site.

Online services tend to pay high percentages, given their low fixed cost of goods sold. Dating services, career services and subscription services pay fees as high as $50 or percentages in the 20's.

In the book category, Amazon is the top offer among affiliate programs, giving 15 percent of any subsequent transactions. Barnes & Noble gives 7 percent. But some argue that this is an equal offer, given that Amazon's site is designed to steal users away from affiliates once they cross over. This prevents the affiliates from receiving as many repeat transactions. The BN.com site is designed (whether purposefully or not) without the same capability of getting users to come directly to their own special BN page, thereby thwarting the affiliate.

Sites in the movie, music and textbook categories give offers ranging from three to eight percent, or sometimes flat fees of around $5 for each new customer. These are the types of offers against which an advertiser's affiliate marketing program must compete.

Another tool to remember in searching for the affiliates of various companies is the AltaVista reverse search. At the AltaVista.com site, type in the text box, "link:website.com," replacing the generic website with the company you desire to query. Altavista will return to you a list of sites that link to the site you typed in.

Decide on the Right Outsourcing Partner

The affiliate program involves many individual elements that could each require automated systems. Most programs evolve to encompass thousands of participating sites. Handling the security, accounting, marketing, technology or even just the check writing element could warrant independent software and a staff of two. While it might make sense to just handle it in-house when the program is small, it becomes practically impossible to hand an existing program over to one of the outsourced companies without service interruptions. That sort of problem can scare away your affiliates.

Most of the companies providing outsourced programs provide these points of value:

- An existing stable of affiliate sites likely to join your program
- Check writing and other income-related issues, like IRS reporting
- Banner serving of affiliate program graphics and HTML
- Automated reporting to both affiliates and the advertiser affiliate program managers
- Technical support to affiliate sites and the advertiser

These services generally charge a startup fee in the low thousands. They then take a percentage of the advertiser's sales through the program—most often two or three percent. Some also have monthly minimums.

Each of the services is different from the others in some minor and sometimes some major ways. It's well worth checking out the web sites of Commission Junction, ClickTrade, LinkShare, ClickXchange, BeFree and Dynamic Trade.

Measure the Results

The data advertisers receive back from affiliate programs can be piled up into a hierarchy of progressively useful information. At the bottom comes the number of affiliates in the program, hopefully a growing figure. But the number of affiliates doesn't put food on the table. The number of active affiliates—those sending viewers over to the advertiser's site—is a better figure by which to measure the growth of the program. But this figure, too, doesn't represent the success of the effort. A smaller list of affiliates: those that send over viewers who then commit the desired act—perhaps purchasing something—is the list that can signify success. These "successful" affiliates are the ones to watch and to make sure they receive all the care and feeding an advertiser can offer.

Inevitably, affiliate marketers find a small minority of sites producing the vast majority of useful transactions. Discerning what makes these sites different from the others will be an important element to the improvement of the program. It might be that those sites enjoy a very specific type of audience. Very often it's the way the site itself implements an affiliate program that makes all the difference. It might be a matter of banner placement, or frequent creative exchange. If an affiliate marketer can determine what makes that site a success, there's a very good chance the marketer can spread that success to other affiliates.

If the program is not adding new sites, or at least not adding new successful sites, the affiliate marketers need to revisit the program's offer and see what the competition might be doing to steal the market. Sometimes a slowdown in new affiliates is simply a matter of having done less program promotion.

Market the Program

Affiliate program marketing can be broken down into three major parts.

The first major step was taken when the program manager chose an outsourcing partner. Programs can get a big head start, depending on the size and quality of that company's existing affiliate network.

The second step involves listing the program on many of the affiliate program directories on the Web. As many as 50 companies have lists of thousands of different affiliate programs most sites can join. A great number of affiliates come through these directories. There is even a special site that manages to list an affiliate program in many of the other directories: Affiliate-Announce.com.

Finally, the advertiser must market the program as though it were a product itself. The program should almost certainly be referenced on the advertiser's homepage. An affiliate section should be posted on the site to give all the necessary information, answers to anticipated questions, and automated sign-up applications. Making it easier to sign up and participate will multiply the number of affiliates attracted to a program.

More active efforts should be made within obvious product categories. If an advertiser sells doghouses, the affiliate program manager should directly contact the obvious pet-related web sites.

The marketing efforts can be geared around the original objectives. If the advertiser hoped to sell 10,000 units a month through its affiliate program, it can back into the number of required affiliates by looking at the average number of visitors coming from the affiliate network and their transaction rates. If the average affiliate sends 100 people to the advertiser's site in a month, and the average transaction rate is 1 percent, then the advertiser will need 10,000 affiliates to make its numbers.

Care and Feeding of Affiliates

Many affiliate program managers put out newsletters—usually by email—to all the affiliates each month. This can be a good idea, especially when there's a lot of information available to help all the affiliates increase their rate of clicks and purchases. But some affiliates complain of vacuous newsletters bereft of meaty content. It seems that more occasional or irregularly-timed newsletters with real content might be more effective than regular newsletters that necessarily contain more fluff.

Increasing the offer to affiliates can reinvigorate the level of care they expend on your program. Sometimes this can even be done in test batches, offering a special incentive to a certain group of sites to see what type of results the advertiser might expect if the new offer were rolled out to the whole market. More and more affiliate programs are stratifying their offers, so that the higher-performing sites get even higher percentages of the purchase. This incents each affiliate to reach for the next level of compensation.

Advertisers must put the same scrutiny and care into the affiliate creative as they do with the advertising creative. Unfortunately, many affiliate programs languish in a creative desert. The creative process for affiliate programs needs to be as dynamic and iterative as the other marketing efforts. Stale creative will work as poorly on an affiliate's site as it will on the site of a media buy.

Weed Out the Fraudulent Affiliates

The affiliate program managers will need to weed out the fraudsters. Every affiliate program will eventually be targeted by someone who will try to trigger payments without delivering real customers. There are a variety of ways they can do this. Here's a common one:

If an affiliate program offers to pay affiliates a dollar for each person they send over to register for a product newsletter, a fraudulent affiliate could exploit the situation using a "Hotlining" technique.

With this technique, the fraudster creates a new web site that contains some sort of information that people seek. A common device is a password to a pornography site. But to get to that password, the user will first have to sign up for the advertiser's newsletter through this "affiliate" site. The fraudulent affiliate might use one of the words on the newsletter's post-sign-up page as the password. In this fashion, it can tell visitors to its own site that they must fill out the advertisers form to get to the page, "where you must use the third word in the first sentence" for the password. Each time someone uses that page to get at the pornography password, the affiliate program advertiser pays the fraudster a dollar.

Precisely because the affiliate programs have become so automated, the industry has become susceptible to these types of practices. Most major programs have a person who spends at least part of his time looking out for these types of tricks within the list of affiliates. They can most times be detected by looking for affiliates that give great traffic numbers, but few subsequent purchases. A list of these can be spit out of many of the automated affiliate program packages.

The outsourced affiliate program management companies do an increasingly good job of weeding out fraudulent affiliates. In the early days of the industry, they had little incentive to reduce the number of affiliates, but now the market features so much competition that this is quickly becoming a major point of consideration among advertisers.

At least one uses a clever application that thwarts fraud by posting passwords to affiliates only in JPEG format. This prevents the automated fraud programs from "reading" the number online. An actual human wouldn't even be able to tell the difference, but a computer looking to access a new affiliate program membership program would see only a graphic file.

ADVICE FOR AGENCIES AND CLIENTS

Since the media people at both the agency and advertiser now control so much of the marketing process online, they need to take into consideration several strategic issues that used to be the territory of the other departments. Media people have more responsibility for growing existing business, winning new business and managing internal resources so as to be able to properly staff up.

Determining the Roles for All the Players

While there's no inherent reason why the media department need to take control of this issue, the media people often find themselves in the best position to know which departments of an advertiser will need to be involved with a campaign. Some campaigns—like branding campaigns—will involve only the marketing folks. Other campaigns—often the ones that sell directly to customers—will need to involve many different groups inside the advertising company, like the sales group, operations, fulfillment, customer service and others.

The information technology group within the advertiser will likely have to interface directly with the media people to figure out exactly which technical metrics need to be collected and presented to make the campaign run smoothly. Campaigns that lack coordination among these departments are doomed to run without the benefit of refinement. They almost always suffer from a lack of quantifiable results that allow the campaign to be termed a success. These types of campaigns seldom win budgets for future iterations.

This brings up a difficult issue—especially difficult for an agency handling this account. Agencies will want to make sure before a campaign starts that each of these participants knows the criteria by which the campaign will be judged. Sometimes there will be more than one type of criteria, depending on the department involved, and this can be difficult. Campaigns with multiple objectives are likely to suffer from diluted creative and imprecise media targeting. Unless everyone agrees beforehand that the metric employed to judge performance is an all-encompassing one, like ROI, the relations between these departments can turn ugly.

Managing Client Expectations

In the online media, there is always some additional element that can be measured or new version of the creative that can be produced. There's no such thing as a completed campaign. Whether it's a company judging its marketing department's performance or a marketing department judging its agency, they have to choose arbitrary limits of scrutiny, above which they will not spend any more supervisory resources.

Marketers used to traditional campaigns, with finite beginnings and endings, will sometimes fall into the trap of allowing a great deal of mission creep into campaigns. If expectations aren't set correctly, a client might demand more and more work be done on a campaign, far above the level of service for which they have paid. The marketing department of the advertiser and the agency must make sure that all stakeholders in the campaign understand the limits from the beginning:

- The number creative iterations that will be used
- How often performance reports will be analyzed
- How often the creative and media will react to the analyses

- The primary objective of the campaign and the measurement used to determine its performance
- What the performance data will tell the advertiser and what knowledge the performance data will not be able to determine

Getting Paid

Media people, and particularly agency media people, need to enforce a certain discipline over the pay agencies receive from clients. If the pay rates and patterns experience in traditional media were followed, agencies would lose money and do a very poor job buying the right media and managing its performance.

Usually, agencies promise too much service to a client for too little money when they first start off on an interactive account. Used to the traditional rates in other media, they can set themselves up for great failure. In traditional media, the staff doesn't have to keep changing the creative, adapting the media mix, collecting data and performing analysis all after the campaign launches. This doesn't even begin to take into account the additional expense of more complex trafficking, contract management and the very high ratio of media buys to manage versus dollars spent.

In traditional media, an agency will conduct all the various services—from creating the creative to planning and buying the media—for about 15 percent of billings. A media shop might charge 10 percent just to handle the media part. There's no great reason why these numbers have been set around these figures, aside from the fact that most agencies can do good work and still make a profit at those rates. Those media are mature enough to provide the stability to frequently make those rates reasonable.

In interactive marketing, there is no such stability. Instead of spending $1 MM on 10 media buys that are done after they appear on television or in a print magazine, that same $1 MM would more likely be spent on more than 100 buys online. And each of those buys would have to be personally managed.

Once, while renegotiating a large agency contract with a client, I stood in front of a whiteboard with the chief operating officer of the company attempting to figure out just what variables should go into the costs an agency needs to cover. Campaign duration, number of creative iterations, type of media purchased, reporting periods and about 35 other variables were fit into an unreasonably-long algorithm before we gave up in frustration. That client had 10 different divisions, and their media spending differed in all these variables. In the end, we agreed to charge for our time, instead of attempting to arbitrarily link our compensation to the media billings.

At the end of the next year, when we looked back at the different agency fees charged to each division, we discovered that the effective percentages of billings had varied from 7 percent (a division that spent an enormous sum on a single media buy) to about 120 percent of billings (a division that spent very small sums on very many niche sites with special targeting). I had no complaints taking 7 percent of the former, and the COO had no issue with me getting 120 percent of the latter.

These contracts need to be revisited frequently to make sure that the people doing the marketing are getting the right resources to do the job. Clients unwilling to do so should be resigned by the agency.

Client Retention

Without listing the typical platitudes on how to retain clients, I can contribute perhaps one useful tactic that interactive folks have a special ability to exploit.

The data that gets collected through these online campaigns is a resource that has the potential to marry a client to the agency, if it's done right.

The performance data isn't merely a commodity. It's a highly proprietary resource that winds up being useful in a very special way to the client whose brand produced the information. We've discovered over these last few years of online marketing that we can't make many generalizations about the creative and media performance of brands. Instead, the very narrow product category, the specific brand image, the style of creative, and all the other elements that make the advertising of one client unique to another, have such a great effect on the performance results that they each client must be considered independently of one another. We can't take the data from one client and then tell another client that they should expect a certain result if they attempt a similar campaign. The little details of difference provide too much interference for such extrapolations to prove true.

There are certain gross things for which we can use aggregated data. We can, for instance, tell one site that they better darned well give us a certain rate for one client because we can see the poor way it performed for another. But when we really want to predict results, we have to have that second client's data.

And these predictive analyses of the data can happen only if we're able to collect the data in a special kind of database. If we just have a bunch of post-buy performance reports, that's not going to allow us to query a database to discover which types of sites or types of creative prove most effective in which types of campaigns. After a few campaigns, it's just too much data for a person to glean off of these paper reports. The data need to be linked together somewhere in a computer, where the performance statistics for each site are matched to which pieces of creative were run when. Better still, agencies should be adding additional information into these databases, like the campaign objective, the type of message employed, the product category and so on, so that these variables may be queried in the future.

With such a database, the client will find it extremely difficult to take the online business to another agency. If the agency merely collects post-buy reports from sites, the client not only can easily move to another agency, they probably should.

New Business: The Threat and Promise

While going out and pitching new clients won't be in the job description of many media buyers, much of the new business an agency receives comes only through the good graces of the media department. Most new business comes from the expansion of existing accounts rather than new wins. Convincing incumbent clients to lay out more money often requires objective success that only the media department can prove.

New Clients Determine Your Agency's Direction

These new clients also determine the growth, staffing plan, and the very identity of the agency itself. Agencies tend to fail to realize this until it's too late. The best example that comes to mind is my own experience with Microsoft. We were tickled to win back the account in 1995, but we had no idea that the trade press perceptions, staffing needs, resource requirements and non-compete clauses would all conspire to hobble our firm's growth. We saw a lot of diversifying opportunities go by the wayside because of the ever-present immediate resource pressures of the "gorilla" account. I recall pitching, winning and then turning away large clients, like Macromedia and Charles Schwab, because of our endless need for more resources to feed the giant client.

This was probably strategic mistake for my agency. The Microsoft business launched us into the pantheon of the biggest online buyers, but it stunted us in the long-term. While we bought one out of every six dollars spent on the Internet in 1997, that agency's reliance on the one large account disallowed it from scaling with the rest of the industry. Today that agency's spending, while larger in absolute dollars, is much less than one percent of the industry's total online budget.

340-TILL

Make a List

You can't just chase the accounts that are currently in review. Many new business folks simply look at that page in Adweek, where they list all the big accounts currently looking for new agencies. But this is like a talent agency hiring new stars based on who's currently out of work.

The work the agency does will be exhibited solely through the approval processes of these companies. The very fact that they have accounts in review suggests they have problems working with at least one agency.

We must make a few lists. The first list should be the unique qualities your agency can employ in the marketplace. Then, based on that list, write down the dream clients that would best exploit these abilities. Think hard because there are a lot of factors to anticipate. You don't want one huge client that will dominate your staff and business. You don't want too many clients from the same category, lest your agency get pigeonholed into a niche. You want clients that will let you do great, cutting-edge work. You want clients that have a culture of working well with other companies and can make your relationship profitable.

You should come up with five or six optimal companies suited to your talents and desires.

Contact Them

You don't need a mutual friend or some other excuse. Go ahead and give the marketing chief a call. Be completely open and honest: it's a great story. You went and made a list, and she's sitting on top of it. This is really quite flattering to them. They won't give you any business right then. They'll thank you for the call.

And then, six or nine months later, she'll call you because they've finally had it with their last agency. And now you're on top of her list. You'll have to pitch, but they'll already know that your own special algorithm of client matching suggests that you're optimally suited for them in particular.

These efforts shouldn't be confined to the new business directors. The surest way to promotion at an agency is to hunt down new business. Agencies have a tendency to under-appreciate existing employees, but that's difficult to do when they have power over clients and billings. I'm quite certain I'd still be an account director somewhere had I not gone ahead and wooed several new leads.

Fire Clients

It isn't all beer and skittles, though. Often it's as important to fire incumbent clients as it is to get new ones. Sometimes the needs of a particular client change and are less relevant to your agency's skills. Sometimes, to be blunt, they just become too much of a pain and cease to be profitable. Cut your losses early. The sooner you do, the sooner you'll put that staff on one of the more optimal accounts. My own experience shows that if I fail to do this early enough, I'll lose the staff itself. People hate working on dysfunctional accounts. And the agency that keeps such a client isn't doing it many favors.

Clients that find their agencies leaving them need to evaluate why this happens. It very well might be due to changing agency priorities and resources. But chief marketing officers need make sure there isn't something wrong with the selection process or the way in which those relationships are subsequently managed.

You can see several accounts that keep appearing in the "currently pitching" lists in the trade magazines. Some seem to appear every six to nine months. I wouldn't want to be on those accounts. I bet the agencies lost money on the relationship to boot.

3340-TILL

The New Business Engine: Media Staff

The real engine of growth in online agencies, however, remains the media staff. A competent group will continue to impress the client into laying out more and more media dollars. This should be encouraged with a little bit of selectivity. Remember the lists we made above? A similar list should be made among your existing clients. Which ones do you really want to expand? Are there any that shouldn't grow anymore? Keep that balance.

As a media buyer, there are three tactics that must be pursued to grow your business:

- The obvious one is to ensure your client likes your firm. To the degree that you impress the heck out of them, this will naturally follow. This also has a lot to do with setting expectations as to what you deliver when. In the absence of well-worn paths in the online world, sometimes clients' expectations become unrealistic.
- Put the client's feet to the budget fires. Ask them the question: why is it that you're spending X in print and TV and only Y in online media? They will very likely not have a good answer.
- Come to them with unique opportunities. Every day there are new and different things being done online. Some of these things will be relevant and useful to your clients' brands. If you keep bringing these ideas to them, you will organically grow the business. I caution buyers, however, on doing neat-o things that look very nifty but give scant metric feedback. There are plenty of rich media doo-dads to do out there that will blow a $100,000 production budget. But, in the end, no one can tell what good it did. To get this organic growth, you need to be able to prove results to continue that program, even as you introduce additional ones.

Scaling

Finally, don't be the dog that catches the car. When you get the new business, it's easy to find yourself with a lot of media to buy and only one quarter the staff needed to do it. We need to be honest with the client as to the timing of how quickly we can scale upward. I've been surprised at how understanding clients have been when we've been forthright with this issue. They appreciate being brought into this very internal and sensitive issue with some openness. I've had clients thank me when I told them we wouldn't be able to handle some business for two or three more months.

Managers should never expect to be able to find four new media buyers and a supervisor in the same month they win an account. Maybe in some other industry or some other labor market, but in this one they're going to need some time. Often the pitch process will be delayed, and clients will want to compress the planning time available for the first campaign. Agencies should accommodate this only if reasonable and if the existing staff can handle it.

The quickest way to turn over your work force is to have them work double-time for their existing clients as well as the new ones. That works during a pitch and for a couple weeks after the adrenaline rush of a win. But a month later, it wears thin. A happy and functional agency is one that scales in anticipation of desired business. This might seem an unnecessary luxury to the agency CFO, but it pays financial dividends over time.

The Role of Senior Management and Other Non-Experts

Problems arise when the traditional media expectations of the senior management are challenged by new needs. For instance, it takes about one person per $1 million of media to plan and buy at an ad agency. In the online world, it takes about four times as many people to plan and buy the same amount. But if the CEO is not advocate enough of the new media to become expert in it, they can remain ignorant of these important subtleties. A lot of the early interactive divisions of traditional companies failed to staff up sufficiently, and they failed to force clients to pay sufficiently for the staffing.

Similar thinking causes some senior managers to direct an agency's new business efforts toward very large consumer goods companies because they're very large, have huge traditional media budgets, and are very, very prestigious. But in the online world, that's sort of like seeking the job to design all the fashions for the Russian military. The work isn't very fun for the staff, and you don't get paid.

Scaling is a major problem for managers who don't understand a great deal of the intricacies of the medium. The systems that we use, like banner servers, trafficking systems and databases, need to be available and need to scale with the work.

In the absence of a desire to learn all about these technical details, the senior managers need to delegate these decisions to a special interactive manager. Given enough leeway to hire, fire and run deficits for quarters at a time, special online managers can frequently succeed where the company's existing structure would not.

THE INTERACTIVE MARKETING CAREER

Marketing careers can face trying times. It's a very cyclical industry, and the online parts of it can be a roller coaster ride. Sometimes it can be difficult to get a good sense of scope on just how good or bad a job situation is. In early 2001 I published a quiz on the ClickZ site, on the Media 101 column I write weekly [http://www.clickz.com/media/buy_101/] to help people determine just how their interactive ad agency job might stand up to the competition.

People emailed back their scores, and it turned out that most hewed fairly close to the important inflection point just between liking the workplace and not liking the workplace. Since some of the variables make some leaps of deduction (e.g., bureaucratic memos sent on colored paper indicating a higher degree of hidebound administration), I was surprised to see how accurately people's scores reflected their actual attitudes that they noted in the text of their emails.

Of course, as media people, it behooves us to try to quantify what is an inherently subjective topic. Here's the quiz. (Eat your heart out, Cosmo.)

Quiz to Determine Interactive Quality of Life

- Does your employer house the interactive group separately from the rest of the agency? If no, score 2 points. If yes, and it's on a floor above the traditional media department, score 8 points. If yes, but it's on a floor lower than the traditional media department, then score only 6 points.

- Without prior permission, does someone in the interactive group have the authority to hire new people in the event a client wants to throw them more business? If so, add 10 points to the score. If unsure, assume the answer is no. Score 2 points.
- When conducting major new business pitches, does the new biz team get the interactive group in on the process as the very beginning? If yes, score 8 points. If they get the group involved only as an afterthought, score 4 points. If not at all, score 2.
- Does a new hire out of college make more money in the interactive group than in the traditional group? If yes, score 8 points. If no, score 4 points. If unknown, then assume answer is no.
- Does the interactive group have a different brand identity or sub-brand from the rest of the company? If yes, score 6 points. If yes, and they've been spun off and offer equity options, then score 10 points. If no, score 2 points.
- What is the average time an employee spends at the company? Less than 1 year will score a measly 2 points. Between one and two years will score 4 points. Between two and 5 years will score 8 points. More than five years will score 1 point.
- How much interactive billings does your agency handle? Fewer than $4 million scores 2 points. Between $4- and $12 million should score 6 points. Between $12- and $40 million will score 8 points. More than $40 million will score 2 points.
- How far from 50-50 is the gender split in the company? A mere 10 percent deviance (for example, a 45-55 split) scores 8 points. A 20 percent deviance scores 5 points. A deviance greater than 30 points scores 2 points.

- What is the ratio of interactive media employees to interactive media billings. A ratio of greater than four people per $1 million scores 8 points. A ratio of one or fewer per $1 million rates only 2 points. Anything in between rates 4 points.
- How many useless memos or emails does each employee receive from the agency corporate staff? If they receive more than 4 official communications a day, score 2 points. If 2 or 3 a day, score 4 points. If only about 1 a day, score 6 points. Fewer will score you 8 points. If they receive a majority of these communications on colored copy paper, with different colors signifying different types of useless memos, then subtract an additional 6 points from the total score.

Interactive workers can score somewhere between 19 and 84 points. If someone scored below or above this range, they missed their calling in the account services department, and they should under no circumstances subject themselves to the math-intensive media industry.

If they score between 70 and 84 points, they should be paying the company to let them work there. If they scored between 50 and 70 points, they probably work in an above-average agency doing above-average work, and I bet they like their workplace. And if, by some chance, they happened to score 70 precisely, and they're wondering which of those two groups to put themselves into, then they're too mathematically anal-retentive even for the media department, and they should consider the database group.

Scoring between 30 and 50 bodes ill. Workers with these scores are either too new to realize it yet, or they've already come to the conclusion that they plain don't like it there. That agency doesn't deserve them. Start interviewing.

The worker who scores between 19 and 30 should go home right now and take a shower. Never go back. You can buy new office supplies and make new friends.

In the interest of reader service, and to satisfy my lurid curiosity, please feel free to email your final score to the publisher (tacticalguide@yahoo.com). If you do, they'll email you back the running average, so you can tell precisely how dismal you should feel relative to your industry compatriots. Depending on your score, the next section might be of great interest.

How to Get an Agency to Hire You

The hiring patterns of agencies in this industry vary faster than the price of corn during October harvest. We're boom and bust and boom and bust all within the space of a city block. One agency thinks it needs to hire 200 people; another lays off 400.

Part of the problem is the way agencies get paid by clients. Agencies are what Wall Street analysts would cynically call "body shops." That is, they sell the time of people. Which means the only way to make more money is to hire more people and get clients to pay for them. This leads to signing large initial contracts and desperately hiring to fill that quota. When those people hired very quickly turn out to not really be necessary to the client, the agency-client relationship evolves, and great inefficiencies develop within the agency. They keep people on payroll without specific billable work to assign them. Or, worse, they foist these people on other clients, even though those clients might be better served by people with different skills.

It's not that these people aren't good at what they do, it's just that the agency happens not to be the place where they can best apply particular skills. Thus, we have the wonderful anarchy that is the interactive agency labor market. Boom and bust, boom and bust.

I've been working in this mess since the early 90's, and I've had six or seven jobs in that time. By an informal census of my friends, this seems to be a bit lower than average for folks with my tenure. Think about that next time an agency offers you retirement plan vesting after four years.

This begs the question of what to do once you find yourself in that unenviable position of being the person standing outside the agency once the music stops, with the agency no longer providing enough seats.

My first recommendation, of course, is to run screaming from the industry. Seriously. Dentistry is a great field where you get to meet all sorts of people, and they tend to yell at you less. Everyone can always go to law school. You can follow the example of famous J. Walter Thompson ad creative in the 1950's, Ed Zern, and become an outdoors writer, traveling the country with bird dogs and shotguns.

After the above quiz first ran on ClickZ, the average reader score proved to be a 48.5. On our grading scale, that falls into (just barely) the category of "That agency doesn't deserve you. Start interviewing." Not a ringing endorsement for the state of our profession.

But, since you bother to read books like this one, you're probably afflicted with an unhealthy curiosity about this interactive thing. You might even see yourself as helping push an envelope that will create new types of commerce, not just for products and profits, but also for ideas and media itself. If this sounds mildly arousing to you, then you have my condolences and my sympathies. Your alternative, alas, is to get back into the saddle and find that next advertising job in the string of advertising jobs you'll have before you finally wise up.

Connecting with Agencies

Some of the old saws are good saws. Always keep a contact file of all the folks you meet in the industry. Get their cards, and keep track of them. If you're using one of those paper systems, throw it out. I have about 4,000 contacts flying around, and I'm not finding anyone without a digital search function. And you'd be amazed how useful this becomes the richer your data grows.

It provides great entertainment later when you can track all the various job paths everyone has gone through.

Importantly, make sure you get the right contacts. I find that the single best people in the industry for job leads are the lower level planners and buyers. The higher ups in the agency hold a great deal of respect for the opinions of the folks in the trenches, particularly when it comes to assessing expertise in media. If I were trying to get a job as a planner or supervisor, I'd rather have my reference come from a buyer than an account director. This, of course, changes when you seek jobs at more senior levels, like head of interactive.

These tactics shouldn't be things to think about when you need to find a new job. You should be doing these things throughout your career. I'm a firm believer that a person is a much better professional when they know they can get another job quickly elsewhere. It gives them the integrity of the "Go soak yourself." Anyone who can tell that to their boss without worrying about their job will be a better, more credible and more respected force within the agency.

Some other old saws: go to the industry seminars and mingle. A lot of regional organizations have sprouted up in most metropolitan areas, some covering rich media, others covering media issues. These are great trolling grounds for people seeking new hires.

Sometimes, though, in some communities, the labor supply is just too anemic. I remember one instance in which we had to hire a new buyer for a major account in San Francisco. We needed that person absolutely immediately, otherwise we wouldn't be able to include the cost of the position in the renegotiated contract. A media supervisor and I went that evening to one of those media buyer meetings down in the South of Market area, where everyone sits around and talks about the imminent death of the banner. I was prepared to make an offer on the spot. We split up and sat in the audience listening to the questions the various buyers from other agencies made. One person in particular asked some pretty insightful questions. I worked my way through the crowd to get to this person at the very end. He was facing the other way. Before he could exit into the next room, where the refreshments waited, I yelled to him, "Hey, excuse me!"

When he turned around, it turned out this fellow was the media supervisor with whom I had come. "What?" he asked, thinking he'd done something wrong.

Finding Agencies That Hire

I've always found that agencies that conduct lay-offs are frequently the ones with the greatest subsequent hiring needs. It seldom fails. The agency finds itself overstaffed. It simultaneously draws up a lay-off plan, it places a hiring freeze, it gooses its new business efforts. Meanwhile, necessary job slots remain unfilled and the long fuse of new business prospects gets lit. This is exactly when the resumes coming into the HR department start to taper off, hearing the news of the initial layoffs.

But then one or two new accounts are won, and the agency suddenly finds itself 20 percent understaffed. These are the great vacuums of our industry. Lots of people get sucked up into these agencies at such times. If you send your resume out to agencies that conducted layoffs within the last three months, you might find yourself subject to desperate calls from their HR departments a few weeks later.

The really clever among the job seekers keep an eye on the high profile, ongoing new business pitches. I've been impressed with people sending me resumes, telling me they'd love to work for my agency if we got the such-and-such account. Provided they have relevant experience, these are people who become top-of-mind once we win a pitch.

The Interview

People in our industry, particularly on the buy side of the fence, tend to see themselves as part of a group. They tend to see things as an us-versus-them situation. It might be buyers versus sellers. It might be interactive folks versus traditional media people. Any way it slices, they tend to have insecurities. Your job in an interview should be to become part of the "us." Rather than sitting on the other side of the desk like a foreign substance, you need to engage the interviewer. You need to wrest out of them the issues that interest them and then engage them in the conversation. You don't have to agree with them on how to handle the issue, but you have to show that you'd be on their side. This isn't a criterion they have in their head for hiring, but it's the stuff on which the intangibles are established. If they think they like you and that you're one of them, they'll fight for you.

Let them talk. I've found that the more a candidate has already won over an interviewer, the more the interviewer wants to talk. If the interviewer wants to spout, count yourself lucky, and don't feel you should interrupt.

Have some very tough questions for the interviewer. To the degree you can put them on the hot seat, you make yourself seem a desirable candidate they must work to win. I don't recommend asking insulting questions, but here are some questions that made me think candidates asking them would be very intelligent employees:

- If I can get my client to succeed and spend more money, can I have the authority to hire more staff to handle this? Or will I have to handle that additional work with the same staff?
- How much authority does the interactive leadership at this agency enjoy? Can the television people take our budgets? Do we have primary client contact?
- Will the agency invest in my keeping up-to-date by sending me to conferences and such?

After Rejection, the Recourse

You will be rejected. That's the industry. Don't take it personally. I know a lot of folks coming out of the Ivy League with magna cum laudes who get the jitters just contemplating their first rejections. Get used to it. I can think of no better lesson right out of college.

But don't take the first "no" as a finality. It may indeed be that a job opening gets cut or that they fill it with someone else. This doesn't mean they don't like you. In fact, most times that I've done a lot of interviewing for a position, I've wound up considering some of the candidates for other positions. Frequently there's an embarrassment of talent riches.

I see a lot of rejected candidates shy away later from that same agency. This is a big mistake. Unless the agency tells you with greater certainty that they just simply can't abide you, keep going back for additional positions. I've hired account executives after they did this two or three times, a couple of which rose to account supervisors within a few years.

This can be taken to an extreme, though. I remember one instance of a woman in San Francisco who kept calling my employees for weeks and weeks. The first couple times was endearing, showing a great deal of persistence. The seventh time made us contemplate a restraining order.

NEGOTIATING FOR AN AGENCY JOB AND SALARY

A lot of people going into the agency business don't realize that they can negotiate an agency's offer of employment. Worse still, they sign employment agreements without fully understanding all the terms, particularly when agencies offer equity. Let's tackle these problems one at a time.

Negotiating

People starting right out of college are going to find that their negotiating power is a great deal less than those with experience. It's easy for an agency to argue that fresh college graduates are relatively interchangeable, and therefor don't warrant differentiated compensation. You might be able to negotiate some extra vacation time or perhaps a moving bonus, but don't push a potential employer too far if this is your first job.

The first thing you want to do is ensure your negotiations are fair. If you are negotiating directly with the employer, that's probably fair. If, though, the employer inserts a hired recruiter to negotiate with you, this is putting you in a weak position. The recruiter is generally not authorized to make many concessions. This means that you wind up getting a lot of sympathy from the recruiter, but little movement from the original offer. If the company does this to you, and you are seeking a high-level job, have the recruiter talk to someone you hire for yourself. It's worth the extra money to hire your own representative—a lawyer who understands compensation equity is usually a great choice.

It's important to realize just what is negotiable. Almost all employers have limitations, where certain areas simply aren't able to budge. For instance, if a board of directors of a company votes on a very particular kind of equity compensation plan, it's extremely unlikely they're going to change it just to accommodate you. Sometimes these plans have discretionary flexibility, but often times they do not. Finding out the dimensions in which the employer can wiggle will put you in a very powerful position.

These items are generally negotiable:

- Salary
- Signing bonus
- Moving bonus
- Vacation time
- Computer allowance
- Hours or days worked
- Quantity of equity offered
- Severance

These items are typically written in corporate stone:

- Health benefits
- 401K and other retirement plan benefits
- Terms of equity offered (we'll go into that later)

I recommend a compensation package negotiation strategy where the potential employee makes the first offer. Make it high. I don't know the employer who will completely break off negotiations just because the first offer was much too high. There will be a counter offer.

When that counter offer comes, you now have the difference between your desired pay and the package they would like to offer. Your next step is to bridge the gap by filling it in with things in which they have great flexibility.

The scenario would work like this:

- You suggest they should pay you $100.
- They express surprise and disappointment at such a high suggestion. They tell you they were thinking more along the lines of $75.
- You express disappointment, but ask for confirmation that they have some flexibility in some other areas like, for instance, on the equity side of the package.
- You counter with $85 and an increased equity package that would make up another $15.
- You accept their next counter offer of $75 and $10 in equity.

Equity

Few people truly understand this area, so don't be disappointed if you find yourself initially confused. There are a lot of legal financial terms and legal language making this complex. Here's the simple version.

Companies will give employees the opportunity to purchase company stock at a set price. Note that this is different from just giving away stock, which is seldom ever done. This kind of benefit is called an option plan. There is a very particular formula to it.

Each of these companies has a set number of shares of stock associated with it. And each of these companies has a financial worth called a market capitalization. When you divide the "market cap" by the number of shares out there, you get the price for each share. So far, it's a simple algebra equation: price = market cap / shares. If a company is worth $100, and it has 10 shares, each share will be worth $10.

The option plan will let you purchase shares after a certain amount of time spent at the company. This is the vesting schedule. Most plans I've seen recently involve you working there for at least a year before any of these options actually become yours.

Most companies will grant you the options over a period of about three or four years.

When you do "exercise" the options that you have earned, you are not given shares of stock outright. Instead, you merely have the right to purchase them at a special (hopefully by this time relatively cheap) price. That price is called the strike price. It surprises a lot of folks who suddenly realize later that they have to pony up serious money to buy their stock.

Here's an example:

- Company gives you options to purchase 1,000 shares at a strike price of $3.
- At the time you start work, the stock is worth $4 per share. The theoretical benefit at that moment in time is $1,000.
- A year goes by, after which you are entitled to one quarter of your options. You decide to exercise them, paying $3 times 250, or $750.
- But in that intervening year, the stock price has gone up to $8, which makes that equity worth $2,000. You make a profit of $1,250.
- Three years later, you've vested all of your equity, but you decide not to exercise any additional options because your company's stock is now at $2.50 a share. We call that being "under water," where it costs more money to exercise the option than the underlying stock is worth. You generally do not have to exercise your options, if they are under water.

Different option plans might differ from this structure. Certainly, the tax consequences of all this will vary based on all sorts of factors, so it's best to get professional help when the time comes.

Unfortunately, to negotiate intelligently about equity you need some very specific information. You MUST know the strike price of the equity. And you MUST know the number of outstanding shares. Without these numbers, you will be unable to calculate the potential value of the offered options.

I see a lot of companies sending out employment offers with equity options for tens of thousands of shares. It looks very generous until the potential employee realizes that the company has tens of millions of shares outstanding, and that each is worth very little. If they involve a high strike price, they stand a great chance of never being worth much at all, no matter how many of them they give.

Worse, sometimes the person with whom you're negotiating doesn't know these numbers themselves. They may never have asked these necessary questions themselves when they were first employed. Do not accept an equity package without knowing these numbers. Or if you do, you must assume the package could be worth nothing.

Do make sure that in the course of the negotiations, you treat everyone with respect. There is never a reason to be impolite. You will likely have to work for these folks, so make sure you don't give them second thoughts. This is one reason why some argue that it's always good to go through a recruiter or a set of third parties.

You will likely learn a lot about your company during these negotiations. How flexible will the company prove in the future? How much authority does your direct supervisor really have? How does the venture value its employees? I've always found that my later discoveries about the personality of a firm have been foreshadowed by the nature of the negotiations.

A DAY IN THE LIFE OF A GOOD MEDIA PLANNER

To get a proper picture of the responsibilities and life of an actual online media planner, we have to visit the habitat of the planner and observe directly. This chapter will detail the day-to-day activities of a composite agency media person. She's not perfect, but she gets the job done, and hopefully in a way that might reveal some of subtleties of why the market works the way it does.

Day 1

Our planner gets up fairly early, waiting her turn for the shower behind her three roommates. Some day she'll go into ad sales and be able to afford her own place, but, for now, she's happy for the camaraderie.

To get a jump on the work, she checks her email remotely from the apartment couch and discovers that her account team has given her the go ahead on a large media plan. It would have to start yesterday to be done on time. The client just now signed the contract.

Anticipating the delay, she's already finished the draft of the RFP and made up a draft list of those sites to which it should be sent.

She did this as an afterthought a few weeks ago when she'd just finished the rough plan outline proposal that the account folks took to the client for approval. She forwards these two documents to her media supervisor for "review" by email, but tells her in the message that if she doesn't hear back in 10 hours, she's going ahead with or without approval.

On the bus on the way in to the agency, she makes a mental list of things to do:

- Make sure the production person, creative person and traffic person all know the timeline for this campaign—and commit to it
- Invent that timeline
- Starbucks
- Ask around the media department to see if there are other major projects falling due just about the same time to prevent impending train wrecks
- Call up her special sales reps to warn them about several specific needs (i.e., favors) she'll require
- Make sure she sees the signed copy of the client approval before anything leaves the office, as these "signed" deals have a tendency to regress to "he said so over dinner last night," after the account team is forced to get specific

She'll spend the next couple hours doing these things. The most important will turn out to be making sure everyone from creative, production and traffic are anticipating the work load that will be pressed upon them when the time comes. It takes her a couple hours only because she gets interrupted frequently:

- Her supervisor told the client the evening before that, yes, it was a great idea to find out how many banners the competition was running in the various sizes. It takes her 5 minutes to show her supervisor how this is fruitless. It takes her 30 minutes to put together the memo anyway.
- Her boyfriend calls once and emails twice.
- Four different media planners independently come in to talk for 5 minutes apiece.

- Two others come by but are quickly disposed of with intent stares at the computer monitor.
- She answers 12 emails. Three of them are for business. 44 get filed into her sales rep folder, unread.

She spends half an hour talking to her supervisor. She then spends another half-hour prettifying the initial RFP and plan documents.

She gets hungry. Normally, she'd grab a friend and walk a block down the street to pick up a small lunch. She could have lunch in any of the most expensive restaurants in the city, any day, if she were to accept the sales reps' offers. But she's just tired of being sold to, and she seldom takes up the offers. Today's different, though. She needs to do some special haggling. She invites a particular rep to invite her to lunch, where she can feign disinterest until she gets the deal terms she needs.

After twenty minutes of niceties in the hallways, 10 minutes to the restaurant, 90 minutes eating and talking, and 10 minutes to get back, she finds it already 3 p.m. She's won the terms she was seeking, but she wonders if it was worth the time.

She has just enough time to finalize the RFP recipient list and blasts it out the door by 4 o' clock. She sits in on a conference call with the client to review the schedules, but she never gets to talk at these things. She presses the mute button and uses the other line to talk with one of her roommates during the call. Occasionally, she'll depress the mute button again to grunt an "Uh huh."

At 5 p.m., she plays a game of darts with some creatives on the other side of the floor, then settles in to prepare some Excel spreadsheets for when the RFP responses come back. At 6:30 she hits the streets again, opting for a quiet evening at home in front of the Internet.

Day 2

The next day, the floodgates open. She has awakened the media rep hoard.

Before our media planner gets to work the next morning, she has four cell phone messages (she was smart enough to turn it off the night before), her roommates tell her three reps called there, her work voicemail is just about full with 18 messages (from 12 reps), and her email shows 38 new messages from people with media company domain addresses.

She sighs as she steps up onto the bus to work. She gets off two blocks early to visit Starbucks, and she orders a Venti.

As she walks the remaining distance, she ticks off in her head the triage she needs to do to manage the rep communications. Her mental list looks like this:

- The people she's most interested in (particularly those from which she's asking favors) have already been called before the RFP went out. She has appointments with these folks already, but she wants to make sure to return their calls.
- The people who called back because she sent them an RFP obviously need to get their messages returned.
- The others? Well, she has to admit to herself that she's really curious to know how they smelled the money and came out of the woodwork so darned quickly. Almost enough to call them back. She decides instead, to call up just a sampling of them.

She doesn't know this yet, but some of the reps on the RFP list (actually, just more than half of them) owed favors to other reps, and they passed on some of the information from the RFP to people who weren't on the list. Everyone thought it would just seem a handy coincidence if the errant site reps happened to call on the day after an RFP was unleashed.

By noon, she's managed to call back all the people important to the campaign. The tough part was trying not to insult them all while turning down their offers for lunch and dinner. She just wants the facts.

Today's lunch is spent talking mostly business over Italian food with one of the "important" reps she called before the RFP went out. This sales person might not even quite comprehend his special status. After all, it really wouldn't help the price much for him to believe his media was special to her.

The conversation wends its way to CPMs. Once she has him committing to a rough range, she then lets him in on some of the secrets. She knows this will hurt her negotiating position, but she's sticking her neck out thinking that he might be able to get her even better targeting if he really knows what she's trying to achieve.

One out of four times, it works, and the sales person is able to concoct something special—perhaps a certain package of inventory or the application of a special targeting technology. Most times, it just puts her over the barrel in the price negotiations. Reps who do this to her don't get let in on the secrets the next time around.

After lunch, she starts filling in her pre-prepared spreadsheets so as to compare the different rates from the different sites. Another column along the spreadsheet is the various creative sizes and other production specs. Some of the sites failed to include these. She leaves them off the list. If she has time, she'll email them one more time, but most likely, she'll just leave them off.

She knocks off at four. The production folks are playing Doom over the net against a large creative team over at another agency. She joins in until dark, then heads home in a cab feeling somehow very empty. She's spent the day with 40 people all trying to get her to give them something that she didn't own, but something that she controlled. She looks forward to the execution stage.

340-TILL

Day 3

The next day, after settling in with a large coffee, our media planner scans the Internet before she jumps into the next stage of the buy. She checks the news, the stock quotes she tracks (she gets a lot of good tips from reps with inside information) and even logs onto eTrade to unload some shares. By 9 o' clock, her supervisor has arrived, and she picks up all the printed spreadsheets from her desk and heads into her boss's office.

After going over the final list of sites that made the buy, the supervisor asks a few questions, nods and says, "Alright. Let's get this signed."

The planner emails the list to the client and confirms the conference call for two hours later. Since they already had buy-off on a very similar list before the final price negotiations happened, she doesn't feel very nervous about the upcoming approval. But there's still a lot to do between then and now.

She walks over to visit the traffic and production folks in person. She gives them each a copy of the site list—this one with the production specs next to each site from the information forwarded in the RFP process. She asks both groups if any of these sites have proven problematic going up on time in the past. She doesn't want to have to deal with another hassle.

Several times before, one site would go up a few weeks late because they gave the wrong production specs (once because they had just changed them, another time because a rep said the agency could use a form of creative the rep's own tech team later refused). It resulted in an unbalanced media campaign that threw off several controlled media tests they were conducting, caused hours and hours of extra discrepancy resolution, and ultimately left the client with a queasy feeling about the whole enterprise.

Sure enough, the 18-year-old production intern points to two sites that they had problems with in the past couple months on other clients.

"Big problems?"

"No, but I can't guarantee it won't happen again."

"Ok, they're off the list. I'll email you all the new version by lunch."

Our planner has a back-up list of sites she would have liked to include on the buy originally, but she didn't have the money. She turns to this list now. She picks out two sites that best replace the particular type of sites she just trashed off the list.

One, she favors because it's the most analogous to the sites left off. The other she chooses because she wants to curry favor with the rep since there's a new campaign in the works that might require a favor from him.

She emails the result (with a very brief explanation) to her supervisor, and then sends copies to production and traffic.

She sits in on the client conference call. Her supervisor answers all the questions, so there's not much use in saying much. The client picks some nits, just to show she's up on the lingo. The planner heads off these issues by turning that discussion into a general discussion about the media market, making sure to show her appreciation of the client's sophistication. The client faxes back a signed approval.

She heads back to her cubicle. She sits back in the chair and thinks for a few seconds. Is she forgetting anything? No? Ok, she sends out the "yes" email to all the folks who made the buy.

When she comes back from lunch a half hour later, half of them have already responded with nice emails (a couple with some subtle gripes about not getting at least 15 percent of the buy and about how important it is that they get at least 15 percent of the buy.)

She then emails out the "no" letter to the remainder of the folks who responded to the RFP. She chooses this time to call her parents. She wants to be on the phone for the next couple hours when the particularly pushy reps start calling up for their "appeals" process. It's an enormous waste of her time to have to field tens of calls from reps trying to not take no for an answer, but she feels sometimes she can't just ignore them. She'll need favors from them sometime later down the line. But for this afternoon, at least, she can funnel them into voicemail.

Day 21: After the Media Begins to Run

Last we left our media planner protagonist, she was overseeing the process of trafficking out ads to the various sites who made the buy. She, her supervisor, the traffic department, and even a couple creatives who happened to walk by at the wrong time, were caught up in a 6-hour battle of matching the right creative sizes with the right sites and making sure the creative actually made it online.

Over the next three days, more and more of the sites began to show the scheduled runs, called "flights" in the jargon. The ones who didn't manage to get the creative up by this point received pointed emails.

Now, in the aftermath of the trafficking process, our media planner slips into work early. It's 7 a.m., and it's the first time all her flights have been up for a complete week. In other words, she can begin to look at the data and see what's happening. Any sooner than this would have been mere speculation (not that she didn't peek frequently). She now has enough data under her belt to avoid misinterpreting trends. The particular day or time of day and any number of other errant factors could have skewed the real results before now.

Her client has been calling every morning since the first ad went out, but our planner refused to divulge any information. Once she stated a clickthrough rate or a cost per transaction, the client would have accepted this as global gospel and demanded immediate reaction. She's played that game too many times before to fall into the trap.

Her first task is to assemble all the data. This involves a number of processes. Her agency employs a third party ad server. This allows a consistent count across sites. Or at least it would if all the sites allowed for all the ad servers, which of course they don't.

Sites owned by the Excite/Matchlogic network are more likely to allow the use of Matchlogic's ad server, and sites from Doubleclick's network are more likely to allow its Dart ad server.

Because of all this, she sometimes has to log onto a special site where one or more publications have special password-protected areas where she can view her client's results. This is a huge pain, slowing down the process of collecting the campaign performance.

If she worked on a huge account with enormous budgets, she wouldn't have to worry so much, but since her client spends only about $100,000 per month, some of the larger sites and networks get a bit uppity in their acceptance policies. The worst part of it is that even when a site allows her to use her own ad server, they won't respect her numbers. If her ad server reports an underdelivery, the site won't recognize the need to grant a makegood unless their own ad server also reports the same discrepancy. So she winds up with two sets of data—one that is more accurate and consistent at the agency side and one that is used to resolve discrepancies from the site side.

This morning, though, she doesn't care about discrepancies, she's seeking truth. She assembles a spreadsheet together by taking the numbers she has from her own ad server and adding in with them (not really a statistically clean policy) the numbers she gets from the sites where they didn't allow her to use her own server.

And then she plays. This is the best part of the job. She's developed hypotheses, she's negotiated, she's done all the work. Now the experiment pays off or fails. There might be 10 different theories she's employed to choose these particular sites. She needs to determine which of these theories proved true, which ones were losers, and what implications this means to her future media buying.

She cuts the numbers in the spreadsheet over and over again, looking for intelligence among the mountain of information. Some stuff is simple, like which creative works better than another in a given time or particular circumstance. Others are rather complex, like targeting people of a special background by combining search term words along with targeted content adjacencies and specially designed creative.

From the morning to the mid-afternoon, skipping lunch, she pinpoints evidence of the success and failure of the theories. This will act as a rough outline for part of the post-buy document that will be prepared after the whole campaign has run.

In the course of doing this, she comes up with seven more theories for the next campaign. This is what excites her. She knows her next campaign for this client will be a better one. This is the very foundation on which the agency's client relationship grows stronger. And she feels pride in being its primary creator.

KEEPING UP TO DATE

The interactive media and the media markets change quickly. This affords the opportunity for media buyers to both take advantage of undervalued new opportunities, and also the opportunity to waste advertiser dollars on outmoded technologies and media and discredited strategies. Keeping up to date requires some regular reading and interacting with the community.

Most people will find free resources on the web sufficient for keeping abreast of the important trends. For people desiring more detail, subtlety and proprietary views, research companies and certain publishers offer alternatives.

Good Web Resources

ClickZ publishes a large series of weekly columns on various relevant issues. I write the "Media 101" column for a how-to approach to online media. Tom Hespos and Jim Meskauskas, two of my favorite online columnists, write buyer-side articles of a more opinionated nature.

Mediapost publishes several sites on the media markets, providing more of a current news approach to the industry. Masha Geller writes a daily column that I consider a must-read.

For a comprehensive review of a large number of online advertising resource sites, the Laredo Group publishes a very up-to-date list. Their reviews of the content of the various sites are succinct and useful. They can be found on www.laredogroup.com.

I-Advertising.com has some great discussion boards for shooting the interactive breeze with people who've done it before.

3340-TILL

Iconocast publishes an opinionated newsletter that often poses controversial views.

EmergingInterest.com concentrates on rich media issues. Bill McCloskey, long synonymous with the East Coast rich media industry edits the letter, providing insight and levity.

CyberAtlas.com, once a division of my Internet Profiles, presents some very useful data on Internet trends and facts.

Ad Age puts up most of its headlines and some of its longer stories on its "IQ" online section, which can be very interesting. Ad Age, along with the rest of the major print trade magazines, sometimes suffers from the editorial malaise of press release rewrites and an unhealthy focus on the personalities behind the companies.

Adweek, Mediaweek and Brandweek provide very current information on their respective markets, with particular focus on traditional media. They sometimes suffer from the same editorial problems as most major print trade publications, as mentioned above. Unfortunately, while visitors can see the headlines for free, the content of most stories requires a special online subscription.

Proprietary Research Tools

Media Metrix and Nielsen/Netratings both offer a few free general reports. The top 50 web sites is frequently a free feature on these sites, an effort to tempt advertisers and agencies to subscribe to the more detailed information available to paying customers.

Other research companies, like Jupiter, eMarketer and Forrester, make analyst reports available on popular topics of the day. If I could level a criticism at these analysts, it would be that they tend to give too much credence to current fads (push, streaming media, wireless ads, etc . . .) and not enough concentration on the brunt of the everyday media work. Their analysts tend to be very young and get much of their practical information from interviews with more experience practitioners in the industry.

Second Edition

A second addition of this book, including new types of advertising as well as expanded and revised existing sections, should appear on shelves in 2002. To that end, the author welcomes criticisms, omissions, comments and advice as to what would prove most useful to readers. Email is welcome for comments and requests for publishing notification at editorial@tacticalguide.com.

APPENDICES

The Online Advertising Process

This list of events describes the life of an online campaign. For the sake of keeping things generic, the example campaign describes an online banner effort—the simplest and most common type of campaign. In real life, the process will vary significantly to fit the idiosyncrasies of each agency and client. Marketers that do not use an agency will generally employ the same process, except they will assign agency functions to in-house staff.

A lot can go wrong in the process. Mayhem will result if some participants disagree on which department or person should be responsible for each task. Each agency or marketer needs to spend the time to put together their own process document to make sure each player agrees on the roles, the order of work and the expectations of what will be produced and when. One small hiccup in the process will often create a cascading failure, setting off a chain-reaction that can be far greater than the initial mistake.

The process itself will then become a critical tool for diagnosing problems with the marketing and with the agency. For instance, only after creating formal processes did most of the large interactive firms discover the inefficiencies of scale involved with trafficking. The priority placed on automating certain parts of trafficking and campaign analysis arose only after it became clear that those parts of the process were often failing.

It will be easy to underestimate the time and attention needed to put together a formal process document. The heads of the media, creative, account service, trafficking and production need to directly participate. And after the process document is created, it needs to be vested with authority. Process documents can be ignored unless there are direct consequences for failing to live up to standards and timelines.

The process listed below is merely a guide to tactical execution. It is by no means a complete list of the interactions between the various parties. There would be a layer of strategy, intelligence and sheer interactive talent that would be missing were these the only activities to take place at an agency. Regular internal planning meetings need to take place to constantly evaluate what interactive marketing is doing and it potentially can do for the client.

Starting a Campaign

- Agency involved in advertiser discussions on need for marketing and marketing objectives
- Input session organized by account management team to ensure objectives suit all advertiser-side players, like product management and sales groups
- Client gives specific direction to agency for the development of rough creative and media briefs
- Account team and media team route initial briefs to other departments for advice
- Modified brief presented to client for final approval
- Upon approval, all internal agency forms for the campaign are generated and made available to appropriate departments
- Traffic or financial department opens up job numbers in the accounting system and informs all groups how they should account for related time and expenses
- If appropriate, accounting department should construct a cost estimate for the client for signature
- Account team constructs schedule and distributes

- Once finalized, both cost estimate and schedule are forwarded to client for signature

Brief Full Team

- Cross-department briefing meeting held to discuss media and creative approaches, resolve any potential differences
- Schedule second internal cross-department meeting for review of initial concepts
- Set times with client for initial creative and media reviews following internal meetings
  Creative Development
- Creatives take brief and develop broad concepts
- Production team consults with creatives to ensure the concepts can be executed with terrestrial technology in the third millennium
- Collect art and other assets necessary for concept execution
- Art buyer gives ballpark figures for suggested art; alternatives found for those with unreasonable prices
- Creatives develop presentation materials, with input from account team
- Creative routed to proofreader
- Work submitted for internal creative department review
- Other departments to look at work to ensure compatibility with media and production needs
- Creative routed to proofreader again to check any modifications
- Work goes to client for approval

Media Plan Development

- Coming out of initial client meetings, supervisor and planners develop first pass at strategies
- They develop a plan with the creatives to conduct initial creative testing with the first portion of the campaign's spend

- A creative testing matrix may be produced at this time to ensure the correct number of creatives and buys are planned and made
- Creatives and media group determine which factors, including qualitative factors, should be tracked along with the typical media metrics (type of creative, campaign objective, etc . . .)
- List of metrics is created and sent to the database group to ensure the correct variables are attached to the right pieces of performance information
- Database team makes sure each creative and buy will be instrumented with the appropriate additional information
- Planners make a rough list of sites from which they will later choose a more refined selection
- Planners consult existing client data on past experiences to add to the rough list
- Planners use research tools and syndicated panel data to add still more sites
- An RFP is created to reflect concerns about the sites given the particular campaign objectives
- The RFP is sent to sites on the initial list
- Responses are collected by the buyer, and most knee-jerk requests for vendor meetings are politely declined
- Buyers meet with reps of those sites that have legitimate additional issues or offers to discuss
- Prices from respondents are compared, and sites with the higher prices are left off the buy
- Sites are notified of their status
- In a formal RFP process, sites attempting to "appeal" the decision to leave them off a campaign are not given a subsequent chance to get back on the buy by undercutting prices of other sites
- Plan is finalized for internal review
- Client approves plan at the same time the creative is approved

Creative Execution

- Upon approval, the art buying group ensures all necessary rights are bought before campaign starts
- After client approval, modifications are made and final versions of creative are produced
- Final versions get sent to client for final approval
- Upon final approval, ads are sent to production department to ensure all proper sizes are created
- All creatives in all sizes are sent to the traffic department for subsequent sending to the appropriate media vendor
- Traffic department names each creative uniquely to ensure subsequent proper data collection
- If the agency employs its own ad server, the ads are uploaded to the system and scheduled appropriately
- After banner server scheduling, unique URLs are logged and sent to the traffic department to pass on to the appropriate media vendors

Media Execution

- Prospective buys are entered into financial tracking system, if appropriate
- Formal estimates are generated by the financial department and passed on to the media people
- Media people obtain client signature for the formal estimate
- Upon receiving signature, the buys are "made live" in the agency's accounting system
- Insertion orders are printed by financial group
- Buyers send insertion orders to the sites
- Buyers ensure each site returns a signed copy of the insertion order. Sites failing to do so are dropped from campaign.

- With final list of sites, a final testing plan is created, featuring a matrix of parts of buys vs. individual creative pieces
- The database group is given the final testing matrix of the buys and executions
- Traffic department ensures all elements are produced in proper sizes, etc . . .
- Traffic sends appropriate creative work to appropriate sites
- Traffic department confirms that sites received creative
- Traffic department responds to problems reported by sites
- Buyers or traffic group checks online that each creative is properly placed on expected media location
- Traffic department contacts any site not properly displaying correct ad with correct links
- Buyers take sites off the buy that fail to comply with trafficking requests

Tracking

- Sites begin to report on performance
- Buyers collect performance reports and collate them weekly
- Reports are forwarded on to database group for entry into agency system, if not done already via automated tool, like a banner server
- Media group responsible for constructing weekly or biweekly tracking reports for clients
- Traffic group responsible for making sure scheduled flights change as per testing matrix
- Buyers contact traffic department to notify of needed adaptations due to performance feedback
- Traffic group goes ahead with these changes so long as they do not conflict with existing testing matrix
- Weekly/biweekly tracking reports delivered to clients, creative team and account team

- Performance checked monthly by buyers against expected and guaranteed media delivery
- Buyers notify sites of necessary makegoods and credits stemming from discrepancies
- After makegoods negotiated, finalize makegood plan with sites, send it for approval to client
- Date set for post-buy analysis to be made to client
- All collected data analyzed by buyer and planner teams
- Post-buy report written and put into presentation format
- Post-buy report internally reviewed by creative and media group
- Post-buy report delivered to client

Lather, rinse, repeat

Interactive Creative Brief

Expected Deliverable

For instance, the creative to put in an upcoming spread in a technology culture magazine

Target Audience: What they currently think and do

Describe the attitude and behavior of the desired target, especially in relation to how they might be likely to receive ad messages.

What should the communications make them think and do?

What is the specific change in thought or action that the creative should cause?

The single-minded proposition

State the simple message the audience should receive

Support points

Features

Tone/manner of communication

Mandatories

Insert here all the must-dos with which the client and its legal department insist on burdening the creatives. This often involves logo treatments and legal wording.

Media Brief

Overall Objective

This should be a brief description of the client's ultimate marketing goals, like sales or share figures, or new product introductions.

Media Plan Objective

Here should be described the specific task this particular campaign should achieve, like awareness levels or a certain response.

Target Audiences

As much targeting information should be given as would prove useful in finding relevant sites. The information should be prioritized by importance, indicating which of the many types of audience data will most likely prove useful to the objective.

Timing Considerations

Seasonality and other marketing efforts should be noted here, as well as required campaign durations.

Geography

Budget

Creative Considerations

Materials Availability (shipping dates)

Competitive Issues

Plan Due Date

Any Additional Considerations

Approvals

____________________ Advertising Manager
____________________ Product Manager
____________________ Marcom Manager
____________________ Account Manager
____________________ Media Manager

Standard Terms and Conditions for Internet Advertising

For Media Buys One Year or Less

These Standard Terms and Conditions for Internet Advertising for Media Buys One Year or Less are intended to offer Media Companies, Advertisers, and their Agencies a voluntary standard for conducting business in a manner acceptable to all parties. This document is to accompany Agency and Media Company insertion orders and represents a common understanding for doing business. This document does not cover sponsorships and other arrangements involving content association or integration, and/or special production.

I. INSERTION ORDERS AND INVENTORY AVAILABILITY

a. From time to time, parties may negotiate Insertion Orders under which a Media Company will deliver advertisements to its site(s) for the benefit of an Agency or Advertiser. At the Agency's discretion, an "Insertion Order" (IO) may either be submitted by the Agency to the Media Company or be submitted by the Media Company and signed by the Agency. Each IO shall specify: (a) the type(s) of inventory to be delivered (e.g., impressions, clicks or other desired actions); (b) the price(s) for such inventory; (c) the maximum amount of money to be spent pursuant to the IO (the "Total Spend") and (d) the start and end dates of the campaign. Other items that may be included are: reporting requirements such as impressions or other performance criteria; any special ad delivery scheduling and/or ad placement requirements; and specifications concerning ownership of data collected.

b. Media Company will make best efforts to notify Agency within two business days of receipt of an insertion order (IO) if the specified inventory is not available. Acceptance of the IO and these Terms and Conditions will be made upon written or electronic approval of the IO by the Media Company and Agency and/or the display of the first ad impression by the Media Company, unless otherwise agreed upon in the IO.

AD PLACEMENT AND POSITIONING

Media Company must comply with the IO, including all ad placement restrictions, so that, consistent with the scope of the IO, an advertisement provided by Agency (the "Advertisement") is provided to the site (the "Site") specified on the IO when such Site is called up by an internet user.

a. Media Company will provide at least 10 business days' prior notification of any material changes to the design or architecture of the Site or placement position of the Advertisement. A material change is defined as any change in editorial content which would change the target audience or significantly affect the ad placement and/or ad unit specified in the IO. Should such a modification occur, Agency may immediately cancel the remainder of the buy without penalty within the 10-day notice period.
b. Final technical specifications, as agreed upon in the negotiations, must be submitted to the Agency within two business days of receipt of the IO. Changes to the specification of the ad units purchased after that period will allow Advertiser to (i) send revised creative, (ii) immediately cancel the remainder of the buy without penalty, or (iii) request that the Media Company resize the ad unit at Media Company's cost, and with final creative approval of the Agency, within a reasonable time period to fulfill the guaranteed levels of the IO.

c. The Media Company will comply with the IO, including requirements to schedule a balanced delivery schedule, unless otherwise specified in the IO. Any exceptions (including bonus impressions) must be approved by the Agency.
d. Ad delivery shall comply with editorial adjacencies guidelines stated on the IO. Failure to comply with editorial guidelines shall be grounds for immediate cancellation of the contract by the other party, without penalty. Advertising that runs in violation of the guidelines shall be non-billable.

PAYMENT/PAYMENT LIABILITY

a. **Invoices**

Invoices are to be sent to: the agency's billing address as set forth in the IO and should include the IO number, the Advertiser name, the Brand name, and any Campaign name, number or other identifiable reference as stated on the IO.

Invoices should be accompanied by proof of performance, which may include access to online reporting, as addressed in this document. Media Company should invoice Agency for the services provided not less often than a calendar month basis with the net cost prorated evenly over the term of the ad buy, unless otherwise specified in the applicable IO.

b. **Payment Date**

Payments will be made thirty days from date of invoice, or as otherwise stated with the payment schedule set forth in the IO. If Agency has not been paid by the Advertiser within thirty days, Media Company may seek payment directly from Advertiser, pursuant to Section IIIc.

c. Payment Liability

Unless otherwise set forth by the Agency on the IO, Media Company agrees to hold Agency liable for payments solely to the extent proceeds have cleared from the Advertiser to the Agency for advertising placed in accordance with the agreement. For sums owing but not cleared to Agency, Media Company agrees to hold the Advertiser solely liable. Media Company understands that Advertiser is Agency's disclosed principal and Agency, as agent, has no obligations hereunder, either joint or several, except as specifically set forth in this Paragraph.

The Agency agrees to make every reasonable effort to collect payment from the Advertiser on a timely basis.

Agency's credit is established on a client by client basis.

If Advertiser proceeds have not cleared for the IO, other Advertisers from the representing Agency shall not be prohibited from advertising on Media Company site if their credit is not in question.

Written confirmation of the relationship between Agency and Advertiser shall be made available to Media Company upon written request. This confirmation should include the Advertiser's acceptance of sequential liability and authorization to have the Agency represent the Advertiser.

If the Advertiser's or Agency's credit is or becomes impaired, the Media Company may require payment in advance.

Should Advertiser consistently be late in payment, Media Company has the right to cancel remaining advertising, as long as Advertiser has been given 10 business days written notice.

II. REPORTING

a. Media Company must provide or give access to reporting, either electronically or in writing, with the initial report within two business days of delivery of the Advertisement, and subsequent reports at least as often as weekly, unless otherwise specified in the IO.

b. Proof of performance, as addressed in the IO shall be a prerequisite to payment for the campaign.

c. Reporting must be broken out by day and summarized by creative execution, content area (ad placement) and other variables defined in the IO, for example, impressions, keywords, and/or clicks.

   Media Company's act of making available the online report shall constitute a certification that the report is accurate.

d. In the event that Media Company fails to deliver a report by the time specified or to make the report available online, Agency may initiate makegood discussions.

   In the event that Media Company delivers an incomplete report, or no report at all, such failure may result in nonpayment for all activity for which data are incomplete or missing.

III. CANCELLATION

a. Prior to the serving of the first impression of the campaign, Advertiser may cancel the campaign with 30 days written notice without penalty.

b. The first 30 days of the campaign are firm. Effective on the 16th day of the campaign, the Agency may cancel the campaign for any reason, without penalty, upon 14 days' written notice, unless otherwise stated in the IO.

c. Short rates will apply to cancelled buys to the degree stated on the IO.

IV. MAKEGOODS

a. Media Company shall monitor delivery of the Advertisements, and shall notify the Agency in writing as soon as possible (and no later than two weeks before campaign end date unless the length of the campaign is less than two weeks) if Media Company believes that an underdelivery is likely. In the case of a probable or actual underdelivery, the parties may arrange for makegood consistent with these Terms and Conditions.

b. In the event that actual deliverables (impressions, clicks, etc.) for any campaign fall below guaranteed levels, as set forth in the IO, and/or if there is an omission of any advertisement (placement or creative unit), Agency will make an effort to agree upon the conditions of a makegood flight either in the IO or at the time of the shortfall. If no makegood can be agreed upon, Agency may execute a credit/refund equal to the value of the underdelivered portion of the contract. In no event shall Media Company provide a makegood or extend any Advertisement beyond the period set forth in the IO without prior written consent of the Agency.

V. BONUS IMPRESSIONS

a. Where Agency utilizes Third Party Ad Serving, Media Company will not bonus more than ten percent without prior written consent from Agency.

b. Where Agency does not utilize Third Party Ad Serving, Media Company may bonus as many ad units as Media Company chooses unless otherwise indicated on the IO. Agency will not be charged for any additional advertising units above any level guaranteed in the IO.

VI. FORCE MAJEURE

Neither party shall be liable for delay or default in the performance of its obligations under this Agreement if such delay or default is caused by conditions beyond its reasonable control, including but not limited to, fire, flood, accident, earthquakes, telecommunications line failures, electrical outages, network failures, acts of God, or labor disputes. In such event, Media Company shall make every reasonable effort within 5 business days, to recommend a substitute transmission for the Advertisement or time period for the transmission. If no such substitute time period or makegood is acceptable to Agency, Media Company shall allow Agency a pro rata reduction in the space, time and/or program charges hereunder in the amount of money assigned to the space, time and/or program charges at time of purchase. Agency shall have the benefit of the same discounts that would have been earned had there been no default or delay.

To the extent that a force majeure has continued for five business days, the Media Company has the right to cancel the flight.

VII. AD MATERIALS

a. It is the Agency's obligation to submit advertising materials (defined as artwork, active URL's and active target site) in accordance with Media Company's existing criteria or specifications (including content limitations, technical specifications and material due dates) as posted on the Media Company's website at the time of the signing of the IO. Any specs stated on the signed IO supercede posted specs. If advertising materials are late, Advertiser is still responsible for the media purchased pursuant to IO.
b. Media Company reserves the right within its discretion to reject any advertising materials that do not comply with such policies, criteria, specifications, or any applicable law.
c. If material provided by the Agency is damaged, not to the Media Company's specifications, or otherwise unacceptable, Media Company shall notify Agency within two business days of receipt of advertising materials.

d. Media Company will not edit or modify the submitted Advertisements in any way, including, but without limitation, resizing the Advertisement, without Agency approval.
e. Media Company shall not, without prior authorization from Agency, display or publish any materials relating to Advertiser or its products, or alter, modify, or change the Advertisement or other materials provided by Agency, including but not limited to resizing. Third Party Ad Server tags shall be implemented so that they are functional in all aspects. Media Company shall use all such materials in strict compliance with any instructions provided by Agency. Media Company will not use Agency's or Advertiser's trade name, trademarks, logos or Advertisements in any form without Agency's prior written approval.

VIII. INDEMNIFICATION

a. Media Company shall defend, indemnify and hold harmless Agency and its Advertiser principal, and their respective agents, affiliates, subsidiaries, directors, officers and employees against any claim, action, liability, loss and expense including reasonable attorneys' fees (collectively "Loss") relating to or arising out of Media Company's breach of this agreement or Media Company's display or sending of any Advertisement other than as approved by Agency.
b. Advertiser shall defend, indemnify, and hold harmless Media Company and its respective agents, affiliates, subsidiaries, directors, officers, and employees against any Loss relating to or arising out of Advertiser's product or the content of any Advertisement delivered accurately, including but not limited to materials that violate the right of a third party; materials that are defamatory or obscene; or materials that would constitute a criminal offense.

IX. NON-DISCLOSURE, DATA OWNERSHIP, AND PRIVACY

a. Any confidential information and proprietary data provided by one party, including the Advertisement description, and the pricing of the Advertisement, set forth in the IO, shall be deemed "Confidential Information" of the disclosing party. Confidential Information shall be kept in the strictest confidence and shall be protected by all reasonable and necessary security measures. Confidential Information shall not be released by the receiving party to anyone except an employee, or agent who has a need to know same, and who is bound by confidentiality obligations. Neither party will use any portion of Confidential Information provided by the other party hereunder for any purpose other than those provided for under this Agreement.

b. All personally identifiable information initially gathered pursuant to the IO regarding individual web users is the property of Advertiser, and is considered Confidential Information. Agency and Media Company may use such information on an aggregated, non-identifiable basis.

c. Media Company, Agency, and Advertiser shall post on their respective Web sites their privacy policies and adhere to a privacy policy which abides by the applicable laws. Failure to continue to post a privacy policy or non-adherence to a party's own privacy policy is grounds for immediate cancellation of the IO by either party.

X. MISCELLANEOUS

a. Media Company represents and warrants that the Media Company has all necessary permits, licenses, and clearances to operate the Media Company's website and post all content contained therein or as given for use outside the Site. The Agency and Advertiser represent and warrant that the Advertiser has all necessary licenses and clearances to use the content contained in their advertising material. All parties' performances hereunder will be in compliance with all applicable laws, rules and regulations.

b. These Terms and Conditions and the related IO constitute the entire agreement of the parties with respect to the subject matter and supersede all previous communications, representations, understandings, and agreements, either oral or written, between the parties with respect to said subject matter.

c. In the event of any inconsistency between the terms of an IO and these Terms and Conditions, the terms of the IO shall prevail. All IO's shall be governed by the laws of the State of [Insert State Here]. No modification of these Terms and Conditions or any IO shall be binding unless in writing and signed by both parties. If any provision herein is held to be unenforceable, the remaining provisions shall remain in full force and effect. All rights and remedies hereunder are cumulative.

GLOSSARY

AAAA's

The Associate of American Advertising Agencies, a trade group of mostly large and traditional media ad agencies.

Action

Any measurable action an audience member can initiate. More particularly, it usually refers to the very specific transaction that the advertising companies wish audience members to do to meet the goals of a campaign. This is a common measure of advertising effectiveness, especially when coupled with cost information (cost per action). Also referred to as a transaction.

Activity Report

A regular report the media vendor sends to agencies and clients regarding the up-to-the-minute performance of the media they purchased. It usually contains impressions and clickthrough data.

Actual The number of impressions ultimately garnered by a client.

Ad Agency

A company that provides the services of either purchasing media for advertiser clients or planning and producing creative messages for that advertising.

Ad Network

A company that groups together many sites so as to offer more efficient operations and sales. Ad networks often allow for the application of targeting and automation technologies across many sites.

Aided Recall
The recall determined by showing an ad to viewers and asking them if they had seen it previously.

ARPANET
A network precursor to the Internet, developed by the Advanced Research Projects Agency in the early 1970s.

Attachment
A discrete document appended to an email message to appear on the hard drive of the recipient.

B2B (also B-to-B)
An adjective suggesting products or services sold by one business to another business.

B2C (also B-to-C)
An adjective signifying the seller intends the products or services for a consumer audience, as opposed to a business audience.

Banner
A graphic file, sometimes animated, that appears on a web site as an advertisement. Clicking on the banner usually sends a site visitor to an advertiser's site. The use of alternative banner sizes and "buttons" that might not provide the same links or tracking data are also considered banners.

Banner
The most common form of creative seen on the Internet, usually a rectangular, animated graphic.

BBS
Acronym for "bulletin board system," a local online service usually servicing 10 to 300 members. It is not capitalized when written out.

Behavioral
A type of measure used for advertising targeting, which indicates the people in the category have either conducted a certain type of behavior or that they have a propensity to do so in the future.

Billings

A figure for measuring the size of an ad agency's business. It comprises the sum of both the media moneys spent by the agency on behalf of the client as well as any fees collected by the agency.

Bot

A server application that queries other web servers automatically, often to catalog web sites.

Buy

This is the media deal an agency strikes with a media vendor. This is a contractually based agreement signifying that the agency owes the media vendor a certain amount of money in return for a certain minimum amount of media.

Buyer

The person at the ad agency or advertiser who negotiates the final deals with media vendors.

Campaign Management Tool

A database system allowing buyers to automate parts of the planning, trafficking and data analysis process.

Campaign

The campaign is the fundamental unit of advertising. It comprises the sum of all the marketing efforts against one particular objective. For online purposes, it is the sum of all the media efforts made on behalf of one goal, whether it be to sell a product or increase brand awareness during a holiday season.

CGI

Acronym for "Common Gateway Interface," a tool for employing scripts and other applications in web sites. It is capitalized when written out.

Circulation Audit

The verification process employed in print to verify circulation figures. In the print media, there is a one-to-one relationship between the number of copies of a publication and the number of times a given advertisement is printed, the circulation figures equate to impression figures for advertisers.

Circulation

The average number of people who view a publication in a given month.

Click Rate

The percentage of people who clicked on an ad relative to the number of times people saw the ad.

Click

One instance of an audience member clicking on a received piece of creative. Also referred to as a clickthough.

Client (agency context)

This is the agency's customer. The client employs an agency to figure out which media to buy and what creative to run. The term advertiser is sometimes used as a synonym.

Client (technical context)

Any program, like a browser or email application, that accesses a server.

Client/server

A type of computing architecture that distributes certain computational tasks out to the applications running on the users' computers and retaining certain other tasks for computation on a central server.

Commission

A percentage of a deal paid to an intermediary, like a salesperson or an agency.

Cookie

A computer file that allows sites to mark certain viewers with a unique identification number and other information. That unique number may then be stored in a database, where it can be associated with profiles and other types information on the viewer.

Cost Per Transfer

A standard measure of advertising efficiency.

CPA

Abbreviation for the cost per action, a typical measurement of advertising performance on the Internet. The action may be a purchase or merely getting a customer to fill out a survey.

CPC

Abbreviation for cost per clickthough, another term for CPC (cost per transfer).

CPM

Abbreviation for the cost per thousand impressions (advertisers use the letter M to denote 1,000 and MM 1,000,000, etc . . .), the standard form of pricing in most media.

CPT

Abbreviation for cost per transfer, a pricing mechanism for campaigns designed to push people to visit an advertising site.

CPX

Abbreviation for cost per transaction, another term for cost per action. The transaction in question does not necessarily refer to a sale. It refers to any server transaction, which could be a purchase or a site visit or any other recordable event on a web site.

Creative

Agencies and clients exploit their media space by placing "creative" for the audience to view, usually comprised of text and graphics meant to garner a particular reaction from the receiving audience.

Curtain Page

An introductory page preceding a site's homepage. Some sites use these to make visitors choose an appropriate language. Others, unfortunately, use it as the place to store gratuitous Flash animations.

DARPA

Acronym for the "Defense Advanced Research Projects Agency."

Daypart

A rigid set of time demarcations used in broadcast media to divvy up the day (e.g., daytime and primetime).

Demographic

A category of people, used for advertising targeting. Demographics involve criteria that the audience is most often unable to change, like gender, age and familial relations. The broadcast and print media have very specific and rigid sets of demographics they use as standard templates (e.g., moms 18-34).

DES

Acronym for "Data Encryption Standard," a security technology developed by IBM and used less today, in favor of the more web-friendly public key encryption standard.

Discrepancy Process

The series of events that follows the discovery of a shortfall in a media vehicle's guarantee. It will often involve a verification process, negotiation process and a makegood execution process.

Discrepancy

The shortfall created when a media vehicle fails to meet its guarantee.

DOS

"Disk operating system," a generic term for the basic computer software that runs your computer.

Double Opt-in

A process of collecting names for an email list by which a viewer must first deliberately choose to join, and the list manager must receive a second confirmation of the viewer's intent.

Download

Refers to an audience member consummating a transaction. If someone clicks on your advertising banner and subsequently requests the software you're trying to sell, it counts as one download. Please note that some agencies use this same term for any goal transaction, whether it be to literally download software or perhaps merely to purchase a service or send for additional information. That use is nonstandard, however, and is more precisely referred to as a "transaction" or "action."

Duplicated Reach
The number of people who see an ad on one media vehicle who also see the same ad on another.
Email
Referring either to a communication, most often limited to text, sent via a special email server. Also used as a verb, meaning to send electronically. Emails with graphics and HTML visible in the body of the message are often called rich email.
Extranet
An intranet that allows users from other companies interact with the proprietary content with specific permission.
Fall-off Rate
The decline in effectiveness experienced by all advertisements over time, as an audience sees an ad more and more times. Care should be taken to recognize that as direct-oriented metrics like clicks and actions might decline, the less measurable branding effects of advertisements sometimes continue to grow.
Flight
A period of time in which ads are running. A campaign might have several sets of flights spaced out between "off" periods. The set of buys arranged for a particular flight time may also be collectively referred to as a flight.
Float
The possession of funds during a transaction. When an ad agency puts client moneys in its account, for instance, and then pays media vendors a month later, they are said to "hold the float." Companies make surprising amounts of money on interest earned from these transactional floats.
Frequency
The average number of times the people who see an ad view it on a particular media vehicle. This is also sometimes called "site frequency," so as to distinguish it from "campaign frequency," the average number of times the people see an ad across all vehicles.

FTP

"File transfer protocol." A method of acquiring computer documents from a server. Applications such as Dartmouth College's Fetch allow Internet users to receive FTP files from FTP servers. Some early Internet advertising applications used FTP to transfer large graphics and forms of rich media. Today it is still sometimes used to fulfill requests for large files, such as new and updated browser applications.

GIF

A common graphics format (Graphic Interchange Format, spelled out), also written as ".gif" when used as a suffix to a file name. The format is owned by Compuserve and is licensed freely.

Gopher

A database network format precursor to the web.

Grandfathered Rate

A price an advertiser may continue for receive in thanks for past business, even as prices rise for new advertisers.

Gross

When associated with a price for media, it connotes that the amount includes an agency commission.

GRP

Gross rating points, a figure used in broadcast media showing the gross percentage of the viewing public who saw an ad, regardless of target universe.

Guaranteed Circulation

The level of circulation a print vehicle guarantees advertisers. If the circulation falls below this number, the media vehicle will often owe the advertiser a credit or a makegood.

Guaranteed Delivery

This is the amount of media a media vendor certifies will be given to an agency and client. Frequently it is a mere minimum that will be exceeded with "overdelivery." If a media vendor fails to make the guaranteed amount, there is a "discrepancy" that must be resolved, usually be credit back to the client or by a "make-good" order to deliver more media later.

GUI

Acronym for "graphic user interface." It is not capitalized when written out.

HTML

Acronym for "hypertext markup language," the primary protocol for the web.

Homepage

The primary intended access point to a web site. Also used to signify the page that a web user employs as the default address for a browser.

HTTP

Acronym for "hypertext transport protocol." This is often found at the beginning of web addresses to indicate to the browser that the document it will find at the address should be interpreted as HTML.

Hybrid Deal

A media transaction that involves more than one form of payment measurement. Most commonly employed to guarantee a minimum payment via a CPM deal in combination with a performance requirement through a CPA or CPC structure.

IAB

Abbreviation for the Interactive Advertising Bureau, a trade group of sites and technology companies convened to promote the interests of sites.

Impression

This is one instance of an audience member receiving the creative.

Insertion Order

The media contract and terms confirmation between an agency and media vendor.

Instrument

An abstract term for a contract that grants rights to one party to purchase media from another party at a specified cost. These are sometimes used by advertisers to lock in prices, just in case short-term demand unexpectedly makes prices rise.

Internet

Used today to encompass any content or application accessible by electronic means. More precisely used in reference to those applications and content accessed via one of the specific Internet protocols, like HTML or FTP.

Intranet

A proprietary, mini-Internet, used for internal purposes and generally protected with passwords.

JPEG

A popular graphic file format that allows for some compression of file sizes. The file names of JPEG format documents frequently have a ".jpg" suffix appended to them.

Keyword

A search term that may be purchased by an advertiser to create an adjacency of its creative to the content that will appear when visitors search for the particular term.

LAN

Acronym for "local area network."

MIME

Acronym for "multipurpose Internet mail extensions." These extensions indicate to email programs that an attachment is of a certain type, allowing the programs to properly interpret them.

M

In advertising parlance, this signifies 1,000. In other industries, the M would indicate a million and the K is employed for 1,000. In advertising lingo, MM is used for a million and MMM for a billion, etc . . .

Makegood

The means of rectifying a discrepancy, the make-good pays back an under-delivered client with additional media weight or money.

Marketplace
The financial environment set by the presence of both buyers and sellers, affecting the commodity prices of media.
Media Incumbency
The right retained by an advertiser to continue purchasing a specific placement.
Media Vendor
The party selling media.
Media
This is the space on the newspaper page or the time on television that broadcasters and publishers allot to paying customers. In the online context, it is usually a small bit of screen space atop most pages that allow for a rectangular "banner" to be placed by an advertiser. It comprises an opportunity for an advertiser to deliver a message to a viewer or listener.
Net
When associated with a price for media, it connotes that the amount does not include an agency commission.
Newsgroup
A particular section (or topic) of the USENET, a bulletin board application long used on the Internet.
Online
An word used to describe any instance where computers are hooked up to other computers. This includes both the "online services" like AOL and Prodigy as well as the Internet. It can also refer to non-computer devices, so long as they maintain some sort of connection to other computational devices.
Online Media
Advertising space that may be purchased, with an audience of people currently online.
Opt-in
A process of collecting names for an email list by which a viewer must first deliberately choose to join.
OS
Acronym for operating system.

PDA

Acronym for "personal digital assistant" (like Apple's Newton

Overdelivery

The amount of media a site delivers over the minimum guaranteed in a buy's contract.

Pass-through

The average number of readers exposed to a copy of a printed publication.

Pivot Table

A two-dimensional table employed to show multi-dimensional runs of data.

Planner

The person at the ad agency or advertiser who decides the strategies to employ in organizing the purchase of media, and then determine which sites will be most appropriate.

Portal

A site design as a jumping-off point for web users when they first get online. They often include search engines, directories, and a host of services web audiences typically use, such as email. When referring to a individual web users, the portal site is determined by the URL address listed as the default page on their primary browsers.

Preference

The degree to which a consumer prefers one brand over another, expressed as a percentage for each brand.

Product

The product is the individual entity being advertised via online media. This may be a literal product, or a service or perhaps even a concept.

Profile

Information gathered on a viewer that may then be applied in future targeting.

Psychographic
A category of people, used for advertising targeting, which indicates a certain mindset (e.g., people who believe the value of individuals can be determined by their salaries). Unlike demographics, an individual might change psychographic categories at will (unless you adhere to Hobbesian Calvinism or Antinomial Puritanism, in which case you're stuck with who you are).

Rates
Prices for media, usually expressed as CPM's.

Ratings
An audience measure often used in broadcast media. In television, expressed as a number that indicates the percent of current viewers watching who are watching a particular show.

Reach
The number of people who see an ad at least once.

Recall
The percentage of ad viewers who can remember seeing an ad and remember which brand was advertised.

Regional Edition
A version of a publication made available to a given region, often with region-specific advertising.

Remnant Media
The extra impressions available on a site after all sold ad placements have taken their share of the inventory. Remnant media is often used to barter with other sites for self-promotional campaigns. Other uses include selling it at a discount, employing it with public service campaigns and using it for in-house campaigns to sell site-branded products.

Request For Proposal (RFP)
A form agencies send out to media vendors seeking pricing information.

Rich Media
A creative form that involves sound or motion or other types of content more involved than a simple banner.

ROI
Abbreviation for return on investment, the amount of profit an advertiser makes over and above the costs of a media campaign.

RSA
A brand of public key encryption protection.

Selective Binding
A publishing process allowing modification of a publication based on individual subscriber information.

Server Chain
The combination of web servers used to call up a particular ad. This can involve a variety of different company's servers, potentially including the advertiser, agency, web site, third party technology provider, rich media creative format provider and others.

Share of Voice (SOV)
The percentage of impressions used by one advertiser relative to those of its competitors.

S-HTML
Acronym for "secure hypertext markup language."

Site
A publication on the Internet.

SMTP
Acronym for "simple mail transport protocol." It is not capitalized when written out.

Spam
The email equivalent of junk mail.

Sponsorship
A package of media on a single site, usually involving a specially-marked status on the site to suggest a close relationship between the brand and a specific section of content.

SSL
Acronym for "Secure Sockets Layer," a common security protocol used by browsers and sites.

SYSOPs
Acronym of sorts for "systems operators," the people who run bulletin board systems.

Tab Delimited
A standard form of output from many computer programs and databases, making it simple to import such information into another system.

TCP/IP
Acronym for the main Internet protocol.

Teaser
A type of creative that doesn't tell viewers the brand or product type of the advertiser. These campaigns necessarily involve future ads that reveal the brand after a buzz has developed. Sometimes this can go horribly awry, as in Amtrak's campaign for the new Acela trains. After spending tens of millions of dollars on teaser ads, the train service was delayed. By the time faster trains ran a year or so later, the teaser campaign was difficult to recall.

Traffic
The communications and creative assets that transfer back and forth between an advertiser, agency and media vehicle during a buy.

Transaction
Any measurable action an audience member can initiate. More particularly, it usually refers to the very specific transaction that the advertising companies wish audience members to do to meet the goals of a campaign. This is a common measure of advertising effectiveness, especially when coupled with cost information (cost per transaction). Also referred to as an action.

Transfer Rate
The percentage of people who arrived at the advertiser's site relative to the number of times people were exposed to the ad.

Transfer

The delivery of one audience member to a receiving site (usually the client's) upon causing that audience member to click on a piece of creative.

TRP

Total rating points, a figure used in broadcast media to show the percentage of the viewing public—who are also members of the specifically-targeted universe—who see an ad.

UI

Acronym for "user interface."

Unaided recall

The recall determined by letting viewers list the ads they remember.

Underdelivery

The amount of media a site delivers under the minimum guaranteed in a buy's contract.

Universe

The number of people within the audience in consideration. For instance, the universe of American women is about 150 MM.

UNIX

An operating system common on Internet servers.

URL

Acronym for universal resource locator, the primary address format for web sites.

USENET

Acronym for the collection of thousands of newsgroups available on the Internet.

Vertical Publication

A publication geared to a narrow audience, often a specific industry.

Vertical Site

See vertical publication

Vortal

A site geared to a narrow group of people, often a specific industry, with all the qualities of a portal. The word is an ellision of the words vertical and portal.

WAN

Acronym for "wide area network."

Web

Common shortened version of World Wide Web.

Web Server

A computer that hosts a web site.

Web Site

A location on the web.

Webmaster

The person who handles the day-to-day operations of a web site, usually of a technical function. Also sometimes seen as "webmistress."

Wireless Media

Advertisements shown on cell phones that sport screens (and now, occasionally, other types of wireless devices).

World Wide Web

Main format of Internet materials. Referred to frequently as the "WWW."

INDEX

Symbols

A

B

C

D

E

F

G

H

I

J

K

L

M

N

O

P

R

S

T

U

V

W

3340-TILL

Printed in the United States
5962